CRIPPING YOUTH MINISTRY

AN INTERSECTIONAL VISION FOR WORKING WITH DISABLED YOUTH

EDITED BY

JUSTIN FORBES AND ERIN RAFFETY

WILLIAM B. EERDMANS PUBLISHING COMPANY
GRAND RAPIDS, MICHIGAN

Wm. B. Eerdmans Publishing Co.
2006 44th Street SE, Grand Rapids, MI 49508
www.eerdmans.com

Published 2026

Book design by Lydia Hall

Printed in the United States of America

32 31 30 29 28 27 26   1 2 3 4 5 6 7

ISBN 978-0-8028-8575-3

Library of Congress Cataloging-in-Publication Data

Names: Forbes, Justin, 1980– editor | Raffety, Erin editor
Title: Cripping youth ministry : an intersectional vision for working with disabled youth / Justin Forbes and Erin Raffety, eds.
Description: Grand Rapids, Michigan : William B. Eerdmans Publishing Company, [2026] | Includes bibliographical references and index.
Identifiers: LCCN 2025033000 | ISBN 9780802885753 paperback | ISBN 9781467470483 epub
Subjects: LCSH: Church work with youth with social disabilities
Classification: LCC BV4447 .C75 2026
LC record available at https://lccn.loc.gov/2025033000

"This book knocked my socks off! *Cripping Youth Ministry* is unlike any youth ministry book I have ever read. Raffety, Forbes, and their team have done nothing less than shift youth ministry's center of gravity. From the title to the artwork to the essays themselves, every line has been crafted with utter fidelity to the book's table-flipping theme: young people with physical and mental disabilities need 'youth ministry' far less than able-bodied ministry needs them. These pages offer much in the way of scholarship and practical wisdom, but they also crackle with these youths' raw, unfiltered, Christ-shaped stories—tilting the axis of youth ministry away from performance back to the practice of being human. I left this book wiser, humbled, and restored."

—Kenda Creasy Dean
Mary D. Synnott Professor of Youth, Church and Culture,
Princeton Theological Seminary

"*Cripping Youth Ministry* is one of those books that curates a conversation that is needed and promises to be enduring. Erin Raffety and Justin Forbes are two of the best guides in all of the youth ministry world to take us into this conversation. The chapters of this book will take up permanent residence in your imagination. This is an exciting work."

—Andrew Root
Carrie Olson Baalson Chair of Youth and Family Ministry, Luther Seminary

"If you are a pastor, parent, religious educator, or practitioner who works with youth and deeply desires to do right by *all* young people (which has always included those who are disabled and differently abled), then you need *Cripping Youth Ministry*! Justin Forbes and Erin Raffety have brought together incredible voices that tell the truth about ableism while also making room for play, joy, lament, and the everyday wisdom of disabled youth themselves. This volume offers a thriving intersectional, theological, and pedagogical vision in which disability, embodiment, and interdependence are not problems to be solved or prayed away, but truly generative spaces of God's presence, communal formation, and liberative praxis and hope. The collection takes us on a beautiful journey through liturgical movements of lament, protest, praise, and prophecy with powerful poetry, art, practices, and questions for reflection. This book is an invitation to transformation, so once you read this, you are now accountable to do the hard work of amplifying these voices to make your classrooms, homes, and churches more welcoming and accessible for *ALL* our young people. While *Cripping Youth Ministry* is the book that adults need, it is also the one that our young people deserve."

—Lakisha R. Lockhart-Rusch
associate professor of Christian education, Union Presbyterian Seminary

"In *Cripping Youth Ministry,* Justin Forbes and Erin Raffety invite readers into a story that is as tender as it is transformative. The book gently dismantles the assumption that disabled young people are primarily recipients of care. Instead, they are revealed as teachers, pastors, prophets, and, above all, friends, whose presence reshapes our understanding of ministry, belonging, and the body of Christ. Warm, honest, and hope-filled, this book is an invitation to slow down, notice more deeply, and receive the good news disabled young people have been preaching all along: *Ministry is not something we do to others, but something we learn with one another.*"

—John Swinton
professor of practical theology and pastoral care, University of Aberdeen

"*Cripping Youth Ministry* opened my eyes to a way of thinking, doing theology, and practicing youth ministry that truly centers our disabled community. I am deeply appreciative of the scholars and practitioners who lent their voices to this important work; their insight, honesty, and lived experience make this book both compelling and transformative. These words challenged me in ways that will forever shape how I see, lead, and serve. Theology should be liberative, embodied, and inclusive, and *Cripping Youth Ministry* does exactly that. It invites us not only to rethink our frameworks but to reimagine what it means to lead and to create spaces where all young people are seen as whole and valued. This book calls all of us into the ongoing work of becoming more faithful allies and advocates, committed to justice and dignity for all."

—Khristi Lauren Adams
author of *Womanish Theology: Discovering God Through the Lens of Black Girlhood*

"Since the publication of *Amplifying Our Witness* in 2012, the conversation around the theology and practice of youth ministry and disability has changed drastically. Given the impact of COVID, new insights about autism spectrum disorder, research on vocation and disability, and a broad, sustained interest in mental health, youth leaders are in need of an updated resource that doesn't only amplify the witness of people with disabilities but centers their voices in all of their intersectional complexity as experts on their own experience. *Cripping Youth Ministry* will prove a helpful guide to youth ministers and practitioners navigating these concerns."

—Benjamin T. Conner
professor of practical theology and director of
the Center for Disability and Ministry, Western Theological Seminary

CONTENTS

ABOUT THE COVER

WHAT IS "CRIPPING"?

Cripping is a verb rooted in disability justice movements and the fields of disability studies and critical disability studies. This term centers disabled experience to expose and challenge ableist assumptions. It begins with the truth that disabled young people already carry wisdom, creativity, leadership, and theological insight. Rather than adjusting the margins of ministry so that disabled youth can be included, cripping invites ministry to be reshaped by disabled youths' perspectives from the start. Cripping is a practice of collective transformation—where everyone's flourishing becomes possible because access and belonging are not afterthoughts but the very heart of faithful youth ministry.

WHY IS JESUS IN A CHAIR?

Portraying Jesus using a wheelchair disrupts the assumption that the divine image must align with cultural norms of ability. Too often, disability is imagined only as a deficit needing cure rather than as a meaningful form of embodied life. By locating Christ in disabled embodiment, the artwork proclaims that disabled people do not merely belong to the church—they reveal God's presence among us. This visual theology reminds us that salvation is not about escaping bodies but finding dignity, agency, and community within them.

WHAT DOES "INTERSECTIONAL" MEAN?

Intersectionality names the reality that each person inhabits multiple identities at once—disability, race, gender, culture, and faith—which together shape how we experience God, community, and the world. Within the body of Christ, these diverse embodied identities are not incidental details but essential expressions of the *imago Dei*. When youth ministry takes intersectionality seriously, it recognizes that there is no singular way of being a young person—and therefore no singular way in which the Spirit forms and calls young people into discipleship. The contributors to this book write from varied social and theological locations, revealing perspectives that challenge and enrich our assumptions. By receiving their insights, we are invited to reimagine youth ministry itself—discovering new forms of belonging and leadership that emerge when the fullness of God's people is honored as gift.

WHERE IS THE ART FROM?

We are grateful to artist Olga Ledis in collaboration with Art for All and to West Concord Union Church, who generously granted permission for this artwork to be shared in this project, allowing the theological imagination of these pages to begin the moment the cover is seen. Her image helps us step immediately into the book's central hope: that disabled young people's lives and leadership transform how the church imagines, practices, and celebrates youth ministry. Throughout the book, additional artwork created by young people with disabilities invites readers to see the church—and God's world—through perspectives that are too often overlooked, yet full of truth and beauty.

AN INVITATION

We invite you to begin with the cover itself—to pause, notice, and allow it to unsettle assumptions about who leads, belongs, and reveals God in the church. As you open these pages, we hope you will remain open to new ideas and new possibilities for what youth ministry can look like when disabled young people are centered as theologians, friends, and cocreators of the body of Christ. May this book spark imagination, deepen love, and move us all toward communities where every young person's gifts are celebrated as essential to our shared discipleship.

Note: The title for this volume, *Cripping Youth Ministry*, was originally coined by Avery Arden as the title for their chapter. Many thanks to Avery for allowing us to use this title!

—Erin Raffety and Justin Forbes

INTRODUCTION

JUSTIN FORBES

I used to say that Michael was one of the pastors in our little church. He never went to seminary, never had a formal title, but his ministry was unmistakable. Michael was a young adult with Down syndrome who had been part of our community since middle school. Over the years his ministry and presence redefined what I believed about the body of Christ, the church, and how I thought about ministry.

One Sunday, years ago now, Michael and I found ourselves sitting on the floor at the back of the sanctuary during the sermon. Michael was grieving the loss of his uncle and quietly wept beside me. He did not hide his sadness at church but instead came that Sunday knowing he would be welcomed and embraced. Before I joined Michael against the wall in the back, I found myself distracted and honestly a bit annoyed. The sounds of his crying were interrupting the sermon—ironically, the topic was about loving one another (I felt like a real winner there!)—and I found myself growing impatient. But then it hit me: Michael was the sermon. He was inviting me to embody the very love the preacher was trying to describe. As I walked back to Michael and sat with him, I realized he was preaching to me in a way that no sermon could. That moment, unplanned and unscripted, was holy. It was good news.

Michael didn't just receive ministry at our church; he offered it. His affection, honesty, and vulnerability were not obstacles—they were gifts. Michael taught and led us, not from behind a pulpit but from within the honesty of his human experience.

This book is full of Michaels. In fact, their names are Chris, Avery, Mo, and Hunter, and they wrote chapters themselves! These are young people whose presence and stories invite us to rethink ministry not in spite of disability, but through its unique witness. For too long ministry has been thought of as something offered to those with disabilities, and I fear the church has missed the voices of these individuals—those who have been operating as pastors, prophets, and companions in our slow, sacred work of becoming more fully human, more like Christ. Why wasn't Michael *a* pastor instead of *like* a pastor? We can do better.

ROOTED IN PRACTICE: THE MISSING VOICES PROJECT

This book did not begin in theory. It began in relationships, in collaboration, and in real places with real people. It grew out of the work of the Missing Voices Project at the Center for Religion and Culture at Flagler College, a project that set out to support innovative ministries with youth on the margins of church and society.

Focused on working with congregations across the state of Florida, the Missing Voices Project started with a theological and epistemological assumption that God is revealing Godself through the marginalized in ways that cannot be learned elsewhere. In other words, marginalized youth would be the sources of insight, understanding, and wisdom in a way that people from other contexts, social locations, or identities simply could not replicate. One source of identity that emerged was disabled youth. We began to realize how few resources existed at the intersection of **disability theology** and youth ministry.[1] We also began to see how profoundly the church was missing out not just on youth with disabilities but on what God was doing through them.

This book argues that ministry with disabled youth isn't niche work. It's not an elective. It's central to the church's call to become the body of Christ in all its fullness. This book is a theological offering born from local ministry, shared **friendship**, and a desire to take seriously the voices the church too often overlooks. In fact, we made a very intentional effort to center the voices of those who self-identify as having disabilities. This is important, as most disability scholarship attending to youth ministry has been written by people like me, an able-bodied white man. While I make no apologies for who I am, I acknowledge that my voice is not the only one that should be heard. I am more than willing to say that I need to hear from other perspectives and social locations to better understand the good news. We need new voices to teach us, but the bigger question is whether we will listen.

CRIPPING YOUTH MINISTRY: WHY THIS BOOK, WHY NOW

Youth ministry has long been shaped by certain assumptions centering those who are extroverted, able-bodied, neurotypical, and emotionally self-regulating. Without meaning to, our ministries can subtly reward youth who "fit the mold" and overlook those whose presence or participation challenges our assumptions.

Disabled youth are not absent from our churches and communities. They are often present but simply ignored. They may be seen but not heard, or heard but not believed. In many cases, they are dismissed with no expectation to lead, teach in, or transform the spaces they inhabit.

This book arrives at a moment when conversations around access, equity, and **disability justice** are growing, but theological engagement with those conversations in youth ministry remains sparse. We are still learning how to listen, how to follow the lead of disabled youth, and how to unlearn the habits of ministry that formed us.

This book is not a how-to guide or a best-practices manual void of context. It is a witness. It is a collection of voices—youth, scholars, and practitioners—who are helping us remember that ministry is not something we do *to* people, but something we do *with* one another. We intentionally gathered a mix of young people, scholars, and practitioners because we felt this more fully represented the reality of our churches and communities. As we talked about the themes and experiences that fill the book, we realized we were being led through familiar liturgical movements of **lament**, **protest**, **praise**, and **prophecy**. As much as Michael's leadership is present yet often eclipsed or ignored, we found faithfulness in being able to lament and protest together what is unjust, while also making space for the praiseworthy and prophetic gifts and ministry of the disabled young people that number these pages.

Finally, as we worked on this project together as a community, we realized that we wanted to include the kinds of practical tools that are so desperately needed. Therefore, the reader will find form prayers, prayer templates, practical activities for ministry, and even art from talented artists who self-identify as disabled. Our hope is to encourage the reader with a bias toward action, a nudge toward what could be in the light of the kingdom of God. We hope this book invites you to move more slowly, to notice more deeply, and to allow disabled youth to lead you toward a more faithful, more human, more Christlike way of being.

Lent 2025
Rev. Justin Forbes, PhD

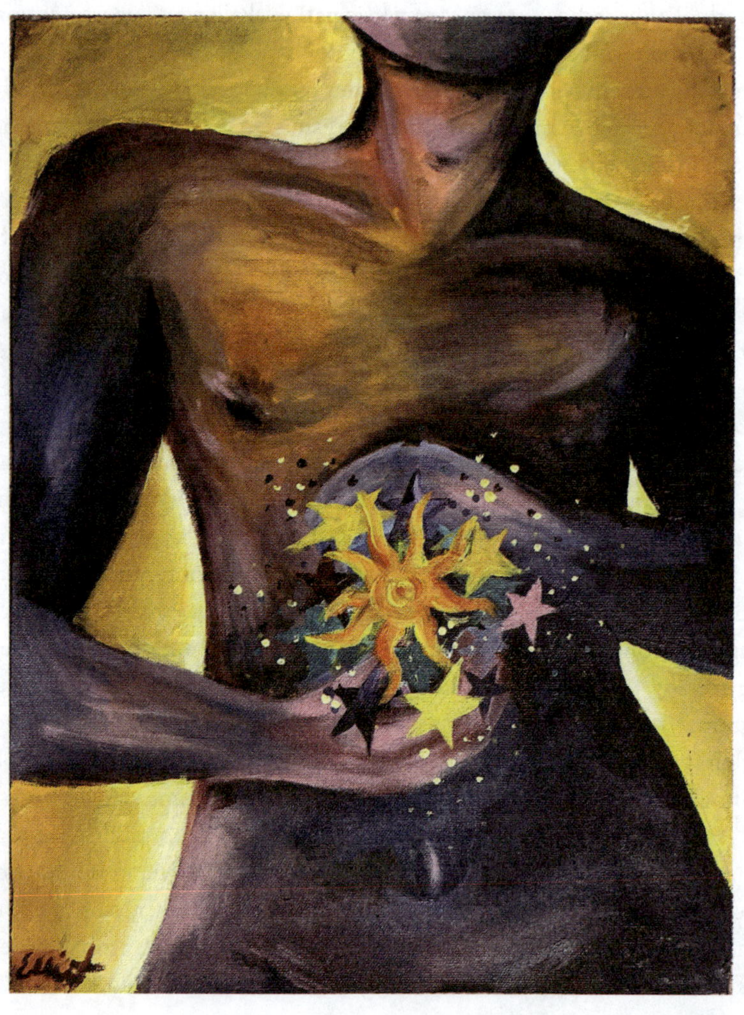

ROUNDTABLE INTRODUCTION

AVERY ARDEN, MORRIGAN CLARKE,
ZACH GRANT, DEBORAH HUGGINS,
AMY JACOBER, SARAH GRIFFITH LUND,
AND HUNTER STEINITZ

We invited our contributors to gather in January 2025. What follows is a conversation, interwoven across youth, practitioner, and scholar perspectives, that identifies laments, protests, praises, and prophecy in ministry with disabled youth.

Thank you to Avery Arden, Mo Clarke, Zach Grant, Deborah Huggins, Amy Jacober, Sarah Griffith Lund, and Hunter Steinitz for coauthoring this introduction.

When it comes to ministry with disabled youth, do you feel most drawn to lament, protest, praise, or prophecy?

Hunter Steinitz: I would have to fit myself somewhere between praise and prophecy, because there is already some really amazing work done by self-advocates, people with disabilities, in their faith communities. A lot of the time those faith communities don't realize that's what it is, but it's right there in front of them. When it comes to prophecy, I think a lot about the example that people with disabilities have had to set just because of the way that we have to move in an ableist world. There is so much excellent trailblazing work happening that the rest of the church just needs to clue into. It's already there. So, it's more a matter of calling their attention to the voice crying out in the wilderness.

Amy Jacober: I feel like I'm probably the elder of the group. "Back when I started teaching," which I feel like I need to be doing in my best, grandma voice, I would beg and beg for there to be conversation around disability, and then, when I was told, "No, that makes people sad," I said, "What about a course?" "Well, no, no, no, because that doesn't have any money in it," and I was like, "What about a weekend seminar?"

And I did get that granted in a few institutions. But I had to raise my own money to do that. I think back now, and I'm like, dear God! I was raising my own money to teach.

So, part of that constant rejection and lament turned into a prophetic space. Because then I just wove it into every course, every time I spoke at a church, everything that I ever did, and even before I knew the phrase "**universal design**." It was just woven in but that was also kind of my spiritual act of protest: You want to tell me no? Watch me. I will find a way to make this happen.

Avery Arden: I see that disabled youth already bring protest, because they experience the world all around them as being full of injustices. So many of us adults become burnt out—capitalism wants us to be too exhausted to have any time or energy left to protest. But young people are more likely to still be burning up with this desire to call out and do something about these injustices. Like, there's a reason Jesus tells us we must be like little children, because young people are constantly asking, "Why? Why is it this way? Why are you saying that there's no changing it?"

Mo Clarke: I feel most drawn to protest when it comes to ministry with disabled youth. As Hunter said, there are a lot of great, amazing things happening through self-advocacy. But I still believe that there are always more things that could be fought for, and it can't hurt to always try to push.

And so when it comes, especially like in my old church, when we had to push for a **Joyful Noise** service, that was a form of us protesting so that more people in our community could get what they needed out of it. And so I feel like it does make a difference if everybody is protesting, not only if one person is protesting.

We asked for stories about youth with intersectional identities that could help us better understand the joys and challenges of this ministry.

Zach Grant: I think about Kendra and Ken, both of whom have now passed away and were disabled leaders in our church and community. Kendra was a communicator. We had an accessible choir, and so she was the person who would always communicate to everybody the information. That was her ministry. And her brother, Ken, would go and help me in ministry at the local high schools. He would sometimes fall asleep because his medication, his blood sugars were not well regulated, and that would put us in interesting conversations with the teachers or the schools that we were going into. And yet he would bring a different vision to the work that we were doing that allowed us to value people in radically different ways. It was absolutely essential. And some of those things he disrupted were just the sort of things that led us into more beautiful spaces.

Deborah Huggins: When we were working on changing part of the constitution of our denomination, the Presbyterian Church USA (PCUSA), we wanted to include "all abilities" in a list of marginalized folks. And a recommendation came through committee that it include "all abilities and all genders," and we knew that that was going to be more controversial. And it was like, how are we going to respond to this? And just knowing, especially with the number of young people who identify as neurodivergent and **queer**, we couldn't *not* do it. We had a self-advocate who's like, "Are you kidding me? I'm also **trans**, like we can't, we can't say all abilities and not say all genders."

It was hard. It was a bigger push. It was a bigger lift. It was less of a sure thing that it would pass. But just knowing how many people have intersecting identities, it was like, we had to be brave and just do that advocacy piece and take a bigger risk. So, it's really important to listen to our self-advocates and our young people.

Avery Arden: When you look at statistics, that something like 40 percent of trans people identify as having a disability, and trans people are also something like three to six times more likely to be autistic, so there's a lot of overlap in our communities. And that shows itself in our church.

A lot of the young people I work with I've known since they were in elementary school or middle school, but watching them gain more confidence and start to have ideas about what they want to do after high school that they're actually excited about has been really life giving for me, particularly as an autistic trans person who grew up without any clue that I was either of those things, that I had so many unmet needs, that the depression and shame that I was experiencing were because I didn't know who I was.

So, to see them learn more about who they are and get that way younger than I did brings me so much joy. By no means am I claiming that our church can take all the credit for that. But I do believe in the way we have tried to cultivate this space where every young person can be themselves whether that means they need to fidget or pace around, or we have to find creative ways to do an activity because one of our students can't stand for long periods. It's affirming youth when they say this is their name, or this is the **pronoun** they're trying out, to grow with them. I know that has some sort of impact on their ability to imagine that it's even possible for them to have communities where their needs are being met, where they're being affirmed in both their needs and their gifts.

Sarah Griffith Lund: I'm a survivor of **suicide** loss. My niece Sydney died at sixteen, and she had ADHD. We don't talk enough about folks with diagnoses or disabilities being at higher risk for suicide because of the shame and stigma. I find a lot of empowerment as a survivor to be an advocate through storytelling and through sharing hope and resources.

But there's a little bit of irony I want to name. Because for me, as a person of faith, my faith and my faith community are what inspire me and keep me going. But what happens when the barriers are *in* the faith community, when they're part of the challenges, the tension, the conflict?

And then we have you all, like, we have this space. I think this feeds my spirit, because it reminds me that God's love and hope and dreams for us are so much bigger than we could ever imagine. And when we feel frustrated in our individual faith communities, I still have hope, and I love that you all are out there doing the work with me.

What most excites you about the book and how it might be used by the people that need it?

Hunter Steinitz: The endnotes, the additional resources that are included in this conversation, are meant for you to go out and look and dig down deeper and find your own local connections to these things, because this kind of stuff is very localized. The kinds of resources that are available to families with disabilities change wildly by what state you're in or by what county you're in. And so really take the extra time to find what's near you, so that you can best embed yourself into what's already going on around you.

Amy Jacober: The Holy Spirit is incredibly on the move. What we have seen historically is people kind of want to lift up their little space, and you are not only widening the tent, you've blown out the sides of the tent and are finding ways to expand it. There's going to be a chapter that somebody's going to read and be like, I would never have bought this book if that person wrote it, but they're going to be exposed to something. And then I think they're going to be reading a chapter, and they're going to say, This is fascinating, I must share this with others.

You are modeling the reality that indeed you can't have lament without protest, praise and prophecy and the merry-go-round of they all are intertwined. I would argue that we're probably more intertwined than perhaps we've allowed the church to talk about previously. I think it's also going to highlight sexism, racism, and **ableism**, and this invites those conversations to say, What does it truly look like to lean into the *imago Dei*?

Sarah Griffith Lund: You may have heard the saying, "The right person at the right place at the right time"? I feel like this is the right book at the right place at the right time. More and more people are disabled. I believe the research supports that globally the most common disability is **depression**.

This book is a life-saving, life-giving resource for the faith community. It is perfect for the newbie, and it is perfect for those who have been doing this for a long time. And I love that it can deepen current community through engaging the conversations in the book, but it can also create new community. I think this is an evangelism tool to share God's love with people who didn't really think the church was a place that cared about them.

INTERLUDE: INTRODUCTION TO DISABILITY

ERIN RAFFETY

When people think of disability, they start with the body. One primary way for understanding bodies in our culture is medicine, and **the medical model of disability** defines disability as bodily impairment, something that limits the function of a part of the body on a regular basis. Although medicine is helpful to many disabled people in providing informational diagnoses, treatments that limit pain, and even technological innovations that may improve disabled people's quality of life, the medical model of disability has historically failed to center disabled people's insights and perspectives. This is because the medical model of disability tends to regard disabled people's bodies as abnormal, in need of rehabilitation, or even as problems that should be cured or avoided through genetics.

In the 1960s and '70s, **disability rights** activists across the globe began to champion another model of disability that they called the social model. **The social model of disability** argues that disability isn't primarily a dysfunction of the body, but rather a result of prejudice that makes society fundamentally inaccessible to disabled people. Many of the early disability rights activists focused on mobility challenges, including the lack of ramps for wheelchair users, embossed curb cuts for blind people, and tangible interventions like accessible transport, access to education, voting, healthcare, and other public services. The landmark **Americans with Disabilities Act** (ADA) and the subsequent **Individuals with Disabilities Education Act**, both passed in 1990, codify disabled people's civil rights in the United States and are achievements of the disability rights movement.

Yet access for disabled people in America is far from equal to that for non-disabled people. Not only is the ADA primarily reinforced through disabled people's litigation, but there are myriad exceptions to the law that continue to inhibit access for disabled people in their everyday lives, including an exception for church buildings. That's right: Churches don't have to build or augment their buildings to be in compliance with ADA if they don't want to. Furthermore, around the time the ADA was passed, a number of disability rights activists noted that whereas legislative change made a big difference for White people with mobility challenges, Black, Brown, **queer**, and chronically ill people were still struggling because their disability experiences differed and disrupted the expected norm. **The disability justice movement**, which aims to both build on and critique the prior disability rights movement, puts forth a broader, more intersectional definition of disability that seeks to identify and examine **ableism** and its relationship to other forms of oppression such as racism, sexism, capitalism, and classism. By ableism, we mean the extent to which the able-bodied experience remains the default or the norm whereby other experiences are made marginal. The disability justice movement argues that it's not just that disabled people were left out of the rights conversation, but that their rights and lives are constantly being affected by prejudice that's endemic to systems like education and healthcare. This is why the disability justice movement centers Black, Brown, and queer experiences of disability as essential to fighting these injustices.

Disabled people's advocacy is bringing new wisdom and understanding to academia, medicine, education, society, and healthcare. One clear example of that is the **neurodiversity movement**, an approach that understands brain diversity as another element of our human variation, and a concept that emerged out of the **autism** rights movement in the 1990s. People who are **neurodivergent**, such as those with autism, ADHD, dyslexia, and other emotional and behavioral diagnoses, noticed that the medical model, especially with its emphasis on therapy to correct their behaviors, was undermining their ways of being in and understanding the world. Yet another area of contemporary advocacy spearheaded by disabled people are the movements for medical research supported by communities of people with ME/CFS (myalgic encephalitis/chronic fatigue syndrome) and long **COVID**. The activism of people who identify as chronically ill and/or disabled is made all the more impressive by the fact that many of these folks live in bodies that tire easily, faint, or even struggle to remain upright. These folks organize and advocate from their beds by calling members of Congress and creatively using social media to raise funds for their medical and legislative needs. Finally, increasingly many people with mental health diagnoses such as **depression**, anxiety, bipolar, and PTSD are embracing their psychological or psychosocial diagnoses as disabilities. They find strength in using accommodations to support their needs, as well as a definition of disability that does not view their mental health diagnoses as deficits or even illnesses, but pursues flourishing life within the symptoms of their experiences.

Of course, these aren't the only models or understandings of disability out there. The fields of **disability studies** and **critical disability studies** are constantly reevaluating these terms and concepts, especially in an effort to center disabled understandings in scholarship and society and to make sure a diversity of disabled experiences is taken into account. Although the language we use for disability is also often in flux, in this volume we use the terms disabled people, people with disabilities, neurodivergent people, as well as Black, Brown, queer, and chronically ill people, seeking to use terms that emerge out of self-advocacy movements and honor the identities and humanity of disabled people. Some people, for instance, many Deaf people, do not identify as disabled, and may prefer to identify by other terms more specific to their communities or diagnoses. In this volume, we also err on the side of self-identification. We let disabled people choose and explain the terms they most identify with to honor diversity of experience and hopefully increase understanding and dialogue. Finally, we don't discriminate against or evaluate people's disabilities. Rather, if people want to be included in this volume, they are! This is important because especially in America, disabled people continue to be disadvantaged in terms of economic status and health. Someone may not have the resources to get a formal diagnosis from a medical professional or get the support they need from healthcare or social services. Disabled youth, especially because they're still growing and learning about themselves, also may not have formal diagnoses.

The field of **disability theology** has been instructive in critiquing some of the passages of the Bible and other religious texts that show that disabled people were prohibited from leadership in religious communities and shunned for fear that their disabilities stemmed from sin. Instead, disability theology emphasizes the goodness in the variety of who and what God has created, charging religious communities with not only extending welcome but also opportunities for ministry and leadership to all people, including disabled people. Although human beings have fallen short in terms of discrimination against disabled people and systems of power that exclude them, our understanding of God's boundless love offers a strong corrective and charge to our present communities.

In addition to teaching about our religious texts in our communities, we hope this volume gives youth workers the tools to teach disabled youth about the compelling history of innovation, justice work, and advocacy that we can see in the social model of disability, the disabled rights movement, the disability justice moment, the neurodiversity movement, chronic illness activism, mental health activism, and the formation of the fields of disability studies and critical disability studies, just to name a few. One reason we, alongside disability activists, embrace the term disability is because it both highlights and resists prejudice. Our understanding of disability, the world we live in, and the world we seek to create, is shaped by disabled people, whose insights we seek to lift up in this volume. We hope youth come to see themselves as fearfully and wonderfully made in God's image and empowered by the legacy and activism of disabled people who have risked it all so that they can be free!

PART 1

LAMENT

A PRAYER OF CONFESSION

RILEY PICKETT[1]

(From the perspective of a queer person pastoring an incarcerated population)

God of Grace,
Each of us in this particular space now offers to you our particular wounds and regrets and mistakes. The things we wish we had done differently, or better, or the things we wish had never happened at all. We place in your tender, loving care our deepest pain and places of shame within us.
May you remind us that we are so much more than our worst mistakes.
We are your children, holy and beloved, and nothing in all of creation can separate us from your unconditional love.
Lord, have mercy upon us. Lord, help us to internalize your grace even as it's beyond comprehension. Work with us and within us to transform more and more into the people you've called us to be in this hurting world.
Amen.

BECOMING UNMASKED

Autistic but Still Worthy in God's Eyes

AVERY WILLIAMS

> ***Guiding Question:*** *How can discovering your own* ***Autism*** *be liberating, freeing you to be who God made you to be?*

My name is Avery Danae Williams. I am an Autistic student at Princeton University, majoring in African American studies with a minor in creative writing. I'm also a multipublished writer with a particular focus on Black **disability studies** and a proud member of Princeton Presbyterians' Undergraduate Leadership Team.

To be honest, I avoided identifying as Autistic at first. I do not fit the stereotype of a "typical" Autistic person: a White, male child. As a Black, female young adult, I was nineteen years old when I discovered I was Autistic. The late discovery answered many lifelong questions: *Why do I misunderstand social cues? Why do I eat the same foods every week? Why do l use comfort objects, like stuffed animals, to soothe myself?*

However, a doctor could choose not to diagnose me because I'm too hard working to be Autistic. For instance, I kept myself busy in high school with Honors/AP classes and extracurricular activities, which caused me to burn out from excessive **masking.** Devon Price, author of *Unmasking Autism,* defines masking as "attempting to hide . . . Autistic traits in order to 'blend in' with [Neurotypical people]."[1]

Besides staying up late to do schoolwork, I ignored my sensory needs. This was especially the case during the pandemic.

Being on camera made me dread going to church. It's worth noting that before the pandemic, my Baptist church in Somerset, New Jersey, was hybrid, although most people went in person. But since my family often lived far from church, we would watch church online. The year 2020, however, marked the first time that *every* program was virtual. I enjoyed tuning into the online services. My pastor couldn't see who was watching, so I was able to unmask (reveal my Autistic behaviors) more easily.[2] I could use fidget tools. I could doodle to focus. I could even log off without anybody noticing. There are roughly five thousand members of my home church, so it was easy to hide behind the screen. Besides, I needed a break from performing on camera seven hours a day, five days a week for school.

My Sunday wasn't over yet, though. I had to log into Zoom Sunday School for an hour. Before dividing us into breakout rooms by class, our Sunday School director had approximately all one hundred students and teachers in the main room. We would go over church announcements. But it was overstimulating because many kindergarteners kept making noises. They didn't know any better; they wanted to have fun. And I wish I had fun understanding these social cues. Zoom fatigue, or exhaustion from back-to-back video calls, was clearly unacceptable.

When we were in our breakout room, my Senior High teachers would repeat, "Put your cameras on! We want to see you; otherwise, you'll be marked absent!" I reluctantly obliged, feigning eye contact and comfort. The more I masked, the more I felt a **meltdown** coming on. So I turned off my camera halfway through.

A meltdown is an Autistic person's intense response to stressful situations, like sensory overload.[3] We often can't control it; the best course of action is to ride out the emotional distress. Despite wanting to scream, sob, and thrash on the floor, I declined the ride; I didn't want to disappoint God for not pushing through my discomfort.

"Avery, can you turn your camera on and share your thoughts on the Prodigal Son?" one of my teachers asked.

"I . . . I don't like being on camera. It makes me very uncomfortable," I said, my voice trembling.

"Okay, no problem," he said.

Hallelujah, I thought. *I'm out of the woods.* That is, until my teachers kept asking me every week to turn my camera on.

Weeks passed, and I stopped logging into virtual Sunday School. I even stopped watching our virtual church service. How could I feel worthy in God's eyes when I was Autistic? I didn't want Him to be mad, reminding me that my sensory needs burdened Neurotypical people (or so I thought). Still, I craved a church community to safely unmask.

Enter Princeton Presbyterians, a progressive, inclusive faith community on Princeton's campus. I first heard about it while working as a Community Action Fellow with the Pace Center for Civic Engagement, where I planned an arts education-based orientation program for the Class of 2027. I knew a lot of the prospective orientation leaders, either from having class together or belonging to the same residential college. I was surprised that one of my coworkers knew one of the students, who did improv comedy with my next-door neighbor. When I learned that all three of them belonged to Princeton Presbyterians, I was intrigued. I still felt nervous that I would go to church and God would be mad at me for my long absence. But at least I could come to church knowing some people. My coworker agreed to bring me to Breaking Bread Worship that Sunday night.

I walked into Nassau Presbyterian Church prepared to meet God's wrath. That all changed when our chaplains, Andrew and Len Scales, welcomed me with open arms. Andrew asked me about my **special interest** in writing. In the Autistic community, a special interest is an intense focus on a particular topic to help us "recharge away from an overwhelming world."[4] Len invited me to go to the Bent Spoon (an ice cream shop on Nassau Street) with her; this way, she could get to know me better. I was pleasantly surprised at the personal attention. After all, I was used to being a number in my home church.

I gradually unmasked more at Breaking Bread. Unlike the blinding blue light radiating from Zoom, the lighting in Niles Chapel was partially dim and easier on my eyes. Plus, we sing several hymns during Breaking Bread. Repeated singing helps me regulate my emotions. I am now the "Rest Guru" on the Undergraduate Leadership Team, and I helped Andrew and Len organize our annual Oasis, a sensory space for students to decompress with baked goods, adult coloring books, and lovely conversations during midterms week. The event was a success. Students left feeling rejuvenated, and I felt joy knowing I could lift some weight off their shoulders.

Reflecting on my two years with Princeton Presbyterians, I realize that God was never mad at me. He wanted me to embrace being Autistic so I could get my sensory needs met at church. And for the first time in a long time, I can say that my relationship with God is stronger than ever.

THREE QUESTIONS OR THINGS I WISH ADULTS WOULD ASK OR SAY TO DISABLED YOUTH

1. Since discovering that you are Autistic, what resources have been helpful?
2. How has being a part of a young adult ministry shaped your Autistic identity?
3. What advice would you give an Autistic young adult wanting to unmask at church?

WHERE BELONGING ABOUNDS

Youth Ministry and Developmental Disability

ERIK W. CARTER

> ***Guiding Question:*** *How might we create communities of* ***belonging*** *for* every *member of the body?*

Amari never felt as though she belonged. She was included fully in the learning and relationship opportunities available throughout her middle school, but it was an altogether different story at church. The ministry model at Northside Church meant Amari was served in a separate program with five other teenagers and adults with intellectual disabilities. No one knew her name or story beyond a few ministry volunteers and "buddies." Although she longed to attend the fall and summer youth retreats, the selected locations were never accessible to someone who used a motorized wheelchair. Despite having deep interest, Amari was never asked to serve or invited to lead. Indeed, her fellow congregants prayed for her more than with her. Why isn't it otherwise?

AMPLIFYING STORIES

As a researcher, I think of myself as a gatherer of stories. These stories are often shared during interviews with youth with **developmental disabilities** and their families, where our conversations explore their experiences in and hopes for the church. Other times they emerge through surveys, where youth and families convey what has been most helpful or hard in their journeys. Our research discerns the patterns that cut across these myriad church stories.

And then we share back what we've learned in ways that we hope honor their experiences and invite a faithful response from the church.

With these stories in mind, this chapter highlights several themes from our research:

- Faith is significant in the lives of most youth with developmental disabilities, even if expressed in unique or unanticipated ways.[1]
- Large numbers of youth with developmental disabilities participate in spiritual practices at home, such as prayer, listening to religious music, and encountering scripture through reading or listening.[2]
- Their involvement in the everyday life of the church, however, can be limited. Only one-quarter of young people with developmental disabilities participate regularly in a youth group and far fewer attend youth retreats or participate in service activities.[3]
- Barriers of accessibility, attitude, and awareness are prominent in many churches.[4] Moreover, the ways churches typically gather, teach, preach, and connect can inadvertently exclude youth with developmental disabilities.
- Many ministry leaders are unaware of these barriers or feel uncertain about how to address them.[5]
- One in three families whose children have developmental disabilities have left their churches because their children were not welcomed or included.[6]
- Although a longing for belonging resides in every young person, it may be amplified among youth with developmental disabilities for whom belonging is rarely assured.[7]

DIMENSIONS OF BELONGING

Churches should be places of belonging for *every* youth, including those with disabilities. While this aspiration is easy to affirm, it is challenging to live out. Nearly one million youth with developmental disabilities reside in neighborhoods across the United States.[8] Despite their deep desire to participate fully in their communities, the opportunities and support needed for them to do so remain rare. As a result, many youth are excluded from the life and fellowship they long to experience.

What might it mean for churches to be places of belonging for youth with developmental disabilities? What practices and postures could help congregations move faithfully in this direction? To address these questions, I draw upon the insights of hundreds of young people with developmental disabilities and their families who have shared their stories through our research.

When we asked them what belonging looks and feels like, ten themes resounded.[9] These ten dimensions of belonging resemble a roadmap for churches—guideposts in the journey from exclusion to embrace. I unpack these important dimensions in this chapter, addressing why they matter and suggesting practical ways to respond. As you read, I encourage you to reflect on your ministry's practices and postures using the tool on pages 31–33. For each area, consider these four questions: *What is your church doing really well right now? How do you know? What could be approached better or differently? What next steps make the most sense for your church at this time?*

Included

Youth with developmental disabilities should be actively involved in the breadth of activities and events that make up the life of your church, from worship services to Wednesday night gatherings, from small groups to service projects. *To be included is to have a presence in the everyday life of one's church.* It is hard for any youth to feel that they belong if they are never or rarely there, always observing from the outside in.

Most studies examining the presence of youth with disabilities in their churches portray something other than inclusion.[10] A constellation of barriers can prevent or limit participation. Common examples include the inaccessibility of spaces, the absence of invitations, the attitudes of congregants, the insufficiency of supports, challenges with transportation, a dismissal of experiences, or a shortage of imagination.

Reflect on the presence of youth with disabilities throughout your church and its programs or ministries. *What barriers might still need to be addressed? What preparation is still needed? Are you including youth with disabilities* fully *in your faith community?*

Invited

The antidote to absence is invitation. *To be invited is to be sought out and summoned by someone else.* One avenue through which churches already invite their community is through websites, social media accounts, and outreach materials. The choice of words, images, commitments, and other information featured in these places signal to disabled youth and their families whether you anticipate their presence. But personal invitations can be even more impactful than mere announcements. Reaching out directly to youth and families to encourage involvement sends a powerful message: *We need you here. Your presence matters. It just wouldn't be the same without you.*

Unfortunately, invitations remain rare for youth with developmental disabilities. A national study revealed that one-quarter (25 percent) of youth with intellectual disability, more than half (51 percent) of autistic youth, and nearly one-third (30 percent) of youth with physical disabilities had *never* been invited to social activities with peers during the past year.[11] Consider how your church might foster a culture of intentional invitation. Encourage youth leaders and church members to reach out to disabled peers and their families. Few churches reference disability or neurodiversity on their websites, nor do they mention support and accommodations available at church. Seek guidance to refine your messaging to be more inclusive and welcoming.

Welcomed

To be welcomed is to be received with authentic delight. It is an experience communicated not only through individual actions and attitudes, but also through the overarching culture and commitments of a community. In other words, welcome is both heard and felt. Simple gestures such as greeting youth by name, listening attentively, connecting them to peers, encouraging their involvement, asking about their week or their interests, celebrating their milestones, learning their preferences, and rejoicing in their presence contribute to creating an atmosphere of genuine acceptance.

The measure of a welcoming environment is not determined solely by the perceptions of those already present, but also by the experiences of those who have not yet arrived. A church may seem welcoming to youth who attend regularly, but has it considered how it feels to those who are new or hesitant to join? Ask youth with developmental disabilities what feels welcoming and what does not. Seek input from those who have left, those who haven't yet arrived, and those who are just beginning to get involved. Welcoming is a dynamic and ongoing effort that requires listening, learning, and adapting to meet the needs of every young person.

Known

To be known is to be understood and appreciated for who you are. It might be evident when people get your jokes, appreciate your quirks, remember your birthday, and can pray specifically about what is really going on in your life. But being known goes beyond mere familiarity. It means recognizing every person as an image bearer, someone of infinite worth. We are to see one another as God sees us—as beautiful, wonderfully made, very good, and called by name.

Youth with developmental disabilities are often known in incomplete or narrow ways. Prevailing views of disability in both the culture and the church portray people primarily in terms of what they cannot do or struggle to do, reducing their identity to a set of "challenges" or "deficits."[12] This is an incomplete way of knowing someone, which flattens the rich and multidimensional portrait of who they are.[13] Like anyone else, youth with developmental disabilities have interests, passions, preferences, personalities, strengths, virtues, and hopes that can enrich and enliven any faith community. However, coming to know them well requires time, attentiveness, and intentionality. It involves asking good questions, truly listening to their answers, noticing their ways of being, accompanying them over time, and learning their stories.

Accepted

Proclamations that "all are welcome" must come without exceptions or qualifiers. *To be accepted is to be embraced just as you are, not as others expect you to be.* Acceptance is sustained by a posture of flexibility, openness, and curiosity—a willingness to adapt and to see the value in doing things differently. Acceptance is evident when a youth group delights in the many ways its members participate, communicate, learn, and lead. It involves recognizing that diversity is an asset that enriches the entire community. Our acceptance must mirror God's: unconditional and expansive.

Yet attitudes about developmental disabilities within churches are often disheartening.[14] The broader culture promotes a hierarchy of bodies, minds, and ways of being in the world, and Christians too often follow suit. Whether unintentionally or overtly, inclusion is often made contingent on being able to communicate, behave, participate, move, or contribute in particular ways. Such attitudes—which can manifest through wounding remarks, judgmental stares, refused support, revoked invitations, denied membership, or referrals to other spaces—can lead to exclusion. In contrast, our attitudes should be different from the world around us. No one should ever wonder whether they belong in our ministries; exclusion is never the way of Jesus.

Addressing **ableism** and attitudinal barriers requires sustained effort. Churches can start by promoting awareness of the obstacles youth encounter within their walls. Offer training and education for ministry leaders and volunteers to build understanding and empathy. Reflect together on your assumptions, language, theology, and practices, ensuring they align with God's vision of inclusion. And celebrate the ways youth with disabilities already contribute to the life of the church, recognizing that their presence is not only welcome but essential.

Supported

The need for support is a universal human experience; no person is meant to navigate life alone. Support for one another should be abundant within the body of Christ and throughout every youth ministry. *To be supported is to receive the assistance needed to participate in meaningful and valued ways.* Youth with developmental disabilities can benefit from a variety of supports—rides to events, accessible materials, help from peers, the right technology, multiple options for participating, or flexibility in expectations. The right support makes participation possible; its absence often leads to exclusion.

Unfortunately, churches inconsistently offer the depth of support youth with developmental disabilities need to participate fully.[15] In our study of congregational inclusion for these youth, parents consistently highlighted a disconnect between the support their child needed and what churches provided.[16] For example, only 18 percent of their churches offered support during religious education, only 15 percent assisted with transportation, and only 11 percent developed individualized support plans for youth with disabilities. These gaps often stem from concerns about costs or capacity, uncertainty about how to offer support, or, most commonly, a failure to ask the right questions.[17]

Good support requires both proactive and individualized approaches.[18] A **universal design** approach anticipates the types of support all youth might need and integrates these into standard practices. This could involve thoughtfully choosing activities, materials, or curricula that allow diverse youth to engage and learn in multiple ways. A responsive design approach builds upon universal design by providing individualized supports tailored to the needs of specific youth. For example, meeting with a young person with developmental disabilities and their family to discuss what kinds of assistance are most important—and when and where they are needed—ensures the support offered is valued and effective.

Heard

To be heard means that others seek out, understand, and value your viewpoint. Being part of a community that yearns to hear your voice fosters a deep sense of belonging. Like anyone else, youth with developmental disabilities want to be noticed, to have a seat at the table, to be acknowledged, to share their opinions, and to influence decisions. Listening to them is more than an act of empowerment. It is a recognition of their God-given dignity and inherent value.

Too often, the perspectives of youth with developmental disabilities are overlooked or dismissed in the church and beyond. Decisions are made for them rather than with or by them. Their insights are undervalued or their voices are silenced. Listening well requires intentionality and patience. It involves paying close attention to the varied ways someone communicates, whether through words, signs, facial expressions, actions, technology, or other means. While some youth can articulate their thoughts verbally, others use alternative ways of expressing themselves. Whenever perspectives are needed, advice is sought, opinions are offered, and stories are shared, make sure youth with developmental disabilities are heard.

Befriended

Peer relationships hold a prominent place in the lives of adolescents. Indeed, the link between **friendships** and flourishing among youth is well documented.[19] *To be befriended means enjoying peer relationships marked by mutual affection and investment.* It involves having people in your life who regularly say, "I choose you back."[20] Friendships should be abundant in the lives of all youth. Belonging grows in the soil of friendship.

Even amid increased inclusion, friendships have remained elusive for many youth with developmental disabilities. A national study revealed that only 42 percent of youth with intellectual disabilities, 29 percent of autistic youth, and 36 percent of youth with physical disabilities got together with friends at least weekly.[21] So many factors can limit opportunities for friendships to form: attitudes that hinder peers from pursuing relationships, segregated ministries that keep some youth from encountering one another, expectations that prioritize learning over relationships, or transportation and communication challenges that keep youth from connecting between Sundays.

Efforts to foster friendship should permeate youth ministry. Ensure that youth with developmental disabilities are invited and supported to participate in every program, event, or gathering your ministry offers. Take time to learn about their hobbies, fascinations, and backgrounds, and intentionally introduce them to peers who share common interests. Foster opportunities for all youth, with and without disabilities, to connect deeply through serving, learning, and worshiping together. Building these bridges can transform your ministry into a place where friendships can flourish for everyone.

Needed

Every person has God-given gifts that make them indispensable in the body of Christ. Youth with developmental disabilities are never an exception to this truth. Their perspectives, passions, strengths, character, talents, and time are needed for the flourishing of the whole community. *To be needed is to be regarded as an integral member of a community, someone whose absence creates a noticeable void.*

Most churches struggle to recognize their need for youth with developmental disabilities. Although a growing number of churches are establishing new ministries *for* these youth, far fewer are supporting ministry *by* these youth.[22] Youth with developmental disabilities should have the same opportunities to contribute and lead as other youth. They might join the choir, read scripture, share their testimony, comfort the discouraged, pray with others, visit the sick, assist their friends, participate in mission trips, reach out to the lonely, or volunteer in the community. As your church seeks to welcome, know, and befriend youth with developmental disabilities, take time to uncover their unique gifts. Then intentionally identify ways those gifts can enrich your ministries and bless the broader community. When churches actively seek out and celebrate the contributions of all members, they model the mutual interdependence of the body of Christ.

Loved

Above all, we are called to be people who love well. Youth with developmental disabilities should never doubt that they are deeply loved by God and by others in their church. *To be loved is to receive the sacrificial and unconditional outpouring of others who deeply desire your flourishing.* Love is the foundation of belonging and the thread that weaves together all the other nine dimensions discussed previously.

Some Considerations

Each of these ten dimensions of belonging highlights actions and attitudes that can lead toward belonging. But a few considerations are important. First, this is not an exhaustive list of what youth with developmental disabilities and their families shared with us in our research (or might share with you). We also heard about the importance of being noticed, appreciated, safe, cared for, respected, trusted, at ease, celebrated, and more. Although the ten themes featured in this chapter were particularly prominent, there may be more that matter. Second, there is no sure-fire recipe for fostering belonging. Youth will vary in the importance they place on each of these areas at particular times, in particular places, and with particular people. This is not an equation but rather an exploration; it is more art than science. Third, belonging is reciprocal. Youth with developmental disabilities should be included, but they should also contribute to including others, welcoming others, befriending others, loving others. Indeed, youth with developmental disabilities can be instrumental in fostering the belonging of their peers. Fourth, these ten dimensions of belonging have similar salience for *every* youth in your ministry, not merely those who are disabled. Belonging is not a special need; every youth longs to belong. The primary difference is that these ten dimensions of belonging tend to be more elusive for youth who have been marginalized and excluded.

MOVING FROM BARRIERS TO BELONGING

What does it mean for churches to be places of belonging for youth with developmental disabilities? This chapter explored this critical question, drawing upon the insights of those who have experienced both exclusion and inclusion within their faith communities. By examining each dimension of belonging and reflecting on your own ministry's practices, you can embark on a journey of intentional action, striving to create a truly welcoming and inclusive community for all youth.

Nila knew things could (and should) be different at Northside Church. As the new youth pastor, she was eager to remove barriers to belonging and create a ministry in which every member knew they mattered. She began by meeting individually with each of the youth and their families, including Amari and her mom, to learn their stories, hear their hopes, and invite their insights. Nila also convened a small team of congregation and community members to reflect together on their ministry models and prevailing practices. Working together with the youth, they celebrated what was working well and prioritized several areas that needed new approaches. Over the next few months, the youth group explored creative ways of worshiping, learning, praying, and serving that were more accessible and engaging for everyone. Nila also strived to connect each youth to the opportunities and support they needed to grow in their faith and friendships. As these changes took hold, Amari experienced church in a whole new way. She still beams when talking about the fun she had on her first youth retreat with friends. With equal enthusiasm, her friends are quick to share how much they needed Amari's presence, humor, prayers, and insights. It just wouldn't be the same without her.

REFLECTION QUESTIONS

1. What does belonging mean to you?
2. What barriers keep youth from experiencing these ten dimensions of belonging?
3. To what extent are believing and belonging prioritized together? How might they contribute to each other?

PRACTICAL TOOL: REFLECTING ON BELONGING IN YOUTH MINISTRY

Dimensions of Belonging	What are we doing **really well** right now?	How do we **know**?	What could we be doing **better** or **differently**?	What should we begin **doing next**?
Included Are youth involved in the experiences and events that are important to and for them?				
Invited Is their presence actively sought out by peers and others in the church?				
Welcomed Are youth experiencing a warm and enthusiastic welcome whenever they arrive?				
Known Are youth known personally and for the strengths and gifts they possess?				

Dimensions of Belonging	What are we doing **really well** right now?	How do we **know**?	What could we be doing **better** or **differently**?	What should we begin **doing next**?
Accepted Are youth received graciously and unconditionally?				
Supported Are youth receiving any assistance needed to participate fully and meaningfully?				
Heard Are their preferences and perspectives being sought on issues that matter?				
Befriended Are youth developing and deepening their relationships with peers?				

Dimensions of Belonging	What are we doing **really well** right now?	How do we **know**?	What could we be doing **better** or **differently**?	What should we begin **doing next**?
Needed Are their talents, gifts, and contributions drawn upon and celebrated?				
Loved Are youth experiencing the deep and unconditional love of others?				

MENTAL HEALTH JUSTICE

Youth Ministry as Suicide Prevention

SARAH GRIFFITH LUND

CONTENT WARNING: SUICIDE

> ***Guiding Question:*** *How can youth ministry be suicide prevention?*

"I am about to do a new thing; now it springs forth, do you not perceive it? I will make a way in the wilderness and rivers in the desert" (Isa. 43:18–19 NRSV). These words of hope from scripture guide us as we create new ways of faithfully ministering to youth that are relevant, meaningful, and lifesaving. Adolescence is a time of emotional, spiritual, and psychological wilderness. What is God saying to the church about the opportunities for us to engage in youth ministry, creating a river of life flowing in the desert of mental health experiences such as depression and anxiety?

I am a disability and **mental health justice** advocate, family advocate, local church pastor, and suicide loss survivor. Our family experienced the tragic death of my sixteen-year-old niece Sydney in the fall of 2020. At a young age, Sydney became our family musician. I've never heard anyone play the ukulele as she did. One time at our great-aunt Joan's funeral in Florida, at the age of thirteen, Sydney spontaneously left the church and went to the car to get her ukulele. Following the memorial service, she came into the retirement community lunch reception and played her ukulele for everyone. We miss Sydney's energetic spirit, her vibrant curiosity about the world around her, and her generous heart. She had an invisible mental health condition, yet at the time we didn't have the tools to understand and best support her needs.

In the aftermath of Sydney's death, I created two resources to help the church, families, and youth break the silence about mental health and suicide: *Blessed Youth,* for adult readers, and the *Blessed Youth Survival Guide,* a booklet for teens with a safety plan to prevent suicide. Working together with children, teens, families, schools, and community partners, the church can be a source of hope and healing.

But **mental health disabilities** and mental health diagnoses that can be considered disabilities, such as attention deficit hyperactivity disorder (ADHD), are often hidden in plain sight. This is because of a "**double stigma**" related to mental health and disability. The double stigma makes the relationship between the two things invisible or causes youth to mask their needs. This is a complex challenge to address because the two issues, mental health and disability, are interwoven. Not all mental health diagnoses lead to mental health disabilities, yet many can. It depends on the individual and the way the diagnosis impacts the person's life. The heightened risk for suicide for disabled youth is not because of the disability itself but because of stigma. **Ableism** blames disabilities; however, what is truly at fault is how disability and mental health symptoms are stigmatized in society. For a person whose mental health reality creates experiences of disability, the stigma and ableism they experience cause them to be at higher risk for suicide. According to the National Alliance on Mental Illness, half of all lifetime mental health conditions and disabilities begin to manifest by age fourteen.[1] This means that teens in youth group are part of the key demographic to experience mental health symptoms that could lead to a diagnosis.

BREAKING THE SILENCE AND ENDING THE STIGMA

United Church of Christ pastor Rachael Keefe is an advocate for disabilities and mental health justice and author of the book *The Lifesaving Church: Faith Communities and Suicide Prevention.*[2] She writes about her personal experience surviving a suicide attempt as a youth:

> When I was 15, I was suicidal and no one knew until I engaged in suicidal behavior that landed me in the hospital. . . . After the crisis passed, people encouraged me to not to talk about . . . the struggle I continued to have with suicidal thoughts and feelings, or about the eating disorder that continued for years after I appeared to be healthy . . . Learning to talk about symptoms

> of mental illness and addictions and the feelings that contribute to suicidality is necessary for individuals and congregations if we want to follow what Jesus taught—or, perhaps more importantly, we want to embody Christ in a way that saves lives.[3]

Rachael was born with both physical and learning disabilities that were not identified until adulthood. She says her disabilities contributed to her sense of inadequacy as a youth because she was expected to do what everyone else could do, but without accommodations and support she ended up feeling stressed out. These feelings of inadequacy were a factor in her suicide attempt as a teen.

As part of my research for this chapter, I interviewed Rachael in her role as a person who survived a suicide attempt and who also identifies as **queer** and disabled. I asked Rachael to tell me about disability as a risk factor for suicide and what the role of the church is in suicide prevention for disabled youth. She said there is an "unspoken theology that says disability is a curse of God. A suspicion of being somehow cursed or judged or punished by God informs our way of being in the world." These unspoken toxic theologies contribute to the shame and stigma of disability in the church.

In our conversation, I shared with Rachael my dismay that the 2024 national strategy for suicide prevention, updated for diversity, lacked inclusion of disability as a risk factor. She replied, "Policies in terms of disability don't change because of these unexamined beliefs. No suicide prevention strategy will be successful until it includes positive and inclusive theology of suicidality, disability and mental health." What would it look like for the church's commitment to **disability justice** to create momentum for advocacy both inside and outside of the church?

LAMENTING THE EPIDEMIC OF YOUTH SUICIDE

According to Surgeon General Vivek H. Murthy's report:[4]

- Suicide is one of the ten leading causes of death in the United States.
- Suicide claimed more than 47,500 lives in 2019.
- From 1999 to 2019, the national rate of suicide increased 32 percent.

- From 2008 to 2017, visits to the emergency department related to suicidal ideation or suicide attempts increased among all age groups.

Within the national crisis of suicide, specifically impacting youth, the numbers ring alarm bells:

- Suicide is the second leading cause of death among people five to twenty-four years old in the United States.
- Suicide rates for this age group increased 52.2 percent between 2000 and 2021.
- Youth and young adults have high rates of emergency department (ED) visits for self-harm.
- The rate of ED visits among girls in 2020 was approximately double compared to 2001.
- In 2021, 9 percent of high school students reported attempting suicide during the previous twelve months.

Yet, missing from this national research and data about youth suicide is the correlation between disability and suicide. Even within the US Surgeon General Vivek H. Murthy's 2024 Call to Action, there is no mention of disability as a reality that makes people at higher risk for suicide, even though university studies are beginning to highlight disability as a key factor. There is more work to do on national suicide prevention strategies when disabled people remain invisible over thirty-five years since the **Americans with Disabilities Act (ADA)** was signed into law. Working to destigmatize disability and mental health conditions can help prevent suicide because with less stigma there will be less pressure to hide these experiences of thoughts of suicide.

The movement that inspired the passage of the ADA also impacted Christian communities longing for greater inclusion. Disability scholar, advocate, and author Nancy Eiesland says, "The liberatory impulse evidenced in the **disability rights movement** has propelled people with disabilities to resist their marginal status in the full range of social institutions, including the Christian church."[5] Eiesland calls for the church to take a leading role in promoting the full humanity of people with disabilities. How might God be calling you and your faith community to join the movement for mental health and disability justice, focusing on removing the stigma?

MENTAL HEALTH DISABILITIES

According to the Center for Disease Control (CDC), the most common mental health realities diagnosed in childhood are ADHD, anxiety, and **depression.**[6] The CDC also reports that youth who experience adverse childhood experiences are at higher risk for experiencing mental health symptoms. Risk factors also include racial/ethnic discrimination. Racism creates stress and trauma for those experiencing discrimination, leading to higher risk for mental health diagnoses.[7] As Christians, we are invited to work to advocate for justice at the places of intersectionality, such as racial justice, mental health justice, and disability justice

Masking is the practice of covering up one's disability. Masking is a coping mechanism to avoid shame and discrimination. This can happen more easily for disabilities that are "invisible," such as mental health diagnoses like ADHD. My niece Syndney experienced stigma related to her ADHD, so she tried to mask at school to fit in and make friends. Yet, masking also makes it harder to get support. Moreover, ADHD symptoms look different among different racial/ethnic/gendered populations and can be misinterpreted. According to a Stanford report, ADHD impacts 7 percent of youth globally and includes symptoms such as difficulty concentrating, paying attention, and remembering details.[8] According to the CDC, ADHD diagnoses among youth have increased over the last decade:[9] Today, nearly one out of every ten youth in the United States is diagnosed with ADHD, an increase also reflected in other nations. This makes ADHD the most common mental health condition among children worldwide.[10] This means we can make the educated guess that our youth ministry will likely include youth with ADHD as well.

Youth with ADHD, like my niece Syndey, have increased risk of suicidal thoughts, suicide attempts, and death by suicide. Within adult populations, research shows that people with an ADHD diagnosis are five times more likely than those without to have experience the risk of suicide. One in four women with ADHD experience the risk of suicide.[11] One study of youth with ADHD found that several factors of ADHD led to increased risk of suicide: interpersonal, academic, and societal challenges; the impact of internal processes such as rumination and emotional dysregulation; and challenges in self-acceptance and self-stigma.[12] Here we see evidence that stigma is a risk factor in suicide for youth.

ADHD is an example of how a common mental health diagnosis can also be experienced as a disability, especially without adequate supports and accommodations. In the context of disability, ADHD can impact a person's ability to engage in meaningful social relationships, experience satisfaction at school, and access the support resources they need to succeed. When considering the high suicide risk of youth with ADHD, we can see how disability is one of the risk factors for youth suicide. But when we destigmatize mental health conditions, creating environments where it is safe to take off the mask, we can perceive diagnoses like ADHD for what they are: disabilities that require resources, support, and accommodations to ensure equal opportunities for flourishing.

DISABILITY AND SUICIDE PREVENTION

To create a culture of suicide prevention in ministering to youth, we need to understand that suicidal thoughts and behaviors are a complex interplay of biological, clinical, psychological, and social factors.[13] We also need to accept the fact that experiencing thoughts of suicide is more common, and not only are youth more willing to talk about it, but we also need to break the silence about suicide in order to save lives. In one case study of disabled high school students in Wisconsin in 2012, results showed that disabled youth were three to nine times more likely to report a suicide attempt compared to their non-disabled peers. For students with multiple disabilities, their risk for suicide tripled compared to youth with single disabilities. The authors of this research propose that disability status added unique risk and may even be a "fundamental cause of suicidal behavior."[14] They call for a need for suicide screening and prevention efforts tailored to address the needs of disabled youth.

Another research project based in Kentucky highlighted that disabled youth experience greater stressors and face issues such as social isolation, discrimination, and ableism. Disabled youth experience higher levels of interpersonal problems, relationship stresses, and financial distress, which all increase risk for youth suicide. Disabled youth who also experience mental health diagnoses and addiction are also linked to suicide behaviors.[15]

BREAKING THE SILENCE ABOUT SUICIDE RISKS FOR DISABLED LGBTQ+ AND BIPOC YOUTH

Disabled youth who identify as queer and Black, Indigenous, and People of Color (**BIPOC**) face the highest risks for suicide. BIPOC and queer youth are most affected by high levels of hopelessness, sadness, loneliness, and suicidal ideation. In 2022, Black youth suicide rates increased 36.6 percent, with Black adolescent girls experiencing the highest increase in suicide attempts. The CDC reported that in 2022, 69 percent of queer students reported feelings of sadness and hopelessness.[16]

Psychologists report in the 2022 National Survey on LGBTQ+ Youth Mental Health that for BIPOC youth, a "national atmosphere of trauma and discrimination affect these young people's suicide risk."[17] The risk of suicide has increased for marginalized youth since the pandemic. The pandemic, mass school shootings, racial unrest, racially motivated hate crimes, anti-LGBTQ+ legislation, and bullying exacerbate the stresses, trauma, and fear youth experience. Experts suggest that adults engage youth in conversations to invite them to voice how these national crises impact them by asking, "What are you exposed to that really bothers you?" This is an excellent question for youth ministry conversations. The key is not only to ask the open-ended questions but to provide enough time and space to listen deeply to youth for their answers.

Youth ministry can be suicide prevention when it is a safe space for queer youth, or youth ministry can be a risk factor if it is not a safe space for queer youth. The Trevor Project, a nonprofit that focuses on suicide prevention in LGBTQ+ youth, identifies increased suicide attempts for youth who report their homes, schools, or churches are not accepting of their queer identities.[18] The risk for suicide is even higher for the 68 percent of disabled queer youth who feel discriminated against for their disabilities. Systemic and individual discrimination, or "minority stress," is frequently tied to higher rates of mental health symptoms, such as depression and anxiety, and experiencing suicidal thoughts among queer youth. Seventy-five percent of disabled queer youth report high levels of stress, 48 percent seriously considered suicide, and 19 percent engaged in suicidal activities.[19] From a theological viewpoint, we begin to understand the spiritual, emotional, psychological wilderness youth face when they experience discrimination and stigma simply for being themselves and how this leads to profound despair.

Viewing injustice, racism, homophobia, and ableism as societal risk factors for suicide focuses the conversation on how communities can combat discrimination as suicide prevention. Suicide experts say that a factor in the rising rates of suicide is that solutions only focus on the individual instead of the systems shaping society.[20] Suicide prevention strategies for queer and BIPOC youth should include getting involved in social movements and advocacy for justice to help increase sense of shared power, agency, and **belonging**. The church can support these efforts with resources and increased focus on community engagement as youth ministry.

FROM LAMENT TO SUICIDE PREVENTION AS VOCATIONAL CALLING IN YOUTH MINISTRY

While we **lament** the increasing rates of youth suicide, we also know that the still-speaking God is calling the church to be a beacon of hope. Youth ministry can shine a light on disabilities and cast out stigma and shame that leads to isolation and disconnection. Embracing youth and their disabilities creates an authentic sense of belonging and dismantles stigma. In the wilderness of shame, through the power of God's unconditional love, we find the river of life. Openly talking about the fears, stresses, and doubts youth face creates a sense of belonging and authentic connection when these emotions and thoughts are held with compassion and care. We create communities of authentic belonging, where it is okay to not be okay, and it is safe to take off the mask of perfectionism.

The first step for suicide prevention is safe messaging. Talking about suicide prevention does not make youth more predisposed to suicide; it helps destigmatize the topic. By creating a space to break the silence about suicide and focus on prevention and learning about risk factors, the church can save lives. There are training tools available through Mental Health First Aid Training that can provide support to adults facilitating these conversations. Youth ministry curriculum and programming can integrate a suicide prevention approach as central to what it means to live a Christ-centered life, create disciples, and save lives.

SUICIDE PREVENTION MODEL OF YOUTH MINISTRY

Key elements in suicide prevention also happen to be key elements of youth ministry: peer-to-peer support and creating a social safety net.[21] We can use the best practices of community suicide prevention and integrate them into youth ministry programs.

The church can help with suicide prevention by learning about tools based on scientific research about what causes suicide. The better educated we are about the multiple causes of suicide, the better we will help prevent it. There is a tool called the Integrated Motivational-Volitional Model of Suicidal Behavior (IMV) that helps us consider the complex and various factors that create the perfect storm of suicide.

According to the IMV, there are background factors and triggering events, and then three levels leading to a suicide death: base level, motivational level, and enactment level. The background factors and triggering events include genetics, personality factors, environment, and life events. Background factors also include identities such as being queer, BIPOC, and/or disabled. The base level includes feeling defeated and humiliated, which leads to feeling trapped, as well as challenges to regulating feelings because of lack of ability in social problem solving, coping, memory bias, and ruminating processes. The motivational level includes intention and levels of risk for suicide: thwarted belongingness, burdensomeness, future thoughts, goals, norms, resilience, social support, and attitudes. The last level, enactment level, includes access to means, planning, exposure to suicide, impulsivity, physical pain sensitivity, fearlessness about death, imagery, and past behavior.[22] Viewing the IMV through the lens of disability and mental health can help raise awareness of risk factors for disabled youth. Informed by this awareness we can intentionally design youth ministries to prevent suicide.

IMV background: When developing relationships with youth and their families, we can pay attention to their family histories of mental health symptoms and suicide, and to the levels of stress in their environments. We can create a culture where sharing the multiple identities of youth (queer, BIPOC, disabled, and/or mental health experiences) is safe. The inventory of adverse childhood experiences adapted for youth ministry could prove helpful. Youth ministry can be a place where life events are anticipated, shared, and supported within a caring community.

Base level: We can create a safe space for youth to express their feelings of defeat and humiliation, of failure and loneliness. Youth group can be a "brave authentic space" where shame is lifted from these common human experiences. Adult leaders can model this behavior through their own ability to break the silence about their experiences with defeat and humiliation. Youth group activities can also explore problem solving and positive coping mechanisms to apply for when youth are feeling defeated, humiliated, and stuck.

Motivational level: We can create a sense of belonging, create goals for individuals and the group, plan fun future activities that include them, emphasize social support with at least one authentic affirming connection, and practice an attitude of gratitude for the simple things in life. Youth ministry includes many of these functions without realizing it, so it is important to understand the value and significance of these activities as fundamental to suicide prevention. (See "Looking Forward Circle" practical tool on p. 44.)

Enactment level: Youth ministry can provide access to resources such as the 988 text/call lifeline, educate youth on the importance of reporting self and peer plans for suicide, emphasize safety related to guns and other lethal means, discuss the finality of death and the long-term pain and suffering caused to the family and loved ones from suicide and tragic death, and help youth create personal safety plans, such as the one in *Blessed Youth Survival Guide*.

Reducing access to lethal means is another crucial pathway to preventing youth suicide. Churches can help communities reduce lethal means by educating church members about gun safety and providing free gun locks. Disabled youth need to be included when it comes to gun safety because they are at risk as well.

The good news is that ministry with disabled youth is lifesaving. The congregation where I serve as pastor created our youth ministry guided by our commitment to suicide prevention using the principles I've shared here. We know of at least one case where a youth has been able to access live saving resources because of the tools they received in our youth group. Sharing God's love with youth means providing the supports disabled youth need to help prevent suicide.

We can learn from researchers in the field of suicide prevention and adapt proven life saving techniques to church youth ministry tools. This is an opportunity to destigmatize disability, mental health conditions, and suicide as we work to build a more just world for all.

REFLECTION QUESTIONS

1. Where have you or others you know experienced racism, homophobia, or ableism in your church or community? What steps can you take to combat these prejudices so that disabled youth feel safer and remove the stigma?
2. How can youth ministry be suicide prevention?
3. What additional resources, education, and tools does your church need to join God's movement for disability and mental health justice to save lives?

PRACTICAL TOOL: LOOKING FORWARD CIRCLE (10–15 MINUTES)

This group activity is based on suicide protective factors: (1) goals for the future, (2) a sense of belonging, (3) feeling appreciated, valued, and respected for the gifts they bring into community.

1. Sit in a circle and invite each youth to think about one thing they are looking forward to in the coming week. It can be anything! Take a couple of minutes to let them think about it. For multisensory and communication diversity options, have some paper and art supplies so the youth can also journal or color about it. Normalize having fidgets in the circle and encourage the youth to use them.
2. Share around the circle the one thing they are looking forward to for the coming week. Give each youth a couple of minutes to share. They can read from their journal, share the artwork they made, or talk about it.
3. Nothing to look forward to? For a youth who doesn't have anything they are looking forward to, ask them, "Is there something you are not looking forward to that you'd like to share about?" Allowing youth to share what is weighing on their minds helps them feel less isolated and alone in their distress and overwhelm.
4. Support youth who don't have anything they are looking forward to in the coming week. Seek out a conversation to follow up with them and make a plan to "look forward to connecting."
5. Keep track of patterns with youth. Youth who don't have something they are looking forward to on a regular basis are at increased risk of suicide. Reflect with the youth about what can be included in the experience of youth group or at church that this young person would look forward to.
6. Find a creative way to make youth group something all youth look forward to in their week. For youth at risk of suicide, youth group might be their only place of authentic social connection and belonging.

TOWARD DISABLED LEADERSHIP IN WORSHIP

Lamenting Loneliness and Cultivating Belonging with Princeton Presbyterians

ANDREW SCALES AND LEN SCALES

Guiding Question: *What gifts do disabled participants bring to the community?*

If you visit Princeton, New Jersey, during the academic year, you'll probably find us, Andrew and Len Scales, sitting in Small World Coffee or outside the Bent Spoon ice cream shop with students. These one-on-one pastoral care meetings often bring up familiar rhythms of university life: feeling overwhelmed by papers and exams, praying for a loved one who is ill, struggles with mental health, a painful breakup or the exciting start of a new relationship, celebration of a job offer or acceptance letter. We get to see students become excited about the stories of the Bible, imagine what the reign of God looks like today, and ask how service to others can remain a meaningful part of their lives after college.

After twelve years of working in campus ministry roles, we've also seen more difficult things that young people wrestle with during their student years. There have been visits to a local in-patient behavioral healthcare center and critical conversations about connecting with the university's Counseling and Psychological Services. Students have navigated the process of attaining academic accommodations for disabilities with varying degrees of success, leaving some relieved and others frustrated. We have lived through a global pandemic with our students and returned to fellowship in person.

What we have not been prepared for is the wave of loneliness and grief that has marked these early post-pandemic years. Surgeon General Dr. Vivek H. Murthy has described an "epidemic of loneliness" in the United States. The pandemic has exacerbated this crisis, but **COVID-19** was not its cause. According to a study released by Health and Human Services in 2023, "The rate of loneliness among young adults has increased every year between 1976 and 2019."[1] The Surgeon General's Advisory observes, "Although risk may differ across indicators of social disconnection, currently studies find the highest prevalence for loneliness and isolation among people with poor physical or mental health, disabilities, financial insecurity, those who live alone, single parents, as well as young and older populations."[2]

For young people who have lived through the pandemic and also live with a disability, the challenge of social disconnection amid a demanding academic program can be acute. Many of our students are also People of Color, some are the first members of their families to attend college, and they are struggling with their mental health. An April 2023 article in *The Daily Princetonian* student newspaper details the present mental health crisis that so many students face. For example, a quarter of the students who have died by **suicide** at Princeton since 1876 have died within the last decade.[3] Seventy-five percent of members of the Class of 2022 and 78 percent of the Class of 2023 have sought counseling or therapy during their undergraduate years.[4]

In 2018, board members, staff, and students developed mission and value statements for Princeton Presbyterians. The value statement *Joy and Hope* says, "Because the Spirit gives us courage in a broken and fearful world, we persevere in the truth that God's Word is Good News for us and for the world. We proclaim in our words and actions that human value is not measured by performance or productivity, but in the steadfast love of the God who made us."[5] For us, living out God's Good News as a campus ministry is a collaborative effort, meaning that the students who participate are not simply objects of ministry, as if our calling is only to do Christian ministry *to* and *for* young people. They are subjects who live out God's story of Good News in the world, shaping our life together through the gifts, insights, and hopes that they bring to the community.

When students become involved in Princeton Presbyterians, our hope is that they discover a sense of **belonging** just as they are. Breaking Bread is Princeton Presbyterians' weekly worship service where we see the most students on a regular basis, and it's a context where students and staff work together to adapt our worship services to become a more welcoming community. Through listening, learning, and adapting our practices from one week to the next, we are creating an alternative community to the dehumanizing narratives and demands of a campus culture that is obsessed with accomplishment.

For this chapter, we've chosen to focus on Breaking Bread, which meets on Sunday nights. What follows is a brief overview of how Princeton Presbyterians functions as a ministry, as well as some details about who participates in our programs and a narrative description of a particular Breaking Bread worship service from Fall 2024. Next, we reflect on how we develop worship services with influences from the Taizé Community. Finally, we offer questions for reflection and discussion for anyone who practices ministry with young people.

AN OVERVIEW OF THE PRINCETON PRESBYTERIANS CAMPUS MINISTRY

Princeton Presbyterians is a Presbyterian Church (USA) campus ministry that serves about seventy students at academic institutions throughout central New Jersey. Most of our students come from Princeton University and Princeton Theological Seminary, but we have also welcomed students from other local colleges and universities. In August 2023, Campus Minister Rosa Ross partnered with Princeton University Presbyterians to plant a campus ministry at The College of New Jersey (TCNJ) called UKirk Ewing, and she engages with about fifteen students regularly.

The Westminster Foundation is the Board of Trustees that oversees Princeton Presbyterians and UKirk Ewing. Along with the Board of Trustees, for the 2024–2025 academic year the leadership of the ministry includes Chaplains and Executive Co-Directors Len and Andrew Scales, Director of Music Megan Coiley, three student chaplains from Princeton Theological Seminary, nine undergraduate student leaders from Princeton University, and UKirk Ewing Minister Rosa Ross.

Grace Matthews, one of our undergraduate student leaders who graduated in 2022, coined the phrase "By Presbyterians, for everyone." To explain this phrase in practice, "Princeton Presbys" is one of two Christian campus ministries at Princeton University that celebrates the leadership of **queer** persons and women. Our students come from around the world and across the United States, and our community includes students who identify as Presbyterian, Catholic, Methodist, Episcopalian, Lutheran, Evangelical, Orthodox, and Jewish, as well as others who do not particularly identify with a faith tradition. We use the language of "progressive," "ecumenical," and "Reformed" in dynamic tension with one another. An image we return to often is the "Beloved Community" that African American civil rights leaders developed in the twentieth century.

Amid a busy academic year, Breaking Bread and the fellowship meal that follows are the anchor of each week. Thirty to forty-five students join us at Nassau Presbyterian Church from different schools. We sing, pray for one another, hear God's Word read and proclaimed, and share the Lord's Supper.

A NARRATIVE DESCRIPTION OF BREAKING BREAD

It's Sunday evening a few weeks into the fall semester, and the Princeton Presbyterians staff is puttering around Niles Chapel at Nassau Presbyterian Church in preparation for Breaking Bread. The worship space is an octagon designed in the austere Reformed style of American Presbyterian churches in the 1950s: cream walls, blue carpeting, and a freestanding panel of stained glass at the back. The gilt lettering of Romans 5:8 emblazons the top of the twenty-foot skylit ceiling. The furniture includes a piano on one side of the glass panel and a small organ at the other, as well as a simple table with a marble top, a slim wooden lectern, and an incongruously ornate baptismal font. There are no pews, and the walls are lined with stacks of blue-padded choir chairs.

We know from the summer wedding of graduate students Mike and Molly Brennan-Smith that Niles Chapel can fit fifty people "butts to butts." Our student chaplains Cece Machado, Taylor Silvestri, and Seunghyun Kim arrange the chairs into an oval with two sides, which manage to face each other and the Lord's Table. Director of Music Megan Coiley shuffles some papers at the piano and plays a few chords to warm up. Cece unfurls a large canvas that students painted three summers ago with swirls of green and sets it as our tablecloth. Taylor arranges a cobalt blue set of communion ware from the Taizé Community on the table with a loaf of vegan and gluten-free bread that the chaplains, Andrew and Len Scales, baked that afternoon. On a table in the hallway outside the chapel, Seunghyun sets out hymnals, bulletins, and magnetic name tags with students' names, **pronouns**, and little doodles they've drawn.

Once everything is ready, the six ministers sit in a circle, pray together, and talk through the order of worship one last time. Megan reminds us to use two-thirds of the lights in the chapel because an undergraduate student with **autism** feels uncomfortable in bright rooms. The softer overhead lighting and the candles that Len lights around the Lord's Table give the room a warm, fall feeling.

Suddenly it's almost 6:30 p.m., and thirty to forty-five students fill the chapel with laughter, cries of recognition, and murmurs of welcome to newcomers. Niles Chapel stands right next to an accessible hallway that opens to a ramp door facing the church parking lot. The *ca-chunk* of the outer door lets us know that more students are about to come up the hallway's incline plane and around the corner for worship.

A young adult patiently waits a few steps down the hallway until no one is standing by the chapel door. He grabs a hymnal, bulletin, and name tag from Taylor and finds a seat at a distance from others so that he can have more personal space. An undergrad with food allergies catches up with his buddy as he takes out a rice cake from his backpack so he can share in the Lord's Supper later. Cece helps a newcomer from TCNJ find the accessible, gender-neutral bathroom down the hallway.

A few minutes after 6:30, Andrew makes a meaningful nod across the room to Taylor. Taylor moves in front of the table and shouts "The Lord be with you!" and students shout back "And also with you!" They share announcements like a location change for Monday's Small Group and remind folks that there's dinner with vegan and gluten-free options just down the hall after worship.

As Taylor takes their seat, Megan moves to the front and leads everyone acapella in singing a brief hymn from South Korea called "Come Now, O Prince of Peace." Avery Williams, a member of our undergraduate student leadership team, and whose youth perspective is featured in this volume, invites everyone to join in a responsive call to worship from Psalm 34. After another hymn, Seunghyun frames our time for confession as a "moment of honesty," when we tell the truth that we need forgiveness and that God has already promised us that forgiveness in and through Jesus Christ.

This week, Cece is preaching on the complicated nature of healing in the Gospel of Mark's stories about Jairus's daughter and the woman with an issue of blood. The long scripture reading is broken up by everyone singing verses from a hymn by William Cowper called "God Moves in a Mysterious Way." Megan takes a moment to explain that the author struggled with mental illness his whole life, and that his hymns speak to painful longing for healing and hope in a mysterious God.

Cece talks about the ways that the woman with an issue of blood faced not only the pain of her physical illness but the injustice of being rejected by her community as an unclean woman. But Jesus sees her and Jairus's daughter as worthy of attention, care, and inclusion in a way that is life-giving and healing. As Christians today, we have a responsibility to ask ourselves how we can undo systems of injustice that exclude our neighbors from full participation in the Beloved Community.

Taylor and Len invite people to the Lord's Supper and offer the Prayer of Great Thanksgiving, and Len recites the Words of Institution with a reminder that the bread is gluten-free and vegan. As Len and Taylor step in front of the table, students come forward to tear off a piece of bread and dip it into the cup of grape juice. We sing a song from the Taizé Community called "In the Lord I'll Be Ever Thankful." Some of our students are immunocompromised or do not identify as Christian, and so they cross their arms over their chest to receive a verbal blessing. When it seems that the meal is finished and everyone is seated, there's a brief pause, and then a member comes forward in an N95 mask and takes communion. Taylor and Len serve one another and sit down, and Andrew steps into the center of the room for the Prayers of the People.

During the Prayers of the People, we invite members of Breaking Bread to share a joy or a concern within a few sentences. Then the worship leader speaks the request again so that it's framed as a prayer of the whole community. The worship leader then concludes the prayer with the words, "Lord, in your mercy," and the community responds, "Hear our prayer." There are prayers for a roommate who needs to travel unexpectedly because her grandmother has died. Someone is celebrating the birth of a niece. Others pray for upcoming exams and their course workload. A student shares about recent struggles with her mental health, and another has a family friend who is beginning chemotherapy. There are prayers for the Palestinian people and an end to the occupation of Gaza as well as for the people of North and South Korea amid escalations of threats that week. Andrew gathers up the things students have shared into a brief summary prayer with a final "Lord, in your mercy, hear our prayer." We sing a final hymn standing in a circle along the chapel walls so that we can see one another as we sing to God, and Cece offers a final blessing before we walk down the hallway to dinner together.

THE INFLUENCE OF THE TAIZÉ COMMUNITY ON BREAKING BREAD

Princeton Presbyterians has made two pilgrimages with students to Taizé in the summers of 2018 and 2023. These trips included students who live with mobility issues, chronic fatigue, **neurodivergence**, and dietary restrictions. In the fall of 2023, Brother Emile of Taizé led worship with Princeton Presbyterians for a service at Nassau Presbyterian Church, which welcomed about two hundred participants. The Taizé Community's practices, music, and spiritual writings and personal dialogue with the Taizé brothers have shaped Princeton Presbyterians' continuing commitment to cultivating Breaking Bread as a community that welcomes students with disabilities.

The Taizé Community is an ecumenical monastery in Burgundy, France, that receives young people as pilgrims year-round for a week of worship, work, and welcome. Brother Roger of Taizé founded the community with his sister Genevieve during World War II, and they helped people flee Nazi-occupied Europe. After the war, Roger and his friends founded a monastic community of Protestants and Catholics devoted to prayer, work, and life together. Young people came from around Europe to seek reconciliation amid postwar devastation and spiritual bewilderment.

After the Catholic Church concluded the Second Vatican Council in 1965, Brother Roger of Taizé began a short book called *The Dynamic of the Provisional*, which emphasizes contemplative waiting on God to provide what is necessary to respond to the needs of today's world. Christians can cultivate a disposition of attentive waiting on God for guidance about how to live faithfully today. Contemplative prayer, communal discernment, ecumenical dialogue, and humility foster a perspective that can acknowledge everyone who comes to a community as a gift of the Spirit.

Whenever a student comes through the doors of Nassau Presbyterian Church, Princeton Presbyterians seeks to welcome that person as a gift from God. There are so many reasons why a college student chooses not to come to Breaking Bread. It's easy to decide to have dinner with friends or catch up a bit on homework instead of walking across campus to a church building to actively participate in a worship service.

We also know that many students come to university with some off-putting or hurtful experiences from religious communities in their past. A possible newcomer may long for a worshiping community, but be unsure whether this fellowship will be creepy, manipulative, or unkind. If they end up not knowing anyone at Breaking Bread, will other students make them feel welcome, or will they feel ignored or dismissed?

For students with disabilities, there are other barriers that can make them feel uneasy. Will there be an accessible entrance to the church and bathroom facilities that can accommodate members with mobility issues? Are there dining options for someone with severe food allergies? Will the language and images used during worship be insensitive to people with disabilities, or will the worship leaders act as though disabled people do not exist in their imagination of Christian community?

Our capacity to change our practices at Breaking Bread is always in dynamic tension with the value of consistency. Consistency helps us build trust with students who have experienced exclusion or judgment from religious communities. Worship leaders take time to explain what's coming up next to reduce anxiety about where we are in the worship service. Over the course of an academic year the sermon themes change, the hymns change, and the meals change, but the rhythms of worship remain broadly constant.

A student who has come to Breaking Bread a few times can expect the same liturgical patterns. A neurodivergent student can anticipate when participants will stand or move around the room during worship. An immunocompromised student can count on distanced seating and the option to receive a verbal blessing at communion instead of the elements.

The dynamic of the provisional reminds us that the Holy Spirit is always at work through people who come to the Breaking Bread community. Students who are disabled, identify as queer, come from different cultures, and belong to diverse religious traditions deepen our commitments to reflect the love of Christ to one another and our neighbors. Sometimes disabled students will bring a particular request that makes the worship service more accessible, such as dimming the lights, providing space for distanced seating, or offering alternatives to the elements in communion (e.g., a verbal blessing, bringing a rice cake). Disabled students share requests during our Prayers of the People about their struggles to obtain academic accommodations from a dean's office, access campus resources for mental health or medical treatment, and deal with uncaring professors. When they offer these prayers, they are bringing these concerns to God, and they are raising awareness for the wider community of students about the difficulties disabled persons face. These themes in turn influence our preaching life, such as when Cece preached about the woman with an issue of blood in a way that invited us to consider the systems of exclusion that kept her apart from her community because of her illness.

When disabled student chaplains invite people to the table, offer the Prayer of Great Thanksgiving before we break the bread and pour the cup, and serve the elements to the community, they are making visible the truth that Christ's body includes, centers, and celebrates disabled persons. When a participant in Breaking Bread shares about an obstacle to their participation or a new way to represent and celebrate an aspect of their identity, it's a responsibility of the community to respond in a way that acknowledges their full humanity and change our practices to make them as welcome as possible.

CONCLUSION

What we've learned about loving students with disabilities has come from the faithfulness and courage that young people have brought to Breaking Bread. Neither of us would describe ourselves as experts in **disability studies**. Our undergraduate student leaders and student chaplains have taught us over the years where we can find helpful resources and what it's like to live with a disability. Students like Avery Williams inspire us as they lead small group conversations, share about their experiences, make space for rest on campus, and engage in activism as disabled persons.

Developing Breaking Bread into a community that can adapt to become more accessible and inclusive is an expression of the Taizé Community's dynamic of the provisional. Each student brings gifts given by the Holy Spirit, whether they come every week or try worshiping with us for the first time. Together, we discern how God is at work among us to love one another and our neighbors as the body of Christ. The leadership of disabled persons as members of Christ's body invites all of us into a fuller expression of a community where everyone joins in the witness of God's love for the world. We are grateful that students have shared their trust, courage, and joy as we work together to transform our campuses into more humane and loving communities.

REFLECTION QUESTIONS

1. We've shared how the dynamic of the provisional is a part of what theologically grounds our welcome with Princeton Presbyterians. What theological commitments shape your practices of welcome?
2. Who are stakeholders who can be transparent conversation partners about their experience in your community?

3. How might you create space for participants with disabilities to lead your community into a more inclusive space?

PRACTICAL TOOL: PRAYERS OF THE PEOPLE

To make prayer more accessible, we have found that asking people to share a prayer request, their joys and concerns, is helpful. We also want to reinforce that the request itself is already a prayer by incorporating it as a part of Prayers of the People in weekly worship. There is no need, however, for this to be situated within a complete worship service.

1. Introduce the prayer time, reminding everyone that God welcomes the things we grieve and the things we celebrate, and that the community also wants to support one another.
2. Invite participants to share briefly something that is a struggle or a joy, a prayer for themself or for the wider world. Explain that you will restate the prayer briefly so they hear another's voice pray alongside them and then you will say "Lord, in your mercy," and all gathered are invited to respond, "Hear our prayer."
3. Ask, "Who has something they'd like to share in prayer?"
4. Listen carefully and reframe the prayer for the community by saying, "We join [name] in praying for [briefly restate the prayer as you might in reflective listening]."
5. Mark each petition by saying "Lord, in your mercy." The community responds, "Hear our prayer."
6. Once everyone has had an opportunity to share, close the time of prayer by lifting up the prayers that have been spoken and those that are unspoken but remain on our hearts.

Consider how this practice might be adapted by offering a time for participants to draw or write their prayers. Then provide space for the prayers to be displayed. Next, the facilitator can continue with steps 4–6 above. How might this translate to a virtual space? Can an online bulletin board be shared among the group, allowing prayers to be offered without being at a physical location at a specific time? We have seen how the practice becomes richer over time as students gain familiarity with one another and build trust.

A PRAYER OF LAMENT FOR YOUTH

CARMELLE BEAUGELIN CALDWELL

Prayer of Lament:

God, there are things in this world that make me feel ______________.
Right now, I am especially thinking about ______________________.
Why, God, do these things happen? I don't know what to do. Could you help me with ______________?
Thank you for listening.
Amen.

God, there are things in this world that make me feel *(emotion: sad, angry, afraid, etc.)*.
Right now, I am especially thinking about *(a situation, injustice, or personal struggle)*.
Why, God, do these things happen? I don't know what to do. Could you help me with *(a request for strength, guidance, or action)*?
Thank you for listening.
Amen.

INTERLUDE: INTRODUCTION TO INTERSECTIONALITY

ERIN RAFFETY

Disability is not a single issue. Disability knows no race, gender, class, or religion. But this also doesn't mean that experiences of disability necessarily unite groups of people. In fact, within the **disability rights movement** in the United States, just like within other social movements, Black, Brown, **queer**, and chronically ill people have been marginalized. The disability rights movement initially focused on White leaders with mobility impairments and passing legislation to effect change for them. Furthermore, the retelling of the movement's history has often edited out meaningful intersections like the Black Panthers critically supplying food to the 504 activists while they staged their government sit-in. As long as we treat disability as a single issue, we will misunderstand not just how the robust intersections between race, gender, class, and religion manifest in experiences of systematic and everyday oppression, but we will also miss out on the wisdom and insights intersectional experiences of disability offer to humanity.

Kimberlé Crenshaw coined the term "**intersectionality**" in 1989 to illuminate the ways in which multiple forms of inequality compound and create additional obstacles that disadvantage people in ways that are not always visible. Ironically, when intersectionality is mentioned, it's often a way of connecting race, class, and gender, and usually disability isn't even part of the mix, remaining invisible. This continues to be the case today with diversity, equity, and inclusion initiatives. Many scholars have written critically about how disability is an oft-obscured and even ignored aspect of diversity. This shows how disability, unlike race, class, gender, or religion, remains at worst pathologized and at best unaddressed. Disabled people are often not imagined into civic or social spaces so much that their absence from diversity initiatives fails to cause alarm. At worst, they are imagined out, because disability is presumed a deficit rather than an informed or beneficial attribute.

Yet the absence of an intersectional approach to disability fails to understand ways in which many disabled people, owing to their race, class, gender, or religion, experience the world. Here are some critical facts: Women and People of Color are far less likely to be diagnosed as children with **autism**, but Black and Brown children are far more likely to be placed in special education classes and diagnosed with intellectual disabilities than their White peers. Disabled Black and Brown children are more likely to be diagnosed with behavioral disorders or even subject to police action inside and outside educational settings than their White peers. Neurodiversity and queerness are intersectional identities that remain misunderstood and, when masked, make youth especially vulnerable to mental health challenges. Finally, resources developed for disability inclusion within religious communities are disproportionately based on and geared toward White, mainline Protestant congregations.

The fields of **critical disability studies** and critical disability theory, which dialogue with the **disability justice movement**, often emphasize a principle they call **multidimensionality**, which highlights the interconnected memberships with which all people live their lives. In acknowledging multidimensionality, scholars make clear that structural privilege can take place along myriad axes, sometimes doubling down in subordinating force. But in valuing diversity, these scholars also point out the subordinated knowledges that folks living at the intersections have to teach us about disability in its multiple dimensions. For instance, disabled folks who have disproportionately borne the costs of climate change, gentrification, war, and refugee crises have developed strategies for surviving and mitigating these crises. Disabled leaders of color have key insights toward resourcing the particular needs and strengths of these communities when it comes to comprehensive care. And, as mentioned above, it is so important to acknowledge the complex identities of queer, disabled youth so that they can flourish in all their intersections, rather than flounder in struggling to conform to neurotypical and heteronormative standards.

In our book, we consider intersectionality vital to understanding, ministering, and leading with disabled youth. In fact, the authors in this book use the term "intersectionality" to encompass both the compounding disadvantages of inequality Crenshaw identifies and the subordinated knowledges that are often formed and flourish precisely in multidimensional margins. Too often youth ministry has been presented as a single issue, downplaying the complex identities of young people or narrowly approaching these identities as tragedies, needs, or deficiencies. Although it is impossible to conceive of the variety of intersections disabled youth experience, we believe that representation matters. Therefore, we hope that the prayers, perspectives, and chapters from youth, practitioners, and scholars in this volume speak truth to power precisely in the nuances of their experiences.

We believe that their particularity **protests** conformity. We invite churches and youth workers to consider where they might have failed not just to understand or honor someone else's story, but to faithfully acknowledge the whole story in its many colors and shades. It is not surprising that honoring intersectionality is a pillar of both the disability justice movement and critical disability studies. What if it were also a pillar of contemporary youth ministry? What if one key to ministering with disabled youth is leaning in to hear and understand their multidimensional stories, especially when they show the church things we've failed to grasp? What if part of ministering with disabled youth involves honoring their protest and what it has to teach us about the gospel?

PART 2

PROTEST

A PRAYER OF PROTEST

Divine Non-Binary

SAMANTHA HOUSER[1]

God of the divine feminine, help me to strip away all that the world requires of me. The smallness, the daintiness, the gentle and submissive tendencies, the beauty standards, the trendiness, the fashion conscientiousness, the norms of cooking and cleaning and caretaking. The expectations of lady-like demeanor.

And instead, equip me with all that I see in you. Remind me of the ways in which I embody intuitiveness, compassion, wisdom, acceptance, forgiveness, collaboration, and reflectiveness.

God of the divine masculine, help me to strip away all that the world requires of me. The greatness, the supremacy, the righteous anger, the norms of being the sole protector and the key provider. The expectations of becoming the one and the only.

And instead, equip me with all that I see in you. Remind me of the ways in which I embody logic, assertiveness, discipline, boundaries, confidence, and objectivity.

God of the nonbinary, help me to strip away the notion of the either/or. The archetypes and the paradigms that divide. The expectations that I must fit into a single category.

And instead, equip me with all that I see in you. Remind me of the ways in which I embody expansiveness, liminal space, inclusiveness.

Help me to trust these qualities, to know them as holy and sacred and worthy.

Amen.

IN TROUBLE IN GOD'S HOUSE

Receiving Every Joyful Noise

MORRIGAN CLARKE

> ***Guiding Question:*** *How can we receive every joyful noise and every family in worship?*

We're sitting in church and my little brother starts to make noises. There are a woman and her grandson behind us. I slowly hear them start to whisper; at first I pay no attention to it, but then it starts getting louder. I start to hear words. She's saying, "That boy needs help," and "That boy is not normal." Her words begin to make my blood boil. Little do I know my mom has experienced this same feeling before.

Gradually my family realized that the traditional church setting wasn't fit for my brother and other disabled youth. Later on I realized people feared what they could not understand and that is the explanation for their actions and behavior, but at the time I didn't and so I looked restlessly for a solution.

My name is Morrigan Clarke. I am fourteen years old and currently going into my freshman year of high school. When people see my family they may notice that J'den, my brother, wears large noise-canceling headphones and **stims**, but they usually don't notice or often misinterpret my minimal eye contact, earbuds, and undivided attention to the game on my phone. J'den has **autism**, and I have severe ADHD. I have learned to cope with it, but at times I still struggle to focus and get my work done. Some of my hobbies are singing and acting. I am also a youth advocate for individuals with disabilities, a girl scout, and an active member of my church community.

Joyful Noise is a big part of my advocacy work in making a positive and more inviting environment for youth with disabilities in our churches. My first encounter with a Joyful Noise service was when I was around six or seven. My parents were informed of this service at a disability-friendly Lutheran church in Hillsborough, New Jersey. They decided we should attend to check it out. After the first service we fell in love with it, especially my brother and I. For example, we didn't have to sit in pews and instead got to sit in beanbags and play with fidget toys. When we did traditional church things, like the Lord's Prayer, we would grab on to this long sensory rope together and pray.

We continued to go to the service, but eventually my mom decided that the commute to get there was too long. We were so disappointed, so my mom thought she should try replicating the service at our church. At the time we could only think of a few families that we knew would attend, but overall we knew how much the disabled youth in the community would benefit from Joyful Noise. Although in the beginning attendance was low, word started to spread and each service kept increasing in numbers until eventually we went from two or three families all the way to ten or fifteen! I would assist at these services by reading and leading songs. Joyful Noise became a place where my family could finally worship freely. Joyful Noise differs from a traditional church service by creating a judgment-free space with few boundaries on how the service is led. With this amount of freedom the environment becomes more comfortable for the families who attend.

Ministry with disabled youth is important because sometimes in the traditional church setting there are experiences that create a negative impact on disabled youth, which can lead to them associating those experiences with church ministry as a whole. A good example of this is not only how my brother was treated, but also how I was treated. As previously mentioned I have severe ADHD; one of the struggles that comes with my ADHD is my ability to keep focus and sit still for long periods of time. I even struggle with this now, but during church I would always have something to do to keep me busy, like paper to doodle on or my mom's phone to play games on.

One day during church I was getting really restless and bored and was starting to lose focus, so I turned to my mom and I asked her if I could play on her phone. To my surprise her answer was no. To some this might seem like a no-brainer—that a child should not need a device to play on in a place of worship and it was disrespectful and rude to do so. But to me that's how I was able to remain calm and occupied in a nondisruptive way. I really didn't want to take no for an answer, so I kept asking until I eventually gave up and decided to entertain myself in another way, to which I was met with a scolding.

But again, I really didn't understand why, so you could imagine how I felt when this started happening consistently.

I started to dislike going to church a lot and started to lose connection to my faith. I was told that God created me to be myself and now I was getting in trouble for being myself in God's house. It made no sense. However now I understand why my mother did what she did, and I don't blame her. At the time I wasn't able to advocate as much for myself as I am now and my parents didn't really know how I was affected by my ADHD and what I needed. It turns out some people in church saw me playing on a device during the pastor's sermon and viewed it as extremely disrespectful and rude, but instead of putting it on me they put it on my mom as a form of bad parenting. This is completely incorrect, because it has nothing to do with her at all, let alone her parenting. My mom felt judged and as if she was viewed badly, so her response was to not have me be on a device, which ended up making the situation worse, but now I understand where she was coming from. I know what it feels like to be judged and feel the need to change my ways to fix it even if it's not under my control to begin with.

This situation is why ministry for disabled youth is so important. When I attend Joyful Noise I am surrounded by engagement to enrich myself, including fidgets, musical instruments, and kind faces. And even when that's not enough, I don't have to sit still! It's such an accommodating environment that allows me to be who God created me to be. I have been able to see my brother worship and thrive in an environment where he is accepted, which goes to show the overall impact Joyful Noise has created for so many young people. I still attend regular church service and yes, I still play on a device to help me remain focused, but now I explain to people why I do, and I do so with confidence and a smile on my face.

THREE QUESTIONS OR THINGS I WISH ADULTS WOULD ASK OR SAY TO DISABLED YOUTH

1. I wish adults would ask disabled youth about their disabilities rather than just assume.
2. I wish adults would encourage youth to be themselves rather than expect them to conform to social norms.
3. I wish adults would ask us what we need rather than them going with what they think we need.

SLOW AND STEADY

The Still-in-Process Growth of the Intersectionality of Theology, Adolescence, and Disability

AMY JACOBER

***Guiding Question:** How does this literature review shed light on our current state of theory and practice regarding theology and disability?*

The path of disability youth ministry and scholarship is not straightforward and has its fair share of dead ends. That path, however, is more extensive than it once was and has far more room for a variety of voices. This chapter analyzes the writing on disability and youth ministry over the years. Each section, like the writings over the years, expresses increased inclusion and belonging. From early paternalistic writings to ministerial practice that moved from "ministry to or for" to "ministry with or by," writings and ministry involve those with disabilities to an ever-greater degree.

Starting Right was the most influential textbook in youth ministry for the better part of the last two decades.[1] While it is difficult to overstate the positives this book brought to the field of youth ministry, it does not even mention disabilities. Youth ministry has two main academic journals, *The Journal of Youth and Theology*, affiliated with the International Association for the Study of Youth Ministry, and *The Journal of Youth Ministry*, affiliated with the Association for Youth Ministry Educators. Both journals have had a handful of articles that address disability and ministry. Both organizations have had speakers present on the need and the biblical mandate for inclusion and **belonging** of disabled youth. Both are receptive, and yet this advocacy has not translated into widespread consideration of inclusion nor belonging.

There are other organizations with conferences and journals where the intersection of youth, theology, and disability have also made appearances. These span from practical theology associations to religious education and disability. *The Journal of Disability and Religion*[2] has published a handful of articles on adolescents over the years. In 2018 there was a special edition of the journal focusing on disability and youth ministry. This was later published in book form under the title *Embodying Youth*.[3] The youth ministry landscape has been shifting and one positive change is increased attention to inclusion.

INTERESTED/INVESTED

Early writings on youth ministry and disability were scarce and tucked into writings that covered disability broadly. Personal biography was a major motivation. Either the author had a disability personally or a loved one with a disability. The writings established the baseline assumption that those with disabilities should be part of faith, church, or some manner of ministry. Consequently, the writings tend to offer a primer on a variety of disabilities and practical advice. Many of these early writings include adolescents within writings that were primarily focused on children.

Joni Eareckson Tada must be included in this review as foundational. Her own story is compelling, beginning with friends visiting her as a teenager in the hospital after she became paralyzed. The presence of friends and **friendship** grounds her theology and ministerial approach. In 1988, Eareckson Tada wrote *Friendship Unlimited*.[4] In 1997, this same book was revised and updated with coauthor Steve Jensen and retitled *Barrier-Free Friendships*.[5] Eareckson Tada emphasizes that it was through friendships amid struggle that she had a profound transformation with God. She writes, "Friends—acquaintances, casual, close, or even intimate—made all the difference in the world."[6] Regarding well-meaning visitors, Eareckson Tada says of those who came to share the love of Christ, "One problem was that those people were more imposing their faith, rather than exposing it."[7] True friendship would share faith, but not make her a project. While there is no documented trail connecting Eareckson Tada's emphasis on friendship to future writings, the term "friend" is found throughout disability writings. The struggle is that the term is used both for those with whom there is an actual relationship and for those who have just met. As a relational term, "friend(ship)" is often neither chosen nor developed over time. Rather, it is frequently imposed upon youth with disabilities. It, too, opens the door for paternalistic interactions with one person declaring friendship and the other presumably having to accept.

Eareckson Tada also holds the theological position that while God hates suffering, he allows it for a greater purpose. She writes, "God delighted in how suffering fit into His plan of good for us and glory for Himself."[8] With her influential early ministry and because she spoke as one from within the disability community, her perspective took hold. Through family camps that included children and youth, the notion that God allowed suffering, including disabling suffering, to bring himself glory was established. To refute this position became difficult. No one wanted to be the person to contradict this incredible woman who was so obviously being used by God to bring hope and the gospel to so many. Yet this was not a universal viewpoint. God can be glorified in suffering but to state that God allows suffering in order to be glorified is problematic indeed.

Five years after *Barrier-Free Friendships*, Jim Pierson wrote *Exceptional Teaching*.[9] His work was primarily local and based in special education with a strong faith conviction. Pierson encouraged the differentiating of impairments rather than lumping all disabilities together. He also makes clear that one's motive in ministry with disabled people should not be pity but dignity. The book largely assumes an integrative ministry during a time when segregated ministries were on the rise. Pierson encourages advocacy for families and participation and leadership for all.

However, there are also paternalistic moments. He writes that it is good to embrace the task of assessing someone's mental age. He goes on to say that one should "determine the student's mental age in order to assess his ability or readiness to embrace faith."[10] His understanding of mental age was determined from standardized intelligence tests.[11] The notion of anyone being able to assess someone's readiness to embrace faith from an intelligence test is presumptuous and harmful. It reduces faith to cognitive assent while simultaneously dismissing the work of the Holy Spirit. Across theological spectrums, this kind of posture has led to exclusionary practices in worship, baptism, and communion. It was meant to be benevolent, but the negative implications are significant.

EXPLORATORY/RAISING AWARENESS

A next wave of writings came from those curious why some teens, particularly teens with disabilities, were missing from youth groups. Early research began with physical disabilities in mind but quickly came to include intellectual and mental disabilities and combinations. In 2007, I published "Ostensibly Welcome," a work focused on the experiences of teens with disabilities within church and youth ministry.[12] It remained broad, not naming any particular disability and covering a range from mild to intense needs for accommodations. Few churches or ministries had experience in youth ministry for those with disabilities, as those opportunities for church engagement for children with disabilities tended to drop off as children became adolescents. There were rare exceptions.

The most prominent at the time of the research was Capernaum, a Young Life ministry founded by Nick Palermo. Other stories mentioned well-meaning leaders sometimes including but often belittling teens with disabilities. My research was intended to focus on the voices of youth, but in naivete, I had not adequately prepared to hear their voices well. Often the parent or caretaker shared stories, while the teen sat close by and agreed. The research then shifted to include the impact on the faith of parents and siblings as they experienced the struggles of their child or sibling. In almost all cases, caretakers critiqued how so much support was shown when their child was young but quickly vanished as they hit adolescence.

Two researchers from the continent of Africa have also recently written on disability and youth within their contexts. In "We Are Forgotten," Seyram Amenyedzi focuses on Ghana, highlighting bright spots of inclusion ministry with more work to do.[13] While her writing is hopeful, it lacks a key perspective: The problem was not that those with disabilities were forgotten, but that they were never included to begin with. There are now those who know better, but inclusion and belonging for adolescents with disabilities is still not widely accepted. Charmaine Manuel offers a similar assessment from South Africa.[14] She writes of the vision for churches to be places of belonging and not shame or blame for those with disabilities, including adolescents. Her research focuses on where, if at all, the work of belonging is happening and how to bring training so that it may continue.

Isabella Novisma, writing in the Indonesian context, is also shaping the international conversation and ministerial practices. She notes in "Decolonizing Ableist Pedagogy" that "the Indonesian education system tends to maintain segregation of students with disabilities from the students who are able-bodied and able-minded."[15] Novisma calls out the charity model of disability ministry, which was created by a colonizing mindset. This model shows up in ministry to and for people with disabilities as opposed to with them. People and especially adolescents who are educated in a system that maintains separation learn that they are not included and should not expect to be. Novisma is calling out this erroneous teaching and practice, transforming the conversation across theological contexts within Indonesia and beyond.

ADVOCACY THROUGH INVITATION

In 2011 Nick Palermo wrote a short article on the future of youth ministry.[16] He invites churches to join in spirit and practice with a ministry he began in 1985. This was long before there were any writings, best practices, or organized conversations regarding youth ministry and disability. He tried to advocate for teens with disabilities to be included not out of charity, but because those with disabilities "have spiritual gifts, talents, and abilities to use for the Kingdom of God."[17] Palermo encourages doing ministry as "Christian 'withness' . . . it's reciprocal ministry. It's 'with' and not 'to' our friends with disabilities."[18] The call of "withness" was an early call for ministry opportunities for those with disabilities not just to be tokens and a deep belief that all have gifts and graces to bring.

Louise Gosbell, an Australian practical theologian, relayed the story about her brother-in-law, John, who has Down syndrome and was known, loved, and served in their faith community. Her brother-in-law was in his late teens when a new minister arrived. "This new minister—without taking the time to speak with John or anyone who knew him—advised my mother-in-law that he did not want John to continue to be involved with the welcoming team. The reason the minister gave was that a person with an intellectual disability does not have the capacity to understand the gospel and so should not be allowed to represent the church in any way, even if that is simply greeting members as they arrived at church."[19] This kind of comment is polarizing, turning some completely from the church. Others focus on refining the inadequacy of current theology, which lacks inclusivity.[20]

FOR AND WITH

Once an awareness regarding youth with disabilities and ministry became more widespread, there were publications that focused on how to create ministries "to and for those with disabilities." Best practices and basic information regarding disabilities were the norm. One notable work was Erik Carter's book *Including People with Disabilities in Faith Communities*.[21] While this book has much to offer, the focus is largely on younger children and adults. Even the sections with youth as the subheading quickly shift to children or never mention youth at all.[22] In particular, *Including People* offers a comment about separate programming with the subheading "Children, Youth, and Adults," but the actual paragraph states, "Although national data are not available, the most common response in congregations appears to be to establish separate religious education classes, recreational activities, and worship services for children and adults with developmental disabilities."[23] Youth ministry goes unmentioned, perhaps squeezed into what is clearly intended for children or adults.

Benjamin T. Conner, a practical theologian, has many writings, two of which are significant for this chapter. The first is his 2012 book, *Amplifying Our Witness: Giving Voice to Adolescents with Developmental Disabilities*.[24] While he is the author, he wrote the book in partnership with disabled youth in his life, especially those with whom he serves in ministry. He also calls for congregations to stop trying to create ministries that he calls "appendix ministries." Instead he writes, "We need a new approach to congregational ministry that includes and amplifies the witness of our friends with developmental disabilities."[25] The second is Connor's 2023 article, "Disability and Youth Ministry: The Book I'm Not Going to Write."[26] In this article he revisits some of what was good and lasting from *Amplifying Our Witness*, but powerfully lays down his pen in order for disabled theologians and leaders, particularly those with intersectional identities, to take up envisioning and enacting the future of disabled youth ministry.

Although Erin Raffety's 2022 book *From Inclusion to Justice* does not focus specifically on youth ministry, her work and teaching with youth catalyzed the 2018 Disability and Youth Ministry Conference hosted by Princeton Seminary's Institute for Youth Ministry, which fostered the special collection of articles on the topic published in the *Journal of Disability and Religion* that same year. She writes a bit about her approach in an article in that collection entitled "The God of Difference: Disability, Youth Ministry, and the Difference Anthropology Makes."[27] Raffety charges disabled youth ministry to consider particular and general differences as things to be celebrated and to guide practice. Youth ministry needn't be about norming youth into a monolith, but should be about journeying with the knowledge that youth are as different from one another as they are different from the God who created them.

THE ADDITION OF MENTAL HEALTH (SORT OF)

The late 1980s and early '90s saw the acknowledgment of mental health as a need, albeit sensationalized and primarily portrayed as a crisis for the family. *Adolescents in Turmoil, Parents Under Stress: A Pastoral Ministry Primer* by Richard Parsons was published in 1987.[28] This book assesses the impact of crisis moments and events and how to support parents rather than youth. Les Parrott wrote the next major offering in 1993, updated in 2000 and 2014 as *Helping the Struggling Adolescent.*[29] This book continued to look at mental health not as part of the disability community but as an isolated issue or problem to be solved. It considers anxiety, **depression**, panic attacks, and schizophrenia alongside drugs, divorce, and more. Nothing was intended to be harmful or patronizing, but it does assume that every issue has a need to be eliminated or solved rather than an opportunity to grow in faith in ways that are not part of the typical mainstream path.

This view of mental health issues as crises to be weathered or solved continued in youth ministry writings. In 2007 *Group's Emergency Response Handbook for Youth Ministry* included grief, depression, stress, and anxiety right alongside abuse, divorce, and other issues.[30] It is intended as a benevolent offering focusing on getting through the inflection points as an emergency rather than considering them as parts of an ongoing reality. In 2025 Monica Kim and Danny Kwon continued the patterns of naming mental health primarily as struggles and crises in *Teenagers and Mental Health: A Handbook for Parents, Pastors, and Youth Leaders.*[31]

INSPIRATION PORN AND OTHER MISHANDLINGS

Every person within the disability community knows what **inspiration porn** is, even if they do not know the term. Stella Young coined the term "inspiration porn," which means the objectification of those with disabilities for the benefit or inspiration of nondisabled people.[32] Many people with disabilities have been groomed to be so thankful for any attention they receive that critiquing that attention feels controversial. Michael Hoggatt takes his cues from Stella Young. In "Night to Shine and Inspiration Porn," Hoggatt addresses popular nationwide youth disability activities and evaluates whether they are authentically serving those within the disability community or rather making those who host feel better about "doing something" for those poor youth.[33] This is a must-read work offering an example of analysis that considers the impact of our actions and what could be better. Two veteran disability leaders, Marc Tumeinski and Jeff McNair, created a rubric when evaluating programming asking, "What, if anything, would be better?"[34] Their rubric would be useful for any youth ministry seeking faithfully to include those with disabilities. It is long past the time for shutting down paternalistic programming and instead building theologically grounded ministries where all belong.

For far too long people with disabilities have been manipulated to fit awkwardly into systems designed for able-bodied people. Many theological contexts hold fast to the notion that disability is something to be cured. Words of faith declared a hospitality that does not exist. In 1987 Dennis Shurter used Fowler's stages of faith as a guide for creating ministerial spaces for "the mentally retarded."[35] Shurter's work codified the infantilization of youth labeled mentally retarded, as if they were trapped being children forever, stating that those with profound disabilities are perpetually at stage 1 (Intuitive Projective, typically ages three to seven; innocent, fluid, and no developed formalized beliefs) and those with moderate to mild impairments will plateau at stage 2 (Mythic-Literal stage, ages seven to twelve; literal and focused on reciprocal cause and effect).

This kind of ill-conceived perception that people with cognitive impairments were never capable of growing up and being treated as maturing humans was the norm. Churches offered simplistic, patronizing programs that treated those with disabilities as though they were children. Michael Langford calls out a parallel practice of marginalization and patronization in his 2018 article "Abusing Youth: Theologically Understanding Youth Through Misunderstanding Disability."[36] In this article he points out the similarities between youth and those with disabilities being outside of what is considered "normal." He addresses the profound misunderstanding of each, offering a helpful corrective that affirms the full humanity and sense of belonging for all.

"NOTHING ABOUT US WITHOUT US"

More recently in the field of disability ministry and youth, two disabled voices have been significant in the advancement of both the differences between and **intersectionality** of disability and mental health: Miriam Spies and Amy Panton. Spies and Panton are PhD candidates at Emmanuel College in Toronto and cohosts of the *Mad and Crip Theology Podcast* and serve as founders and editors of the *Canadian Journal of Theology, Disability, and Mental Health*. Each scholar writes from within the disability community, with Spies describing herself as "a Crip theologian whose research aims to challenge the church in how it views leadership and who it desires to fill those roles." Panton describes herself as "an out-survivor of the psychiatric system . . . exploring the intersections between mental distress and spirituality."[37] They are reshaping the theological conversation around disability and ministry in general and offering models for youth.

CONCLUSION

Youth ministries have long included those with disabilities at varying levels. The levels, however, have varied from hiddenness to tolerance, acceptance, inclusion, and belonging. Thankfully, the ratios that have shifted over time. Over the course of this chapter there has been movement from individual interest to a broader theological mandate. Individual interest is a great place to begin and is often a result of a personal relationship that raises awareness. Once that interest is present, it is difficult to not notice how accessibility impacts almost every area of life for those with impairments and their friends and families. Adolescence is often the developmental stage where lifelong theological convictions are formed. This makes youth ministry crucial not just for the six years or so adolescents are involved but also for the foundation they carry into their adult years. As youth are formed, they mature and influence the church at large. When youth ministry functions as if they are not complete without people with disabilities, the church will follow suit. As youth ministry has moved from hiddenness, to cure, to ministry for, to ministry with, and now to the cusp of seeking full equality, so, too, must the church move from disability ministry as an appendix to a fully inclusive ministry where people with disabilities can minister and lead.

REFLECTION QUESTIONS

1. What theoretical point raised above impacted your understanding of theology and disability?
2. How might you use that idea to affect your practice in ministry?
3. How does the theory and practice of theology and disability affect ministry that is not explicitly about disability? How should it affect it?

LEADERSHIP DEVELOPMENT FOR DISABLED BIPOC YOUTH

Examining Black Spirituality and the Black Church

LAMAR HARDWICK

> ***Guiding Question:*** *In what ways does the ministry of Elijah John Fisher and the Black church serve as examples of spiritual* ***protest*** *for ministry with disabled youth?*

Between 2010 and 2019 I was the pastor at a church in LaGrange, Georgia. LaGrange is south of Atlanta and just north of Columbus. I have fond memories of my time there. While I initially joined the staff at New Community Church as the youth pastor, my role eventually shifted to lead pastor.

The city of LaGrange has become a special place for me because it is the city where I was serving as pastor when I first discovered and disclosed my **autism** diagnosis. I've written extensively about my journey to discovering I was autistic, but I have never paused long enough to appreciate the environment that provided me with the courage and the commitment to make that journey. It was in LaGrange, Georgia, of all places, that my feet were set on the path to exploring my diagnosis and the ways in which having a developmental disability affected my church experience and my understanding of faith, God, and the Bible. The city of LaGrange would prove to be a place where I had opportunities to begin my exploration of the intersections of disability, race, and religion.

However, my experience as a disabled pastor serving in LaGrange is by far not a unique story. In fact, one of the most pivotal figures in Black church history was a disabled man by the name of Elijah John Fisher, who was a pastor born in the very city where, centuries later, I would become a disability activist. Henry Mitchell writes:

> Elijah John Fisher is best known as pastor of the famous Olivet Baptist Church of Chicago, where he served from 1903 to 1915. Born in LaGrange, Georgia, he was the youngest of eight boys in a family of seventeen children. He was "hired out" by his master to serve in a Baptist parsonage while he was a small child. Thus, he received early exposure to Christian teachings and was baptized before he was six years old. His father was an unordained "floor preacher" in the Black congregation that met in the Whites' church building. Thus, his exposure was intensified.[1]

Fisher had a rather impressive history as a scholar and leader in the Black church. He was among a small group of Black clergy in his day that, through determination, became shining examples of those who were able to access formal education in addition to being self-taught ministers. Fisher earned a college degree in record time, and when he entered Atlanta Baptist Seminary he successfully appealed to the institution and was placed in the senior class. He was such an avid reader that he was able to pass the required examinations to do so. Fisher was so advanced that in his only year of formal seminary training he managed to study both Hebrew and Greek, and due to his discipline and dedication to his theological studies, he was known to spend hours studying in his library. Fisher was known in the Black church as an intellectual giant, a man who was as wise as he was knowledgeable.

When Fisher was approximately twenty-one years old he answered his call to ordained ministry. Prior to serving at Olivet Baptist Church in Chicago, Fisher served several small rural churches, including the First Baptist Church of Anniston in 1883, the First Colored Baptist Church in his hometown of LaGrange, Georgia, and Mount Olive Baptist Church of Atlanta in 1889. After seminary Fisher served for two short years in Nashville before heading to Chicago.

At the age of twenty-one Fisher was boarding a train and fell, causing him to lose his leg. He would recover after surgery and go on to have an extremely successful career as a pastor and civil rights activist. Fisher was a prophetic voice of his time, often speaking out against violence against Black bodies, and he even was known for publicly speaking out against Black churches and pastors that remained silent on issues of racial justice. He spoke out publicly against

Booker T. Washington because he believed Washington was too quiet on issues of racial justice, namely, violence against and lynching of Black people. That violence often led to Black people becoming physically disabled. As a local church pastor, Fisher baptized nearly twelve hundred people in a two-year period, and during his twelve years as pastor of Olivet Baptist Church in Chicago (1903–1915), he was believed to have built the largest Protestant congregation in the world at the time.[2] Not only is Fisher a shining example of leadership development in the historically Black church, but he is also a shining example of young disabled **BIPOC** leadership in the church and the community.

Fisher's life and ministry serve as a powerful portrayal of what protest means for BIPOC-disabled youth who are searching for their place in the world. Protest thrives on images of what exists despite oppression and of what is possible in the face of systemic discrimination. Fisher is a portrait and a symbol, and it is important to know, understand, and implement structures that can provide portraits and symbols to inspire young disabled BIPOC youth. In Fisher's case, it was the brilliance of the Black church that shaped him into a portrait and symbol of spiritual protest.

THE HISTORICALLY BLACK CHURCH AND PROPHETIC TRADITION

From its inception the Black church operated as an open prophetic protest to early colonial theology that attempted to disempower and disenfranchise Black people. The civil rights movement and the passing of the Civil Rights Act of 1964 (CRA) should be considered the crowning achievement of the Black church, but not because they resolved the problem of racism and discrimination in the United States. Instead, they should be viewed the same way the musical influence of the Black church helped give birth to new and creative ideas for expanding the pursuit of the American ideal of equality, equity, and justice for all. The CRA would eventually influence the expansion of this movement to include the Voting Rights Act, which outlawed the discriminatory voting practices adopted by many southern states post–Civil War. There was also the subsequent ban on employment discrimination based on race, color, religion, sex, and national origin passed in 1966, as well as the expansion of the CRA in 1967, which outlawed housing discrimination on the same basis.

There were several expansions of civil rights throughout the late 1960s and early 1970s. Among the most notable for the disability community were the

Rehabilitation Act of 1973 and the Education for All Handicapped Children Act (later renamed the **Individuals with Disabilities Education Act** in 1990). **Section 504** of the Rehabilitation Act protects qualified individuals from being discriminated against on the basis of disability. Section 504 forbids organizations and employers that received federal financial assistance to deny disabled people opportunities for employment and access to employer program benefits and other services.[3]

Thus, the Black church's success at securing the passage of the CRA led to the pursuit of a broad piece of legislation by disability activists that would ensure the rights of people with disabilities. In the 1980s disability activists began developing similar strategies employed by Black Americans to make their case for civil rights legislation to protect their community from discrimination.

Black spirituality was born into a story that shaped its thirst for equality. In many ways, Black Christians practiced a faith that demanded a level of patriotism that most White Southern Christians had not tapped into. The plight of the Black church was, in essence, the plight of the American Dream. Despite efforts to portray civil rights leaders and Black churchgoers as unworthy of full citizenship in America, the Black church and its leaders argued for America and not against it. "The movement's aim was not to destroy America's constitutional democracy but to make it live up to its ideals. The nonviolent nature of the movement addressed the sense of justice of the majority, and the fundamental idea of willing social cooperation among freemen was, in the view of the community as a whole, expressed in the Constitution."[4]

The goal of becoming full citizens of America and thus having the security to enjoy the protections of the Constitution was fueled by an unshakable belief that God had also created Black bodies to be citizens of his holy kingdom. Black spirituality deserves the right to claim its long-standing influence on the civil rights movement and, ultimately, the **disability rights movement**. The mixture of faith, blood, and tenacity propelled the worn bodies and minds of Black people in America who, despite being overwhelmingly oppressed, garnered enough spiritual and political power to mold the nation into a slightly more just version of itself. This power isn't merely political savvy. This power was a result of a piety that transcended the evils of slavery and Jim Crow. It is for this reason that both the civil rights movement and the disability rights movement must acknowledge the legacy of Black spirituality and theology at the core of its success.

To engage in a robust discussion of how BIPOC spirituality served as the incubator for the emergence of young disabled leaders like Elijah John Fisher, we must further consider two essential elements of early Black spirituality and theology that helped shape the contribution of the Black church's spirit of protest for civil and disability justice: the adaptation of religious practices and language and alternative views of health and wellness.

ADAPTATION OF RELIGIOUS VIEWS

For many enslaved Africans, the journey to the New World was one of trepidation. Imagine being corralled into holding cells and separated from your parents or your children. Imagine being held in captivity with no knowledge of what your captors wanted or where they might take you. Imagine hearing moaning and weeping over the physical brutality of being rustled like livestock onto ships bound for a land that would become synonymous with pain and despair.

Contrary to what some believe, the transatlantic slave trade was more than an operation built on brute force. While slave sellers, slave traders, and slaveholders practiced unconscionable brutality, perhaps the most brutal aspect of slave trading was the intentional destruction of all aspects of African culture to gain control over the minds and bodies of enslaved Africans. The late Albert J. Raboteau, a scholar of African and African American religions, writes about this in his seminal book, *Slave Religion: The "Invisible Institution"in the Antebellum South*, saying, "In the New World slave control was based on the eradication of all forms of African culture because of the power to unify the slaves and thus enable them to resist or rebel."[5]

Slaveholders understood the significance of eradicating African culture to maintain control over their slaves. In addition, they understood the power that culture has to motivate resistance to oppression. This is important to note because while much of the language, social and political systems, and family structures of enslaved Africans were intentionally destroyed during slavery, one aspect of African culture that adapted and survived the horrors of slavery was African Traditional Religion(s) or ATRs. Raboteau writes, "One of the most durable and adaptable constituents of the slave's culture, linking African past with American present, was his religion."[6]

Adaptation is perhaps the most important aspect of the story of Black spirituality because it shows the necessity of evolution, as it relates to religious beliefs and practices, for surviving oppression. Adaptation is, in fact, a hallmark of the Black church, and this aspect of Black spirituality has the potential to influence the Christian church in America by providing a path toward a more significant role in the anti-ableist movement.

Suppose you're anything like me and you have had any significant time submerged in Western evangelical culture. In that case, you know that preserving "pure orthodoxy" is one of the highest pursuits, if not the highest, of American evangelical theology. Here in the West, we are often challenged to play the role of gospel guardians and gatekeepers, believing that it is our duty and distinct pleasure to determine what is considered orthodox and use that criterion to measure the sincerity and accuracy of a person's Christian faith and fidelity.

If that has been your experience, then hearing that enslaved Africans kept their religion alive by engaging in syncretism may be a cause for pause. No matter the denominational affiliation, most branches of Christianity in the West rely heavily on their certainty that they remain doctrinally pure. I also used to hold this position; I mean, one way we have been taught that we can prove our loyalty to Jesus is to shun syncretism and remain as orthodox as we can be. But I believe we believe this because we have overlooked the natural progression of religion, including the evolution of Christianity in particular.

The idea that faith evolves may feel uncomfortable. However, many people have had significant life experiences that have caused their faith to develop not suddenly but subtly. When I was diagnosed with cancer in 2020 and again in 2022, my faith needed to grow in order to manage the new challenges that I was facing. Evolving faith often requires the need to accumulate new resources and new ideas and attempt to answer uncomfortable questions. While my story is one that many people who face life-altering circumstances share, the same was true for the children of Israel, and the biblical text is full of examples of how the nation's faith developed over the years.

Evolving faith is the process by which our ideas about God change, often in ways that feel like progression, strengthening, or clarity. In addition, growing faith means that we often find new ways to talk about God and our relationship with God. We discover new language, new imagery, and new definitions to describe our understanding of God and how God relates to the world. Growing faith is not an abandonment of core beliefs and ideas about the Christian faith. Evolving faith is the recognition that adjustments are a necessary part of faith, and in embracing the need to adjust we are, in fact, respecting the enormity of God's power and presence in the world because we ultimately confess that our language about God is limited and in constant need of expansion and evolution.

ALTERNATIVE VIEWS OF WELLNESS

Adjustments and accommodations are an important part of the story of the development of the historically Black church in America. Enslaved Africans could adopt Christianity (although it is possible few had already had some contact with Christianity in their homeland) and adjust their traditional religions to accommodate Christian ideals. They also had an approach to health, wellness, and wholeness that also played a role in the evolution of the Black church.

Health and wellness have been the pursuit of most cultures and religions throughout history. Nearly every religious system has guidance in its sacred texts, rites, and rituals that point toward a life of health and wellness. While there is a universal pursuit of health and wellness, the definitions of health, wellness, and wholeness often vastly differ between cultures and religions.

This is especially true of the differences in ideas about health and wholeness between most African cultures and religions. "Traditional African societies had their own unique culture and religion. . . . What they believed to cause disease and disharmony, how they also approached the promotion of health and harmony, how they experienced and expressed illness, pain and disorientation of being, what therapeutic solution they sought, and the places they sought this therapy were all determined by their culture of which religion was an integral part."[7] Although enslaved Africans had to contend with many new ideals being forced upon them, many Africans enslaved in America held to the idea of a supreme being, the supernatural and divine order, which influenced their ideas about health. For many West African traditional religions, the concept of health and wellness leaned heavily on the communal nature of their religion. "Sickness in any individual in the African society is viewed as sickness to the entire community because of the communal system that is operated in Africa, thereby necessitating the healing of that community."[8]

African culture and religion also shaped their connection to each other and the world. They believed that all of life was interconnected and that the world was united both spiritually and physically. For them, all of life was connected spiritually, including the spirits of both the living and the dead. Health or wholeness was the product of maintaining harmony between the spirit(s) that affected life and well-being. With the emphasis on community and fluidity as a central aspect of defining health and wholeness in ATRs, the role of healing in ATRs takes on a much larger task than simply curing an individual. "To Africans, health and wholeness can only be attained when all issues that affect and influence man are addressed."[9] What this means for the historically Black church is that ideas about health, wellness, chronic illness, and disability have been deeply informed by the views passed down through ATRs. They also posit a more communal definition of disability, versus the focus on the individual promoted by Western culture.

CONCLUSION

The transatlantic slave trade was not only a system of brutal physical oppression but also a calculated effort to erase African culture, including religious traditions. However, enslaved Africans adapted their spiritual practices, ensuring their survival and transformation within the New World. The resilience of ATRs amid oppression illustrates how faith itself is an evolving force—one that has historically resisted dominant power structures. This adaptability remains central to Black spirituality and has implications for contemporary faith communities, particularly in their engagement with disability justice.

A key theological insight from this history is the challenge it presents to Western evangelical notions of "pure orthodoxy." Many faith traditions prioritize doctrinal purity, rejecting syncretism as a deviation from authentic Christianity. However, just as enslaved Africans reimagined their spirituality under oppression, faith today must evolve to confront new realities, including the intersection of race and disability. Theological paradigms that exclude disability fail to reflect the full image of God. Black liberation theology, which has long challenged racial injustice, must also address ableist interpretations of faith that marginalize disabled individuals within Black church spaces.

Elijah John Fisher's story exemplifies how historical narratives can inform contemporary strategies for empowering disabled BIPOC youth in faith communities. His life demonstrates that leadership is possible despite structural barriers, yet churches today must take intentional steps to nurture and elevate disabled voices. This requires more than passive inclusion; it demands mentorship programs, ministerial training, and theological education that affirm disabled individuals as leaders and theologians in their own right.

Furthermore, accessibility in faith communities must move beyond logistical accommodations (e.g., ramps and sign language interpretation) to become a theological commitment. Fisher's story challenges churches to see disability not as a condition to be overcome but as an integral aspect of the body of Christ. To enact this vision, faith communities must create platforms for disabled youth to shape theological discourse through preaching, teaching, and advocacy.

Ultimately, this history argues that faith is not static but adaptive, shaped by lived experience and historical struggle. Just as African spirituality evolved to resist oppression, churches today must embrace an inclusive, justice-centered theology that fully integrates race, disability, and faith. By doing so, contemporary churches can not only honor historical resilience but also model a faith that is expansive, transformative, and liberating for all.

REFLECTION QUESTIONS

1. What can we learn from the life of Elijah John Fisher about the role of disabled leaders in the church?
2. How do you interpret the idea of faith evolving over time? How can faith communities better accommodate the changing needs and experiences of BIPOC-disabled youth?
3. In what ways does spirituality serve as a form of protest against systemic discrimination and how can it inform faith and inspire activism today?

PRACTICAL TOOL: LET'S TRADE SHOES (10–20 MINUTES)

Read Galatians 4:12–13.

In this passage, Paul asks for his fellow Christians to put themselves in his shoes, and in doing so he references his disability and cites it as the reason he had to discontinue his missionary travels.

This group activity promotes creating space and opportunities to learn from others. The goal of the session is to begin the journey of learning from others who are different from us as a spiritual practice.

Supplies: You will need a few storage totes, masking tape, blindfolds, and several black markers.

1. When the group arrives for the session, have each of them remove their shoes at the entrance and place them in one of the available storage totes.
2. After everyone has placed their shoes in the storage totes, have everyone sit in a circle.
3. Give each participant a blindfold and ask them to put it over their eyes, ensuring that no one can see. After everyone is blindfolded, dump all the shoes from the storage totes in the middle of the circle.
4. Instruct the participants to position themselves on their hands and knees. At your signal, they should crawl to the middle of the circle, grab two shoes from the pile, and crawl backward until they think they are back in their original spot.
5. Once everyone has at least two shoes, ask them to remove their blindfolds and reorganize themselves into a better circle.
6. For the next several minutes, ask each person to say a few words about the shoe they are holding. What type of person does it belong to? Are they short or tall? What is their gender? What color hair might they have? What color eyes? Be sure to stick to questions about appearance.
7. After about five minutes, have the participants return the shoes to their correct owners. Do not allow this to take too long. Once all the shoes are returned, have them return to the circle. From there, break the larger group into groups of two or three, depending on the size of the large group.
8. Once participants are in smaller groups, have each person hold their own shoe while sharing with the smaller group one thing about their life that most people wouldn't know about them or their family.
9. After each participant shares, have them pass their shoe to the right. Then, have the next person use masking tape and a marker to write down one adjective or one word to encourage the person who just spoke.
10. By the end of the exercise, each participant should have the same number of pieces of masking tape stuck to their shoe, each with a word encouraging them.

11. To close, bring everyone back to the larger circle and have one or two people share their experience doing this exercise trading shoes. How did it feel? What did you learn? How can this exercise help us follow Paul's encouragement to put ourselves in the shoes of those with disabilities, chronic illnesses, or mental health issues? How can this exercise help us value the stories and experiences of those who are different from us, including BIPOC who are disabled?

MODELING POSSIBILITIES

Integrating Crip Wisdom to Fuel Protest and Pride

AVERY ARDEN

> ***Guiding Question:*** *How do we equip our youth to imagine more just futures into reality?*

This mural created by West Concord Union Church (WCUC) in Massachusetts places members of the WCUC community alongside nationally renowned disability rights activists. The mingling highlights the connections between great acts of justice and the small but significant actions of everyday people. Resistance and change come at multiple levels; daily life catalyzes movements, while movements affect daily life. The following descriptions are adapted from WCUC's descriptions of their mural.

(Clockwise from top left)

JENNIFER KEELAN-CHAFFINS (1961–PRESENT) became an iconic symbol of the disability rights movement at age eight, when she insisted on leaving her wheelchair behind to participate in the famous Capitol Crawl. This demonstration is considered the final action that led to the passage of the Americans with Disabilities Act.

SANDRA JENSEN (1961–1997) was born with Down syndrome and a heart defect. Without a heart-lung transplant she was likely to die, but doctors did not believe that someone with Down syndrome would be able to follow a strict postsurgery routine. Disability rights attorney Michael Kluk worked with Jensen to secure a spot on the transplant list, and on January 23, 1996, Jensen became the first person with Down syndrome to receive a major transplant.

OLOF JOHNSON (1944–2016) shared his musical talents in WCUC's worship and fellowship for over twenty years.

LINDA BROWN (1963–2019) of the WCUC community served as an acolyte of the Church of the Good Shepherd in Acton, Massachusetts, for over twenty years. She was an active participant in Special Olympics, Girl Scouts, and Open Door Theater, where she was in more than twenty productions. She was one of the first employees at Roche Brothers Market in Acton, starting there the day it opened.

MARCA BRISTO (1953–2019) was paralyzed from the chest down at age twenty-three, after which she soon lost her job, income, health insurance, and stair-filled Chicago home. Within three years, Bristo formed what is now Access Living, a Chicago nonprofit organization. She went on to play a key role in drafting and passing the Americans with Disabilities Act of 1990—and then, after receiving a presidential appointment, helped ensure it was enforced.

BRADLEY LOMAX (1950–1984) experienced significant accessibility barriers after moving to Oakland, California. He worked to establish a chapter of the Center for Independent Living in collaboration with Ed Roberts and the Black Panther Party. In 1977, he and fellow Black Panthers supported the Section 504 sit-in by providing food and supplies to the protesters.

(Clockwise from top left)

DENNIS LIN (1998–2018) was an energetic, beloved member of WCUC, where he frequently served as greeter or liturgist. At church, on trains, and at elementary schools where he did volunteer work, Lin loved bringing people together.

REV. WADE BLANK (1940–1993) organized the historic 1990 march of disability rights leaders from the White House to the US Capitol that ended in the famed Capitol Crawl, where disabled people crawled up the Capitol steps and were arrested while demonstrating in the rotunda. The Americans with Disabilities Act passed in July; without the courage and skills of Blank and his colleagues, the world would not have had its first comprehensive civil rights law for people with disabilities.

FRED FAY (1944–2011) was determined to demonstrate that a person with quadriplegia could own an apartment, drive a car, get married, have children, and earn a PhD. He accomplished his dreams while also working as a disability policy adviser, helping pass several crucial disability rights acts from 1973 through 1997. Fay was also a pioneer in assistive technology and was instrumental in the development of adaptive computer technology. For millions of people, Fay's innovations provided access to the world around them.

JUDITH HEUMANN (1947–2023), a wheelchair user, was denied her New York teaching license because the Board of Education did not believe she could get herself or her students out of the building in case of a fire. She sued them on the basis of discrimination and became the first wheelchair user to teach in New York City. In 1977, she and Kitty Cone led the longest sit-in at a federal building in history, organizing over 150 people to occupy Senator Joseph Califano's office for twenty-eight days, which resulted in the signing of two landmark laws ensuring the right to an education regardless of ability.

CHRISTINA PICKARD (1945–2020) AND JOHN MARTINO (1954–2022) of the WCUC community met as children at Fernald State School in Waltham, Massachusetts. Pickard had complications at birth that resulted in weak muscles on her right side, hearing loss, and paralyzed vocal cords. Martino was Deaf and learned to sign at Fernald. He and Pickard both came to live at a Minute Man Arc group home after Fernald closed.

ED ROBERTS (1939–1995) is often called the father of the Independent Living movement. After the University of California, Berkeley, attempted to rescind his acceptance to their school upon discovering that he had quadriplegia, Roberts had to advocate admission and accommodations. His admission broke the ice for other quadriplegics to attend Berkeley; these students eventually named themselves the "Rolling Quads," to the surprise of nondisabled observers who had never before heard a positive expression of disability identity. In 1976, Governor Jerry Brown appointed Roberts director of the California Department of Vocational Rehabilitation—the same agency that had once labeled him too severely disabled to work.

Jesus as the Disabled God
By Olga Ledis, commissioned by Rev. Melissa Tustin at West Concord Union Church in October 2017

In the fall of 2019, members of all ages and dis/abilities at West Concord Union Church (WCUC, in Massachusetts) took up paint brushes, scissors, and glue to create a new art piece for their sanctuary entrance.[1] Now, all who enter WCUC for worship are greeted by a unique representation of divinity: Surrounded by twelve "disability saints," Jesus sits in a self-propelled wheelchair with slanted wheels, perfect for a disabled savior on the go. As members worked on the mural, they also learned about the "disability saints" it depicts. Ranging from a second grader at the 1990 Capitol Crawl to several members of WCUC,[2] these "saints" encapsulate the vital place disabled people hold (or should hold) in our politics, in equal rights movements, and within our own communities. Meanwhile, the image of a wheelchair-using Jesus challenges ableist assumptions about the incompatibility of disability and divinity, the conflation of disability and brokenness.

If images of a **disabled God** greeted us at the entrance of every sanctuary, would more churches find room in their budgets for ramps, sign language interpreters, and disability workshops? Would there be more openly disabled ministers, teachers, and elders guiding our communities? Most importantly, would the church finally become a place where all of us can bring our whole selves—including our limitations and vulnerabilities?

FROM SHAME TO NEUROQUEER PRIDE

I spent my teenage years dissociated from my body and other people, beleaguered by anxiety and a shame I lacked the language to name. In college, I met **trans** and proudly Autistic people and my world opened up: There were whole communities of people like me! Guided by their experience, I made life changes to honor my nonbinary, Autistic self (or, to use a term emphasizing how my gender and **neurodivergence** mutually inform one another, as a **neuroqueer** person).[3] Gradually, I became more at home in my **bodymind**—the indivisible unit of body and mind that is *me*[4]—and consequently in God's good, embodied world.

MAKING A FUTURE OUT OF NO FUTURE

I vividly recall the time my wife mentioned that she'd always assumed she wouldn't make it to twenty. My reaction: *"I'm not the only one?!"* What makes it nearly impossible for many marginalized folk to imagine a (positive) future for ourselves?

For disabled people, this impossibility is fueled by the overwhelming presence of "stereotypical stories of pity, helplessness, and victimhood."[5] These narratives influence children's self-esteem. Such was the case for wheelchair user Becky Tyler, who at age twelve struggled to believe God loved her—until her mother read her Daniel 7:9, which depicts God's throne with wheels.[6] That image transformed her outlook: "Having a wheelchair is actually very cool, because God has one." Adding positive representation to the slew of negative images does not solve everything, but it does equip youth to combat society's lies. To this end, I encourage ministers to retell Bible stories in ways that uplift specific marginalized experiences. The following section exemplifies what an identity-specific retelling might look like.

JOSEPH'S NEUROQUEER DREAMS

Joseph is seventeen when his[7] story opens, yet the text calls him a boy (Hebrew *naar*; Gen. 37:2). In his culture, a *naar* should have become an *ish* (man) by that age,[8] but Joseph's family—his doting father, his jealous brothers—still treat him like a child.

Autistic teens and adults know what it is to be infantilized; some people even react with shock upon learning we can have careers, **friendships**, children, and sex lives.[9] Because we don't always behave according to "age-appropriate norms," we are denied autonomy and opportunities.

According to Jewish midrash, Joseph is also "boyish" in his presentation: "He behaved like a boy, penciling his eyes, curling his hair, and lifting his heel."[10] Here, nonconformity is depicted as something a boy grows out of (something people still assure parents of gender-creative children today), but Joseph does not. Additionally, that walking with a "lifted heel" reads to me as a neuroqueer trait, a merging of Autistic toe-walking and an effeminate flounce in the step. I picture a modern-day Joseph(ine) at a gay bar, eyeliner on point as they sashay onto the dance floor.

Joseph neuroqueers his movement through the world, and his father Jacob shows support with the gift of a princess dress (Gen. 37:3; Hebrew *ketonet passim*). Often translated into something like "colorful robe," the only other biblical figure to wear one is David's daughter Tamar, where it is described as what "virgin daughters of the king" wear (2 Sam. 13:18)—a princess dress, indeed!

Unfortunately, when his brothers see Joseph approaching in that girlish garment, they conspire: "Here comes this dreamer! Come on, let's kill him . . . and we'll see what becomes of his dreams" (Gen. 37:19). They seize Joseph, rip away his beautiful dress, and sell him into enslavement (vv. 19–28). Like all too many queer and disabled persons,[11] Joseph endures familial rejection and assault.

Despite continued traumas, Joseph survives and even finds ways to thrive in the land of his captivity. Egypt responds to his gift for dream interpretation not with abhorrence but awe, and Pharoah empowers Joseph to avert famine (Gen. 41). Ultimately, the very thing that Joseph's brothers loathed is what saves not only them, but the entire (biblical) world.[12] When trans and disabled people share our gifts, those blessed to share community with us are enriched. Unfortunately, we are often denied that chance.

EXPANDING IMAGINATION BY MODELING POSSIBILITIES

The summer before I started seminary, a church leader made an offhand comment about a young man who wanted to be a pastor. She just couldn't see it happening. Why? "I think he must be somewhere on the spectrum," she confided, and my stomach dropped. "I'm Autistic, too," I wanted to say. "Am I not fit for ministry either?"

A year into seminary, I interviewed for a field education position at a More Light congregation.[13] My interviewers asked awkward questions about how being trans would "impact" my internship (I hadn't even dared to disclose my **autism**). Afterward, I learned that they went with a different student partially out of concern that church members would struggle with my **pronouns**. Instead of seeing my partnership as a chance to learn and grow, they opted for a "safer" choice. Their imaginations failed them, and they failed me, a member of the community they claimed to advocate for.

Whenever such moments take place, I am tempted to give up on church. But then I remember my desperate, unmet need for possibility models growing up.

"Possibility model" is how trans actress and activist Laverne Cox describes what she represents for many trans people, particularly Black trans women. Rather than simply being a role model to emulate, she hopes to inspire people to pursue their *own* goals: "The idea that I get to live my dreams out in public, hopefully will show other folks that it's possible."[14] Being loud and proud about my neuroqueerness is a political decision as much as a personal one: I risk visibility so that no one like me grows up assuming ministry is closed to them.

Overall, choosing to stick with Christianity has brought more joys than griefs. The church leader who made that offhand comment has been one of my staunchest supporters. Meanwhile, I joined More Light Presbyterians in 2021 to help them develop more educational opportunities for affiliated congregations. This progress lets me look back on painful experiences and notice where they slot into a fuller narrative, fueling me to persevere.

Scripture also models possibilities of disabled leadership. I know of a teenager who dreamed of being a pastor but assumed that his stutter was an insurmountable obstruction to that goal. When he mentioned this "impossible" dream to a friend's mother, she fired back, "You know, Moses had a stutter too." His eyes widened in revelation. In that moment, the sense of vocation he had dismissed solidified into something real.

Like that teen, Moses could not believe God would call him, a man with a speech difference,[15] to be God's voice. Rather than altering Moses's speech, God accommodates his stated needs, making Aaron his cospeaker and providing miraculous signs (Exod. 4:1–16). Moses performs a "sign" for us today: He models disabled vocation made possible when support needs are met and shame and stigma are stripped away.

INTEGRATING CRIP WISDOM INTO YOUTH MINISTRY

As we dare to imagine new futures with disabled youth, ministers can look to the past and present by drawing from crip wisdom—a term for all the "brilliance and experience of disabled people" who have had to innovate ways to survive and thrive in a society not built for them.[16] Much of this knowledge is shared informally, from one disabled person to another (*"Here's what worked for me . . ."*). However, much of it has also been preserved in performances,[17] books, social media posts, and more, available to any who go looking for it.

What follows are ways to integrate crip wisdom into youth ministry. The resource list at the end of the book offers further guidance.

Universalize access. Rather than reserving support needs—from flexible deadlines to permission to fidget or occasionally withdraw to a quiet space—for diagnosed disabled persons, open them to everyone.[18] Along with its benefits to all students, a universal approach ensures that *all* disabled youth—not just diagnosed ones—have access to what they need for an equitable experience. This is a matter of intersectional justice, as any child who is not cis, straight, White, male, and middle/upper class is less likely to have access to screening.[19] Furthermore, if disabled youth cease to be the only ones with "special" needs, those needs will cease to be special, closing some distance between abled and disabled peers.

Enter crip time. Because disabled people are often unable to predict what our energy or pain levels will be, or else depend on often-unreliable accessible transportation, or simply complete tasks more slowly than others, we frequently cannot keep up with society's frantic pace. We must live by "**crip time**," wherein a slower pace and reduced productivity become acts of resistance.[20] Indeed, I can think of few things more dangerous to capitalism, because while capitalism demands that we bend our bodyminds to the clock, "crip time bends the clock to meet disabled bodies and minds."[21]

What better place than church to practice resisting the world's frenzy for Sabbath's slowing down? Here are some ways to embrace crip time in your ministry:

- Welcome latecomers with gratitude that they made it at all and sum up what they've missed.
- Instead of cramming as much information as possible into a session, prioritize equipping youth to acquire knowledge on their own (e.g., teach them how to use free online tools).
- Accept that you may not get through everything you hope to. Focus instead on ensuring everyone has room to process what you did get through.
- Design your lesson plans with a closing activity that can be left off or carried over to the next session. Schedule occasional "catch-up" days.

Make space for special interests. One perceived disruption crip time accommodates is infodumping: the enthusiastic, detailed sharing of knowledge about one's special interest/hyperfixation.[22] A neurodivergent youth's avalanche of information about whale species, prehistoric weapons, or pre-Raphaelite art is not always the non sequitur it seems: Autistic people process and engage through our special interests.[23] Pay attention for connections. For next-level affirmation, you might even *invite* an infodump. Occasionally,

I found ways to incorporate a teen's interest in the Byzantine Empire into an upcoming lesson. He usually became more engaged the rest of the session.

Mess up, but don't give up! Sometimes you'll fail, flounder, or feel like a supreme jerk. Do not let these moments defeat you! To embrace the crip wisdom that all humans have limitations is to accept that that includes *you*. Review what went wrong (ideally with a trusted colleague), brainstorm actions to take in future, make any necessary apologies[24]—and keep trying!

MODELING "FAILURE"

To counteract narratives that disabled people are helpless, disabled activists emphasize "presuming competence": starting with the assumption that, if their support needs are met, a given disabled individual *is* capable of a given activity.[25] Nonetheless, to avoid overcorrecting into a different ableist narrative—that anyone can overcome their disability through sheer hard work[26]—balance is also necessary. Presume competence and ensure access to accommodations but also respect a disabled person's self-knowledge when they say they *cannot* do something or would prefer help.

A young disabled person may still be figuring out what they can and cannot do on their own. Subverting normative ideas about success and failure may help them unlearn shame and protect their energy for what they can do. Let me share my own failure to live up to normative expectations—and why I am glad to have "failed."

I graduated seminary in May 2019; by that fall, I had completed everything I needed to be ordained, apart from accepting a call (i.e., job offer). Seven years later, I am no closer to ordination than I was then. In fact, in 2024 I withdrew from the process entirely after admitting to myself that my ordination goals had shrunk down to two things. First, I wanted the credibility that the Reverend title would bring to my ministry. But I needed to remember that I don't need institutional validation to confirm God's approval. It is more important that I accept my unique strengths *and* limitations, rather than try to satisfy expectations of constant availability and productivity that would bend my neuroqueer bodymind till it breaks. I am proud of the work I do, grateful that *because* my ministry is unorthodox, I can reach trans and disabled persons who have no offine access to affirming community and theology.

The second reason I remained on the ordination track was a sense of responsibility to model possibility for other trans and/or Autistic Christians. After some wallowing, I got over myself—I am not the first or only person in the world to model people like me in ministry! Indeed, the "Autism Pastor" himself, Dr. Lamar Hardwick, appears in this volume directly before my chapter; I also personally know multiple incredible trans and neurodivergent pastors and counselors. I am grateful they are out there, so that I can model a different possibility.

RESISTANCE FROM WITHIN AND WITHOUT

My "failure" to get ordained has freed me to model faithful **protest** against the injustices still deeply embedded within the institutional church. I denounce that churches fought for and still maintain exemption from the **Americans with Disabilities Act.**[27] I resist the Christian perpetuation of ideologies that objectify disabled people into moral lessons and symbols of sin and faithlessness.[28] I protest the obstacles that queer, trans, and disabled people continue to face when seeking to be ordained and/or hired within their denomination.

When youth are equipped with a broad range of possibility models, they can better imagine how they want to show up in God's justice movement. Your job is to equip your young people with stories that ignite their imaginations, cultivate equitable spaces where they can learn and dream together, and actively have their backs wherever the Spirit leads them. Who knows? Maybe, one day, *your* youth will be the models that awaken future children into new worlds of possibility.

REFLECTION QUESTIONS

1. How can you support youth engagement in advocating for and helping enact changes to your church, whether that involves structural changes to improve access, alterations to language and rituals used in worship, or increased opportunities to learn from disabled persons?
2. What is one way you could embrace crip time in your ministry, no longer making your and your youths' lives bend to the clock but instead bending the clock to meet your bodyminds?

3. How can you adapt this chapter's biblical interlude or another disability-resonant biblical passage for use in your ministry (e.g., a lesson plan or a sermon)?

PRACTICAL TOOL: REIMAGINING THE DIVINE BODYMIND

Objective: The purpose of this lesson is to stir up the images of Jesus in our heads and expand our minds to fit a more diverse array of images.

What you'll need:

- A projector on which to show multiple visuals
- A whiteboard, blackboard, or other large writing surface.
- Around five to eight illustrations of Jesus that portray him as a variety of races, cultures, sexualities, dis/abilities, etc. The art pieces listed below are intended as examples of applicable works; if a link is broken, try internet searching the artist's name and art title. You may also do your own search for more art: try phrases like "multicultural Jesus art" or "queer Jesus art."
    - A wheelchair-using Jesus and disability saints (pictured in chapter), https://tinyurl.com/mszzamdw
    - "Luke 14 Banquet" by Hyatt Moore, 2016, https://tinyurl.com/3mt96376—real people with a range of dis/abilities posed for this portrait
    - "The First Supper" by Susan Dorothea White, 1998, https://tinyurl.com/2mb7j3cm—Jesus as an aboriginal woman
    - "Emmaus," Emmanuel Garibay, 2012, https://tinyurl.com/43z38aaz—the risen Jesus as a woman in a red dress
    - Jesus displaying his top surgery scars to three disciples in *id:TRANS* by Elisabeth Ohlson Wallin (2018), https://tinyurl.com/3pn44rke
    - *The Passion of Christ: A Gay Vision* by Douglas Blanchard, https://tinyurl.com/yar7n7du
    - "Advent Attention" by Scott Erickson, https://tinyurl.com/9evfzmtj
    - "Diptych with Mary and Her Son Flanked by Archangels, Apostles and a Saint," fifteenth century, https://tinyurl.com/ywab5b45—image is about halfway down the web page.
    - "Jesus in the Temple Teaching" by Jyoti Sahi, https://tinyurl.com/ynn6fakk

- "Jesus Welcomes the Children," Jesus MAFA, 1973, https://tinyurl.com/pbh2f5s9

The Lesson

Ask youth to share words or phrases that come into their minds when they think about Jesus. Write their answers on the whiteboard.

Then ask them what words they would use to describe Jesus's physical attributes; write those responses.

Ask the group what they notice about the words chosen to talk about Jesus. Do any seem contradictory? Do any patterns emerge?

Tell the group that today you will be looking at images of Jesus from different artists and from around the world and thinking together about why the artists made the choices they did and what these pictures say about Jesus and about God.

Display the first image on the projector and announce its title and artist. Describe the image or ask the group to describe it so that anyone who is blind or has low vision can participate.

Then lead with these guiding questions:

- What are the first things you notice in this image? What feelings come up inside you as you look at it?
- Does this image of Jesus have any similarities to you? What about differences?
- Why do you think the artist portrayed Jesus the way they did? How do you think *they* would describe who Jesus was and what he cared most about?
- What does this version of Jesus tell us about who Jesus is or about who we are?

Repeat for every image. Finally, ask the group how it felt to see so many different images of Jesus. Is it possible for more than one to be "true"?

Closing Prayer

Creator God,

When you made humans in your image, you made us diverse enough to reflect the infinity that is you. You delighted in all our different sizes and skin tones, our countless ways of thinking and moving and showing up for each other.

Open our hearts to share your delight, so that we will look for you where Jesus told us you would be: among the people everyone hates or ignores and in the faces of those we think of as strangers, as too different to be family.

When at last we recognize our oneness in diversity, our mutual need for one another's unique gifts, we will know your kin-dom has come fully down to earth at last.

Amen.

A PRAYER OF PROTEST FOR YOUTH

CARMELLE BEAUGELIN CALDWELL

God, I want to change the way things are.
When ________________ experience(s) ___________________, I often wish I could ___________________, but I don't always know how.
God, how can I help change ______________________?
Please, show me what to do. Help me to be ___________________, so that I could share Your peace with _________________________________.
Amen.

God, I want to change the way things are.
When (*I, a loved one, a community etc.*) experience(s) *(an injustice: discrimination, poverty, exclusion, etc.)*, I often wish I could *(a desired action: fight back, speak up, create change, etc.)* but I don't always know how.
God, how can I help change *(a specific issue: unfair laws, oppression, violence, etc.)*? Please, show me what to do. Help me to be *(a characteristic: brave, wise, strong, compassionate, etc.)*, so that I can share Your peace with *(a person, a group of people or a community)*.
Amen.

INTERLUDE: INTRODUCTION TO NEURODIVERSITY

ERIN RAFFETY

Much as the **social model of disability** moves away from individual or medicalized notions of disability, *neurodiversity* approaches variations in thinking, sensing, and experience as yet another element of our human diversity and seeks to depathologize many conditions previously perceived as disorders from the standpoint of human variety. By depathologize, we mean to move away from understandings of diagnoses that regard them as abnormal or problems. Although the conditions that fall under the umbrella of neurodiversity are increasingly broadening and shifting, the **neurodiversity movement** is often associated with **autism**, because it emerged out of the autism rights movement in the 1990s. However, people who have diagnoses such as ADHD, dyslexia, Tourette's syndrome, sensory perception conditions, high sensitivity, and synesthesia often also identify as neurodivergent. Finally, some people with mental health diagnoses like **depression**, anxiety, or bipolar disorder may also identify as neurodivergent.

Neurodiversity, a term coined by Australian sociologist and autistic self-advocate Judy Singer, refers to not only the spectrum and diversity of autism spectrum conditions, but the total array of brain makeup of the human species. Within this variety, people with neurodivergent behaviors or experiences, **neurodivergences**, that often lead to a diagnosis are neurodivergent, whereas people who do not have neurodivergences are categorized as neurotypical. Of course, there is no typical brain, just as experiences of neurodivergence are unique and varied: Therefore, it is helpful to remember that neurodiversity refers to the whole of humanity and does not just offer another label but valorizes and makes space for our collective humanity.

The move toward depathologizing differences in sensing, experience, and behaviors has led to more self-knowledge, self-acceptance, and pride among neurodivergent people. This is important, not only because an estimated 20 percent of the population is neurodivergent, but especially because when neurodivergent people are constantly made to conform to neurotypical environments, it can cause them great stress, pain, and even comorbid mental health conditions. Thanks to the neurodiversity movement, for instance, we now know that the more typical presentations of autism, ADHD, and sensory and sensitivity conditions in boys and men are not shared in girls and women. Girls and women who have become adept at fitting in, thus **masking** their neurodivergence, often experience anxiety, depression, and other mental health conditions. The concept of **neuronormativity** can be helpful in identifying assumptions and practices about attention, bodily comportment, and respectful behavior that implicitly judge or devalue different behaviors, like **stimming**, fidgeting, repeated speech, and intolerance of certain foods or smells.

The increasing acceptance of neurodivergence through the neurodiversity movement has also helped identify ways in which neurotypical norms in environments, cultures, customs, and institutions, such as education, healthcare, and employment, just to name a few, can limit creativity and appreciation for the gifts and insights of neurodivergent people. A classic example of this are the contributions of Temple Grandin, an autistic academic and inventor, whose personal experiences of autism led her to imagine more humane practices and treatment for livestock. Neurodivergent people are responsible for everyday innovations that also serve neurotypical people, such as fidget spinners and poppers. Many neurodivergent people, especially highly sensitive people, and even autistic people like Grandin, confront the stereotypical presentations of autism and ADHD in that they are astutely attuned to their environments or hyperfocused. As these sensitivities are better understood, they undoubtedly lead to better knowledge about one's own experiences that are transferable not just to human beings but even to animals and to nature.

Within Christian scripture there is repeated emphasis on the richness of diversity, variety, and goodness in God's creation. We can think of not just ourselves, but even our brains, following educator Thomas Armstrong's metaphor, as **brainforests**, ecosystems that grow and stretch, yet need nurturing and acceptance to exist within the larger ecosystem of creation. This metaphor may help make space for youth whose behaviors or expressions diverge from the norm, but in so doing offer something rich and vital to the ecosystem of our churches and communities. As mentioned in "Interlude: Introduction to Disability," because many youth are young and still growing, they may not yet have formal diagnoses. And because medical approaches to neurodivergence have often been limited and stigmatized, both older and younger people may lack formal diagnoses. The neurodiversity movement teaches us that experiences of neurodiversity are quite broad and different, and whereas some people experience certain aspects of their condition as symptoms, others are simply ways of being that make them unique.

Youth workers can help by engaging youth in conversations about their thinking processes, their routines, and experiences of their environments in nonjudgmental ways. Youth workers can also help by educating youth groups on various aspects and experiences of neurodiversity to build knowledge, understanding, and acceptance. Providing a variety of ways to experience God and connect with others at church activities, such as incorporating more embodied practices, quiet options for engagement, and even videogames, can be ways to move away from neuronormativity that inhibits self-expression and connection with God. Many neurodivergent people have talked about how confusing and off-putting basic Christian practices are to them, such as prayer and worship, so demonstrating a wide variety of good and right ways to engage with these, and even letting young people develop and invent their own practices, can be affirming.

Some argue that the language of neurodiversity seems overly academic or abstract, but it is important to remember that this is language that autistic people themselves developed, and other disabled people have found it meaningful and expansive to connect with a broader experience of humanity. Thus the movement does something exciting in moving away from labels, especially those that are imposed, and toward affirming the insights and gifts of diversity. But just as with any language, we should learn to use the terms that people prefer in order to honor and dignify their experiences. As **intersectionality** teaches us, there can be wide variety even across like diagnoses, especially in terms of gender and race. Returning to the theological underpinning of marvel at the truly infinite diversity of God's good creation gives us a starting point not only to better accept and learn from one another but to grow in faithfulness to God and one another.

PART 3

PRAISE

A PRAYER OF PRAISE

We Give You Thanks, O Lord Our God

JOSHUA TAYLOR[1]

(Can be sung to the tune of "Amazing Grace")

We give you thanks, O Lord our God,
for body, mind, and soul.
We bear your love in human form
our lives divinely whole.

We're not alone within our role,
we stand among the saints,
Like Jacob served through labored stroll
our praise knows no restraints.

With eyes as dark as Isaac's sight,
we seek to see your face,
and offer lives for your delight,
and seek your mighty grace.

Like Moses or Elizabeth,
our path may not be straight,
but you have readied us to birth
the hope for which we wait.

Like Dorcus, Sarah, those who strive
to meet us on the way,

for allies who support our lives,
we join our hands and pray.

Our bodies fully join the throng
of those who led the way.
We offer now our faithful song
today and every day.

Through disability and pain,
our faith stands unrestrained,
so, use us Lord for heavn'ly gain,
our lives for you ordain.

THE WILDERNESS OF TRANSITION

Becoming My Own Advocate

HUNTER STEINITZ

> ***Guiding Question:*** *How can faith communities support students through the wilderness?*

"For you formed my inward parts; you knitted me together in my mother's womb. I praise you, for I am fearfully and wonderfully made" (Ps. 139:13–14 ESV). I live only by the grace of God. I was born with a very rare genetic skin disorder called Harlequin Ichthyosis, which makes my skin bright red and flakey. When I was born, the doctors told my parents that I would not live to see my first birthday. As I write this I am approaching my thirtieth birthday, and what a wild ride it has been. I believe that my Creator knit together my being, Ichthyosis and all, in love and with purpose. There were lots of unknowns in those early years, but one thing we did know was that I would go to public school and be educated alongside my peers, consequences be damned.

I was blessed to be born in the United States after the passage of the Rehabilitation Act of 1973, the **Americans with Disabilities Act** and the **Individuals with Disabilities Education Act** (**IDEA**) both passed in 1990. These laws formed the foundation of our special education system, and it is thanks to them that I was able to attend public school in my hometown of Pittsburgh. I had an **Individualized Education Plan**, which allowed me to receive services such as occupational therapy that helped me learn fine motor skills like fastening buttons, zippers, and grasping a pencil. I also had a 504, based on the Rehab Act of 1973, which allowed me reasonable accommodations, like permission to leave class to do skincare when needed.

Because of these supports I was able to learn in the same classroom as my nondisabled peers, which gave me the closest thing to a "normal" upbringing as possible given my unique medical needs. Clearly I would not have been able to do all that for myself as a child; I needed someone who could advocate for my needs and hold systems to task when they wanted to skirt their responsibilities under the law.

My mother, Patti, was a strong and capable woman who took no crap from anyone. She served as a Pittsburgh police officer for over twenty years, and she knew how to get what she needed. She was my biggest advocate. When the district wanted to bus me across the city instead of paying for the accommodations we requested, she held them accountable. When I faced extreme bullying from both peers and teachers, she wouldn't tolerate such abuse.

My mom was also a woman of faith. She grew up in a Roman Catholic family but left the Catholic Church when I was a toddler. Through the recommendation of one of my night nurses we found our way to Riverview United Presbyterian Church when I was about four and never looked back. I was raised in the Presbyterian Church (USA), in a church already rich with disability advocates who insisted on accessibility even when it was unpopular. As I grew up alongside other peers both in school and at church I learned how to advocate for myself, explain why I looked the way I do, and how I am just like everyone else, with hopes, dreams, and interests. I relied on the steady foundations underneath me to continue growing.

In 2008 Mom got sick. After a number of procedures we learned she had pancreatic cancer. As her health deteriorated over the next several years all that self-advocacy practice came in handy, because I needed to speak up for myself and my needs in her absence. In October 2011 I was a junior in high school. Any high school junior is thinking about life after graduation. What college do I want to apply to? When do I have to take the SATs? How do I apply to the schools on my list? Those questions intensify for students with disabilities. Because all of those supports that I relied on before were going to disappear, and I needed to prepare for that eventuality. And right in the middle of all that, on October 19, 2011, my mother lost her battle with cancer.

My advocate was gone, and I was fast approaching what we in the disability community call "the cliff." Every student transitions out of high school, regardless of ability. But for students with disabilities that transition is critical. Up until that point students are required by law to receive accommodations so that they receive what the IDEA calls "free appropriate public education." Once you leave high school, all such regulations go away and unless families prepare themselves and their students they will find themselves looking over the edge of the cliff, full of potential but nowhere to go.

"And behold, the LORD passed by, and a great and strong wind tore the mountains and broke in pieces the rocks before the LORD but the LORD was not in the wind. And after the wind an earthquake, but the LORD was not in the earthquake. And after the earthquake a fire, but the LORD was not in the fire. And after the fire the sound of a low whisper" (1 Kings 19:11–12 ESV). Navigating this transition can feel like wandering in the wilderness with no clear path forward. In a chaotic and confusing environment with big and distracting events (like fires, earthquakes, or college applications), scripture reminds us where to look for God's presence. We find that Presence in the quiet in-betweens. When transitioning out of high school, there is so much to plan for and it can be difficult to know where to turn. Since I no longer had my advocate by my side, I was afraid of the future and doubted my ability to succeed. When I didn't think I could go to college, my faith family reminded me that I had done this before. I had faced insurmountable odds before and by the grace of God and with the support of others I paved a path through thick wilderness. They showed me who I was when I had lost all semblance of identity.

Riverview wandered with me through my transition in the wilderness. They taught me that the church does have a role to play in supporting young people with disabilities through their transition journey. Some of those ways are intangible, like emotional and spiritual support and being present. Other ways of support are much more tangible, like providing meaningful work for disabled youth in a community of kindness that can foster disabled youth as they grow into themselves.

As an adult I now work as a disability advocate. Through that work I have learned that there are many different ways that faith communities can take advantage of opportunities through various national agencies to support a disabled person in their midst. All fifty states and six other territories receive federal funding for **vocational rehabilitation (VR) services.**[1] These VR agencies exist to "assist disabled individuals with obtaining, maintaining, or advancing employment."[2] VR agencies work with community groups and business partners to provide their services. They need pillars within the community to step up and work with them to support people with disabilities within those communities. Through those partnerships, new doors open not just for disabled folks but also for the communities around them.

One example here in Pittsburgh is Brother André's Café,[3] which is a local café staffed by individuals with **developmental disabilities**. "At Brother André's Café, we serve much more than gourmet coffee, baked goods and handcrafted Christian gifts. We serve Christ . . . , we provide employment opportunities for adults with intellectual and developmental disabilities . . . , promote products from vulnerable communities in developing countries and provide a place of community and Christian fellowship," their website reads. This little shop is just one of many places around the city where people with disabilities can find gainful and meaningful employment within their communities.

Churches can be active participants and partners in VR work. If local businesses, schools, and companies offer positions to people with disabilities, VR can help cover the cost of adaptive equipment needed to complete tasks. VR agencies can educate your staff on best practices for supporting people with disabilities in your area. Congregations are uniquely positioned to support disabled people in their congregation in this way. And when you open your community not only do you grow, but so does the body of Christ.

REFLECTION QUESTIONS

1. What do you know about the vocational rehabilitation services near you?
2. What types of jobs would disabled youth in your community like to have?
3. Who in your community would be open to the support of vocational rehabilitation resources so that they could begin hiring disabled individuals?

CALLED?

A Theology of Disabling Vocation

DEBORAH HUGGINS

> ***Guiding Questions:*** *What calls have you experienced in your life? What resources would help bring them to fruition?*

Every December, our church hosts a living nativity. The whole town shows up to see animals, kids, and adults act out the story of the birth of Christ. We re-enact the nativity in four scenes, each one growing in excitement and pageantry until we get to the final moment—scene four. Grace plays the role of Mary. Grace started with scene one, the annunciation, and has been the scene four Mary for the past three years. She is beautiful, gracious, alert, and attentive. She lovingly cares for the baby Jesus, and gazes angelically at the crowd. She welcomes the wise ones, accepting their gifts. In that moment Grace embodies not only the mother of God, but also the full star power that is truly hers, on display for the whole town to see.

Grace, aged fourteen, said, "The first time I played Mary, it was not how I envisioned it. She was all alone—in her room. Anxious and afraid. It was awful. I felt invisible. The next year, I was Mary in scene four—and I went from anxious to fulfilled. It was exactly how I envisioned Mary from the Bible—from the costumes, to the narrator, the adorable animals. I felt fulfilled. I said, 'that's what God is. I am experiencing God.'"[1]

In our town, the school plays are big. People come from the neighboring towns to hear the kids sing, dance, and act. Some of the kids have Broadway credentials. The costumes and the sets are award winning. Our schools are under enormous pressure to perform. To get prizes. To be the best. To place students in top colleges and top programs. But all this excellence comes at a cost. There are a lot of kids who do not make the cut: kids who can't afford coaches and dance classes; whose first language isn't English; who have the wrong body type, hair texture, or gender identity; and who have disabilities. When Grace was in middle school and wanted to be a part of the drama club, she was told that because of the level of supports she uses at school to accommodate her disability, if she tried out she would not be chosen as a main character or a member of the ensemble, and she could not be in the crew or help with the costumes. In the middle school play for Grace's public school, her role, she was told, was to usher—with support from an aide.

Yet Grace's embodiment of Mary in the living nativity is palpable. The first year, during the annunciation, she wept, fully living into Mary's fear and loneliness. In scene four she emanates God's fulfillment and presence, inviting the audience and actors into her experience of the holy. Grace's sobbing in the first scene was as genuine as her fulfillment and joy in the fourth scene. Grace's charisma radiates through not only that scene but the whole nativity.

In this chapter we praise the work of the church to proclaim the gospel through disabled lives and we articulate a disabled theology of vocation within the Reformed tradition. The chapter features three guiding disabled people who are young church members, self-advocates, and leaders in their churches: James, Sydney, and Grace. James is a young adult and Sydney and Grace are both youth; they each have moderate to intense needs for support.

VOCATION

James[2] is proud of where he works. He's proud of his uniform and the excellent reviews that his boss gives him and that his job coach only comes for monitoring. He is successful in his competitive employment setting. This is the fulfillment of years of hard, focused work and support.

James articulated the power of liturgy in worship when he made the connection between his work and the way that the congregation worships: "Um, they [the congregation] follow the leader and they—they do a specific routine, every time. And just like I, I do at work." In the Reformed tradition, vocation or call holds a distinct role. Vocation is not limited to or even primarily focused on clergy. Instead, each believer is given strengths and talents by God and then called by God to their work where they will use their gifts to serve the world.

In the classical Reformed tradition, vocation is not only joining into God's redemptive work in the world, along with prayer and worship, but it is also essential to how we experience God, feel God's presence, and know the assurance of grace and salvation when we join in God's work.[3] Vocation is extended to people of every age, gender, field, ability, and station of life. This leads to a sense of duty and obligation that goes beyond the need to please a boss or an organization. For the believer, work even becomes a way of showing devotion to God.

In his book *Wishful Thinking*, Frederick Buechner states, "There are all different kinds of voices calling you to all different kinds of work, and the problem is to find out which is the voice of God rather than of Society. . . . The place God calls you to is the place where your deep gladness and the world's deep hunger meet."[4] Buechner articulates vocation as a simple equation. We can illustrate it this way:

Your Gladness + The Worlds Needs = Life Lived with God

As we examine Buechner's definition of vocation through the lens of disability, we are invited to challenge several of our assumptions around call, especially as we consider the affirmation of gifts, the role of independence, and the ways that we fulfill the needs of the world.

According to Buechner, call starts with our deep gladness: our passion, our giftedness, our source of joy. This gladness is what each person has to contribute, our gifts. Affirmation of these gifts is often more complex for disabled people in their faith communities. Benjamin T. Conner[5] describes the affirmation of gifts in the church by looking at the abilities of different swimmers: a young child as she works to make a competitive swim team, a young adult swimming for Special Olympics, and a high schooler breaking a school record. All three swimmers are gifted, swimming to their capacity, making improvements, and striving toward goals. All three swimmers are gifted athletes, and all three fall far short of an elite Olympic swimmer.

According to Conner, when we just look at the elite athlete we are in danger of missing the gifts of the other three. When considering gifts, disability challenges the church to examine how we see and affirm the gifts of our members. Disabled people have much to teach us as we seek to affirm diverse gifts. During her first year as Mary, Grace cried during the scene. The organizers assumed that she was distraught because of a problem like cold weather or boredom. Only in conversation with Grace did they come to understand the depth of her interpretation and the fullness of understanding that she brought to the role. Grace was not unhappy; Mary was unhappy. Grace's interpretation challenged the church to not only explore recruitment practices for casting children in a pageant, but to further understand the depth of Mary's feelings. Grace invites the church to a deeper understanding of God.

As the church moves to affirm the gifts of disabled young people, we are invited into a stance of listening, humbleness, and patience as we affirm the deep gladness of disabled youth. The church needs to learn to look past easy affirmations, which so often function to affirm the gifts of only a few in our congregations, and enter into the wilderness of affirming the diversity of voices called to serve the diversity of needs in the world.

The next part of Buechner's arithmetic is the "World's Need." As we look to the needs of the world we quickly become overwhelmed unless we can focus on one area of importance. We can't, after all, address all the needs of the world. Which, then, do we prioritize? The way that we connect is often out of our own stories and experiences. In her article for *Time Magazine*, Martha White urges savvy donors to do the autobiographical work of clarifying their own values, experiences, and interests before engaging in philanthropic work.[6] This advice highlights that the stakes are high when it comes to who defines the needs of the world. If vocation is the interplay of the gifts and skills of a community or an individual with the needs of the world, who defines and sees those needs is essential. In our churches, we must listen to the needs of the world as they are interpreted by a wide range of people, including the needs seen by disabled people.

With two parts of the equation set, we now look at the addition sign to achieve the goal: life with God. This action, in its deceptive simplicity, may, however, be the most radical part of a disabled theology of vocation. Rather than completing a solitary action, the disabled believer knows that they will act in community. The addition sign is interdependent. Conner names the importance of understanding interdependence in disabled theology.[7] Interdependence is a difficult concept for those raised in a country and culture that celebrates our nascence as *Independence* Day, and enshrines our Declaration of *Independence*. The shift to interdependence moves us into supported engagement, leadership, understanding, and functioning—learning alongside disabled people.

Vocation, living life according to our call, participating in God's work in the world, leads not only to a sense of fulfillment and purpose, but also to an assurance of grace[8] and a deep sense of **belonging** in the household of God. Looking at belonging in an intentionally inclusive faith community, we found that the primary ways that disabled youth found belonging in their churches were with leadership, within their family's religious identity, and with the rhythms and rituals of the rites of the church.[9] These dimensions of belonging illustrate the disabled theology of vocation that we are articulating.

LEADERSHIP

Leadership among marginalized groups is often nurtured, refined, organized and activated in faith communities. The prominence of the historically Black church in the civil rights movement of the 1950s and 1960s in America stands out,[10] but this connection was no less true in the work for the abolition of slavery and women's suffrage for previous generations. The twenty-first-century church is poised to use its financial, human, and architectural resources to support the leadership of disabled people. However, this will necessitate a decisive move away from the charity model of disability and toward advocacy and work for justice.[11] We must embrace ministry *by* disabled people, not just *with* disabled people.

In our conversations we found that formal and informal leadership roles were highly valued by young disabled people, their families, and the communities they served.[12] Self-advocates mentioned the reading of scripture in services multiple times in their interviews, and they chose images of themselves reading in worship to illustrate belonging in their church. James and Sydney both expressed something poignant about the preparation for reading, the act of reading, and the congregation's witness of their reading that they identified as signifying, nurturing, and creating belonging and growth in faith. Sydney stated, "I like I feel like I'm included in a way because I have like have a role that I uphold and. . . . It . . . will keep me doing something so I'm not just like sitting and doing nothing . . . like if we don't have I don't have any jobs to fulfill like we won't really even go."[13]

This particular finding was reinforced by family members and church leaders.[14] Holding visible leadership roles in worship created a sense of belonging in the community, helped disabled youth feel closer to God, and created deeper, wider spaces for other disabled voices in the church.[15] John Calvin asserted that vocation is affirming of our faith, giving us a sense of assurance of God's love because we are aware that we are joining into God's work in the world. As Calvin taught, our agency connects us to God's, we feel God's presence deeply, and we are assured—confident of our salvation.[16]

Visible leadership roles were crucial to those we spoke to for nurturing belonging and faith, and are evidence that vocation is something that happens between people, God, and the faith community. The value of visibility is echoed in Grace's story and is especially poignant given her exclusion from more visible roles in her school. As leaders look for ways to support and encourage disabled youth to lead, we should notice what is common and valued in our communities, and we should be conscious of the need for disabled youth to be visible and valued in these spaces. In articulating a disabled theology of vocation or call, it is important that disabled voices are centered and attended to, perhaps especially in worship and times of great celebration.

RELATIONSHIPS

Photovoice research uses photographs taken or chosen by participants followed up with interviews to assess the meaning of the image.[17] In our photovoice research, we asked James to show us pictures that depicted belonging for him. James brought in a picture of his family at church. James, his two brothers, and his father were all dressed in jackets, two in navy, two with a subtle plaid, the pants and belts all matching. Mom's curly hair and bright eyes were matched on the faces of her three boys as clearly as any uniform. All five members of James's family held the gaze of the camera, looking confident and happy.

James carefully showed me each member of his family. Naming them and telling me their birth order, what they love, and where they live. "[A good title would be] 'Evans Team,' because it shows me . . . belonging to my family, so, and they belong to St. Thomas."

In contrast to other findings,[18] our research did not find deep and meaningful relationships extending beyond church programs between peers with and without disabilities as central to the experience of disabled youth in the church. For our participants peer relationships at church tended to be only at the surface, while family was essential. Our participants shared that even when someone was your friend at church, that did not mean they were your friend at school or in the community. In contrast to peer relationships, our participants identified strongly with their families within the church context. They identified family with closeness to God and highlighted the joy of serving communion to and praying and worshiping with their families. While talking about James's photograph, his father explained that James identifies with his family above everything else, highly valuing not only the support but also the identity of being a brother and a son. Team Evans is not just the title of the picture but an explanation of how James lives life.

This highlights Conner's assertion of the value of interdependence as we articulate a disabled theology of vocation. For Sydney, James, and Grace, family relationships are part of the interdependent experience of vocation in service, fellowship, and worship. For our participants it may be that interdependence is not something to pretend does not exist or treat as a hindrance, an obvious support needed to accomplish their goals. They name their connection within their families and the call of their families to worship and serve the Lord. As readers we can recognize the authenticity of their insight. Vocation, or joining with God in God's redemptive work in the world, is rarely a solo task. Named or not, our gifts and strengths include the gifts and strengths bestowed upon us by communities of love and care, and it is in bringing these gifts into the world that we are affirmed in our faith and assured of God's grace in our lives. Rather than considering vocation as an individual spiritual experience, **disability theology** challenges both the preference and even the possibility of independence and chooses instead to make the relational nature of receiving and following God's call obvious.

ROUTINES

In her photovoice interview, Sydney showed me a small, dark statue, rough hewn, depicting a man with a hood and outstretched hands. In his wooden hand he is holding a paper bulletin. Sydney placed it there and then took the photo. Sydney wasn't sure if the statue was a saint, Jesus, or just a man. She explained the photo in this way: "Maybe just sense of like welcoming everyone. Like, not letting. . . . I know it's a statue so it's not, like, a real human being. But, like, maybe just, um, the, the welcoming factor that's, like, everyone can be, like, be involved."

Faith communities are often characterized by our adherence to and interpretation of routines and traditions. Many leaders bemoan the phrase "that's the way we have always done it," but one of our greatest strengths in including disabled people in the church is those routinized interactions. The value of routines in the education of disabled people is well documented, and foundational strategies like task analysis rely on them.[19] In faith communities, we know that routines are very important not only in worship but even in fellowship, religious education, and small groups. Routinized behaviors allow for complex levels of participation, like choreographed rising, singing together, choral reading, and partaking in rituals like communion. Routines support the engagement of volunteers in every facet of faith community life. Novice volunteer church members can meet God's call to the work of the church in all parts of community life—whether it's setting up for coffee hour, teaching Sunday School, or taking care of the building, churches rely on routines and routinized behavior to equip volunteers to meet God's call in their community. In worship, routinized language and movement, called liturgy, even includes elements of call and response, modeling not only how we might come to God in personal prayer, but even our expectations for God's answers.[20]

The routines of worship were essential to Sydney and James; they both mentioned where people sit, how they engage socially, and how they come through the building as essential parts of their experience.[21] Rather than seeing it as part of the furnishings and decorations of the church, Sydney's experience of that little statue that sits outside the sanctuary doors is one of deep comfort and profound love, of welcome. Her experience of the routines in church life is neither stodgy nor unyielding. They are not empty or merely human; they are an essential source of support, without which Sydney's experience in church would be limited or nonexistent. Using the lens of disability theology and the language of supports, the routines and rhythms of church life can finally be named and leveraged as powerful tools to help our congregations experience and hear God's loving voice. Using the lens of disability theology we see our routines not as empty, human constructs, but as the way, the map of the journey that we are traveling on, and the "how" of following God's call in our lives.

IN PRAISE OF THE SPECIAL LOCATION OF THE CHURCH

In our example, Grace did not find "her people" in the theater club. Yet Grace, Sydney, James, and countless others have found belonging and meaning in the church. The church is supporting them as they develop a sense of belonging and purpose, and they support the church as leaders, participants, and worshipers. Thus, vocation is at the heart of religious experience, bringing meaning and identity to our work, and offering not only assurance of God's grace but the sense of joy and hope that comes in knowing that we are engaging with God and others in God's work in the world. As we work together to understand vocation through the lens of disability theology, we find not only a theology that embraces disabled people and affirms their call and voice but a theology that encourages shared leadership, interdependence, and routines that invites and affirms God's presence and grace. This is truly a source of **praise** and celebration for the Holy Spirit's blowing in our faith communities as the gospel is preached by disabled bodies and disabled voices.

REFLECTION QUESTIONS

1. How did God affirm Grace's call in the nativity? How did the church affirm God's call? How did Grace affirm her own call?
2. Leadership is a fairly easy place to understand call, but how about relationships? How about routines? What can you learn about vocation by looking through these lenses?
3. What resources do you need to do a better job nurturing, resourcing, and affirming call?

SINGING THE LORD'S SONG

Possibilities for Praise amid Experiences of Depression

MICHAEL PAUL CARTLEDGE

> ***Guiding Question:*** *How might ministry with young people suffering from* ***depression*** *lead the church to deeper practices of* ***praise****?*

To explore the challenge of praise amid depression we ask with the psalmist, "How could we sing the LORD's song in a foreign land?" (Ps. 137:4 NRSV). Experiences of depression put young people in an unfamiliar world that complicates the authorship of their stories. But even amid depressive suffering, young people are capable of theological reflection, and the church has theological language and resources to listen to, support, and guide young people in their reflection. If congregations come to see theological reflection as a practice of praise, even amid suffering, they will be better prepared to accompany young people and learn from them.

THE DEPRESSION EPIDEMIC AND YOUNG PEOPLE'S EXPERIENCES

The Problem of Depression

Even before the **COVID-19 pandemic**, the World Health Organization had already identified depression as the leading cause of disability around the world.[1] According to the most recent trends report from the US Centers for Disease Control and Prevention, four in ten high school students reported feeling "so sad or hopeless almost every day for at least two weeks in a row that they stopped doing their usual activities."[2] Persistent feelings of sadness or hopelessness are more prevalent among young women than young men, and LGBTQ+ youth are more likely to experience these symptoms than cisgender and heterosexual young people.

Alarmingly, it is estimated that over half of the young people suffering from major depression are not receiving any professional mental health care, such as counseling or medical treatment.[3] In recent years, young people have found various kinds of support online through social media platforms like TikTok and Instagram. While online posts can help with raising awareness and providing a sense of community, there are significant downsides, such as misinformation and the potential for incorrect self-diagnoses.[4]

(Co)Authoring Our Stories

There are countless changes that occur during the period of life called "adolescence."[5] Navigating the many mental, emotional, social, and physical changes young people face can make them more susceptible to mental health challenges.[6] Amid all these changes, young people are constructing their identities and interpreting their world.

Ultimately, these are acts of storytelling. Writing about youth development, Michael Nakkula and Eric Toshalis put it this way: "Being human requires the authoring of one's life, of one's life story. . . . But although identity development and self-construction are sometimes viewed as individual endeavors, they are thoroughly interpersonal or interrelational processes. We do not construct our life stories on our own. We are, rather, in a constant state of cocreating who we are with the people with whom we are in closest connection and within those contexts that hold the most meaning for our day-to-day existence."[7] Of course, this experience is not unique to young people. We all tell stories to construct our understandings of self and world. But experiences of depression can negatively affect the authorship of our stories because it can dramatically alter our understanding of and relationship toward our world.

THE STRANGE LAND OF DEPRESSION

What Is Depression?

It's not uncommon to hear someone say they are feeling depressed to signal feelings of sadness, exhaustion, or aimlessness. But the criteria for depression—especially from a clinical perspective—are much more specific.[8] Our indiscriminate use of the term has led to a "linguistic thinning" and "flattening" of depression.[9] When our definitions of depression are flattened, we can fail to see the unique kind of suffering that is often experienced in depression.

It's common to think of depression in quantitative terms. For example, we might think of depression as feelings of increased sadness and decreased happiness. But this is a thin description that ignores the unique experiences of depressive suffering. Philosopher Matthew Ratcliffe draws on firsthand accounts of depression to better understand this human experience from the inside. Ratcliffe says the reason depression is so difficult to understand is because it "is qualitatively different from what many of us regard as 'everyday' experience. The depressed person finds herself in a different 'world', in an isolated, alien realm."[10]

Within this strange and isolated world, our perception of what is possible often becomes limited. Belief that these experiences will pass becomes difficult, and belief in God might also become challenging.[11] How can young people carry out the construction and interpretation of their stories when all possibilities seem to be closed? How can a young person develop a coherent sense of self in this isolated, alien world?

A Theological Resource for Understanding Depression

Systematic theologian Jessica Coblentz builds on Ratcliffe and other philosophers' work to develop a constructive, theological account of depression. Coblentz shows how the biblical story of Hagar's suffering in the wilderness provides a lens to understand the alien world of depression. In Genesis 16, the enslaved Hagar is given to Abram (Abraham) by the barren Sarai (Sarah) so that they might conceive a child. As Coblentz summarizes, "Upon the conception of what will become Hagar's son, Ishmael, Sarah jealously turns against Hagar, dealing with her 'harshly.'"[12] Pregnant with her son, Hagar runs away into the wilderness, where she encounters "the God Who Sees" (*El-roi*) (143). There, the angel of the Lord tells her, "I will so greatly multiply your offspring that they cannot be counted for multitude" (Gen. 16:10 NRSV). In Genesis 21, after Hagar and her child had returned to Abraham and Sarah, and Sarah had given birth to Isaac, Sarah demands that Abraham cast Hagar out into the wilderness with her son Ishmael.

It is important to state that Hagar's experience of suffering, shaped by sexual abuse, social marginalization, and trauma, cannot be directly equated with experiences of depression. But Coblentz's reflection on Hagar's story offers a possible theological framework to talk about the kind of suffering one might experience in depression. First, Coblentz shows that Hagar's story "represents suffering in a Christian frame without justifying it before God. This suffering *just* is" (170). Although we often look for justifications, there may be no theological purposes behind depressive suffering (171). The isolated wilderness of depression is often experienced as meaningless, and the scriptures make space for this experience. Second, Hagar's story offers us a glimpse of who God is and how God acts amid such wilderness experiences: God is present, and God sees (173). As Coblentz puts it, "The story extends no theological resolution. What God does bestow is presence, and with that presence, Hagar gains the perception of possibilities previously unrecognized" (168).

As those walking alongside young people, our role is to bear witness to the God who sees and is present. Coblentz argues that Christian leaders ought to expand and diversify theological resources for those who are suffering from depression (223). Coblentz's account of Hagar's story is an example of one such resource. The church has theological language and resources at our disposal to better understand the strange world of depression and to speak of how God meets young people in their wilderness. How might we participate with God in meeting them there? As coauthors in their stories, how do we accompany young people in these experiences, and how do we open ourselves up so they might coauthor the stories of our communities?

YOUNG PEOPLE SINGING THE LORD'S SONG

Young People as Theologians

Practical theologian Friedrich Schweitzer has advocated for what he calls an "adolescents-as-theologians approach" to ministry with young people.[13] Schweitzer says young people "are asking, thinking, and communicating theologically when they are trying to make sense of ultimate questions and to understand what, for example, the idea of God really means."[14]

Schweitzer outlines a three-dimensional framework for seeing young people as theologians.[15] The first dimension focuses on the theology *of* young people. We might call this the personal dimension. As young people are authoring their stories, they are likely doing some theological reflection. They aren't simply relying on the stories they have been given. Start asking a young person some questions and you're bound to find some theological presuppositions.

The second dimension focuses on theology *with* young people. We can call this the interpersonal dimension. We often view theology as an individual endeavor. But just as the authorship of our stories is an interpersonal or interrelational process, we do theological reflection in community and within a particular context. Others help us in our reflection by raising questions or offering preliminary answers. There is always a relational component to this work.

The third dimension focuses on theology *for* young people. Schweitzer acknowledges that we might be hesitant with this view, as it sounds too prescriptive. Wouldn't doing theology *for* young people assume an authoritarian dynamic? But I think it is helpful to see this as a pastoral dimension. As mentioned above, there are many theological resources available to young people, and these resources within our traditions should be shared. Traditional forms of catechesis may no longer be effective, but the intention is still important: "equipping young people with what they need theologically."[16]

Our Role in Young People's Theological Reflection

I bring attention to this three-dimensional view of young people as theologians because it tells us something about the role of the church in accompanying young people in their theological reflection. First, the personal dimension calls us to *acknowledge, recognize,* and *listen to* the theology of young people. We must first acknowledge that young people are capable of reflecting theologically on their experiences. Then we must try to recognize when that theological reflection is going on. This means we must commit to listening closely to young people.

Second, the interpersonal dimension calls us to *accompany* and *offer support to* young people and to *raise questions* about their theological reflection. Often, this simply looks like being present. As we walk with young people, we should not be too quick to offer answers to big questions. Sometimes it is more helpful to raise questions with them or provide some possible, preliminary responses in support of their reflections.

Finally, there is a pastoral role for us to play in doing theology for young people. It is important to remember this is not theology *at* young people. Rather, this dimension calls us to *introduce* young people to and *equip* them with the theological tools of our traditions, and *guide* them in their use. It may be helpful to introduce young people to interpretations of scripture that are relevant to their experiences, like the story of Hagar above. In doing so, we can equip young people with their own theological resources to aid them in their reflections. Pastorally offering some theological guideposts can "enrich and extend" theology *of* and *with* young people by ensuring they have good and helpful resources on hand.[17]

If doing theology, broadly speaking, involves reflecting on ideas, convictions, and experiences of God and faith, young people who are suffering from depression have the capacity to think theologically. They have a lot to offer the church, and we should listen closely. Likewise, we have much to offer in equipping young people to think theologically. In taking this approach, we are inviting young people to coauthor our stories, and we are co-creating with them. How might this open new possibilities for praise within our communities?

PRAISE AND PLAY BEFORE GOD

Theology as Play amid Suffering

Reflecting on the horrors of war, famine, and torture, theologian Jürgen Moltmann asks, "How can we laugh and rejoice when there are still so many tears to be wiped away and when new tears are being added every day?"[18] His response points to playing games as "liberation from the bonds of the present system of living."[19] Authentic play has no purpose beyond freedom and joy. Christian theology, he says, can be understood in the same terms: "On first glance Christian theology is indeed the theory of a practice which alleviates human need: the theory of preaching, of ministries and services. But on second glance Christian theology is also an abundant rejoicing in God and the *free play* of thoughts, words, images and songs with the grace of God. . . . The freedom to talk with God and of God is being opened by God's joy."[20] Theological reflection, at its core, is about enjoying God in the freedom of God's grace. But Moltmann's understanding of freedom stands in stark contrast to the supposed freedom that arose out of late modernity. Young people have endless opportunities and unlimited choices, and they are told this is freedom. But it's exhausting, oppressive, and burdensome. In fact, this modern understanding of the self fosters the kind of social context in which depression can flourish.[21]

True freedom is a gift. Inviting young people to reflect on ideas, convictions, and experiences of God and faith is a way to play and rejoice in God's grace; a way to experience the gift of God's freedom together. Practically speaking, this is a way of being with young people. It is not a program, but a posture we take toward ministry. Theological reflection by, with, and for young people is itself a practice of praise and play before God.

Joy and Praise amid Suffering

The Psalms remind us that sorrow and **lament** are not incompatible with joy and praise. Theologian J. Todd Billings puts it this way: "Praise, petition, and lament in the Psalms are all tightly woven together in prayers that help us recognize and rest in God's promises."[22] He continues, "Even the most shocking psalms expressing outrage, fear, and despair are doing so *before God*—and that is praise."[23] So we might define praise as what we do before God in light of God's grace, even amid experiences of suffering and in times of lament.

As we practice praise through theological reflection, we are opened to God's joy. But how can we speak of joy in the context of depressive suffering? How should we understand joy theologically? Just as depression is not simply intense sadness, joy is not just amplified happiness. Theologically, joy is best understood as "resistance *within* the struggle."[24] Joy is not something we conjure up. Joy is the very presence of the God who sees and reveals Godself in Jesus Christ, who enters into our suffering and promises our "pain will turn into joy" (John 16:20 NRSV).

Understanding joy as collective work is important. In depressive suffering, joy can feel like an impossibility for the suffering individual. This is why the shared practice of coauthoring one another's stories is essential. In the strange land of depression, Jesus can seem distant and joy out of reach. In this context, we need others to listen to, support, and guide us.

The Gift of Going Second

In my research on discipleship amid depression, I spoke to one young adult named Kara who struggled with depression throughout her youth. Reflecting on her experience in the context of church, Kara said, "I always felt like I was completely trapped in my mind. I was really desperate for someone to help me get out of that place, but I couldn't talk about it. And when I did talk about it, people said to pray more or read the Bible more." When I asked Kara what might have helped, she said she wished she was given "the gift of going second." This was a phrase she had heard a few times in ministry contexts, and it stuck with her. It is something she now practices in her own life and ministry with young people. Kara described it this way: "The idea is, when I share my story first, it allows other people the freedom to say it second. . . . The more I talk about my experiences, the more other people are willing to share."

For Kara, the gift of going second is about cultivating an environment where coauthorship can take place. This practice models the three-dimensional view of young people as theologians. It requires us to listen to the stories of young people like Kara who are talking about their experiences. This practice also offers a concrete way to accompany and support young people by "going first" and reflecting on our own stories. It can also give us opportunities to guide young people toward theological resources and interpretations of scripture that equip them to practice the kind of reflection we are modeling. The goal is not to find meaning in suffering through our stories, but to "play" in freedom as we talk with and of God in the context of community.

THE UNIQUE ROLE OF THE CHURCH

The church has much to learn from the stories and experiences of young people. But I hope it's clear that the church has a lot to offer young people as well. First, the church can offer deep and meaningful relationships to young people. As we commit to listen to them and accompany them in their theological reflection, we are committing to being in relationship with them. This offers young people deeper connections than what they might find through online support, for example. Second, the church can offer consistency. Amid all the changes that take place in young people's lives, the church has an opportunity to offer consistent support, raising questions and modeling theological reflection. Finally, congregations can provide a grounding within a particular theological and ecclesial tradition, which equips young people with resources for reflection. In an age of information overload, the church can offer a kind of support that is grounded in scripture, tradition, and community.

Singing the Lord's song with young people in the strange land of depression looks like listening to, supporting, and guiding young people as they are authoring their stories and raising big questions. It looks like praising God for their witness and giving thanks for the humbling privilege of coauthoring their stories. It looks like offering them the gift of going second and remaining open to learning from their experiences. As congregations join young people in coauthorship and the free play of theological reflection, we open ourselves up to new practices of praise.

REFLECTION QUESTIONS

1. Who are some people who are coauthoring your story, and how are you coauthoring theirs?
2. How might you help young people reflect on the interconnectedness of praise and lament in their faith journeys?
3. How can you practice giving the gift of going second? Can you find ways to share parts of your own story and model theological reflection for young people?

PRACTICAL TOOL: PRAISE AND LAMENT JOURNALING

Objective: Participants will come to recognize that praise and lament are deeply intertwined in the lives of those who follow Jesus. Young people will practice authoring their stories, and youth leaders will listen to, support, and guide young people in this process.

Instructions:

1. *Introduction*

   In scripture, we often see people bring both their joy and pain to God. And in our faith, we don't have to pretend everything is okay all the time. God invites us to bring our true selves before God, which is itself a practice of praise.

   Explain how we might use journaling to express and process our experiences honestly before God. When appropriate, the youth leader might share how journaling has helped them in their own faith journey.
2. *Scriptural Reflection*

   Read and quietly reflect on a passage of scripture that highlights both praise and lament. For example, you might read portions of Psalm 13 or Psalm 42.

   Briefly discuss how these passages show us that even in the depths of our suffering or despair, turning to God with honesty is an important part of our faith.

3. *Journaling Activity*

   Invite young people to start by writing about the things they are struggling with right now. Encourage them to be honest, as God already knows what we are feeling. You can use prompts like:
   - "God, I'm feeling . . ."
   - "I don't understand why . . ."
   - "I'm struggling with . . ."

   Next, ask young people to reflect on where they might have seen God in their lives. Even in difficult times, there may be small moments to give thanks for. If this is challenging, you might ask young people to write about how bringing their experiences before God makes them feel. You can use prompts like:
   - "God, one way I've seen you in my life is . . ."
   - "I praise you for . . ."
   - "Reflecting in this way makes me feel . . ."

   Alternatively, you can invite young people to draw a picture that represents both their praise and lament.
4. *Group Sharing (Optional)*

   Young people may share parts of their entries if they feel comfortable. You could say: "You don't have to share, but this is a space where we can listen to and support one another, just as we bring both our praises and challenges to God." Leaders can model what this looks like, giving young people the gift of going second.

   If someone shares, encourage everyone to listen without interrupting or offering advice. This is about bearing witness to each other's experiences.
5. *Closing and Follow-Up*

   Conclude by explaining how God is present through all our experiences. Offer a closing prayer that acknowledges both the joy and the pain in the room.

   Encourage young people to continue using praise and lament journaling as part of their personal spiritual practices. Emphasize your own willingness to support young people in this practice.

PRAISE!

Reflections on Kin-dom Camp

PEPA PANIAGUA

> ***Guiding Question:*** *Where is there room in your ministry or context to adapt and expand so that more might experience* ***belonging*** *and be empowered to offer* ***praise****?*

The concept of kin-dom has emerged in recent decades as a way to reconceptualize the kingdom of God as a community marked by interdependent relationships, love, and inclusion. "Some Theologies say it is not an individual but a collective people who bear the image of God. I quite like this," Cole Arthur Riley writes, "because it means we need more diversity of people to reflect God more fully. . . . But if we embrace shalom—the idea that everything is suspended in a delicate balance between the atoms that make me and the tree and the bird and the sky—if we embrace the beauty of all creation, we find our own beauty magnified. And what is shalom, but dignity stretched out like a blanket over the cosmos?"[1] Kin-dom camp was a dream that had been born out of the awareness of how transformational a camp experience can be and a desire to offer a specialized camp for LBGTQIA+ youth ages twelve to seventeen. Operating in the Bible Belt and surrounded by conversion therapy "camps," our hope was to create a space that would be an unapologetically affirming alternative. We wanted to celebrate youth in all their **queerness** and offer them a space of liberation and rest from the wearying world they live in each day.

QUEERFULLY AND NEURODIVERGENTLY MADE

It was daunting to open registration for the first year of kin-dom camp. This camp was an idea that had been a conversation starter just two years ago. Our hope was to provide a community and sanctuary for youth who often decide that death is an easier path than living in a world so unwelcoming to who they are. We would come to learn after our first session of kin-dom camp that over 75 percent of our campers (forty-one of fifty-four campers) had attempted or seriously considered ending their own lives. Our goal was to save at least one life. But as we approached the official opening of registration, we wondered and worried. Would anyone sign up? Would people trust us with their kids? Were we really going to do this?

After over a year of planning, when registration went live, I felt a sense of excitement and anxiety. And as registrations started to come in, I had never been more grateful for the extra questions we had added to our registration process.

While I had fifteen years of youth ministry experience, when it came to setting up and running a camp I was out of my depth. And I was most certainly out of my depth when it came to offering specialized and intentional support to neurodivergent campers. Luckily, the kin-dom team included Andy Hackett and Garrett DeGraffenreid, both of whom had extensive camp experience as lifelong camp attendees and as camp counselors and staff in their young adulthood. They knew the ins and outs of camp and helped put some much-needed meat on the bones of my understanding.

As we began planning, we constructed a Google form for registration and took a template from a local camp as our starting place for what the form needed to include. As we began constructing our registration form, Andy expressed a need to capture more in-depth information in our registration process. He helped create a registration form that included basic questions like age, **pronouns**, name, and guardian name, but he also insisted that we ask questions that allowed us to know much more about the campers we would welcome. He had attended a specialized camp for children with Celiac disease, so he knew that a basic registration form would not capture these broader needs of youth.

So, with guidance and wisdom from Garrett and Andy, we made sure to have additional spaces on the registration form:

- Legal name and preferred/chosen name
- Has this camper ever stayed overnight at camp before?
- What makes the camper most excited about camp?
- What makes the camper (or you the guardian) most nervous about camp?
- What else would you like us to know about your camper?

And possibly the most important question:

- What special needs/accommodations does kin-dom camp need to be aware of?

Initially, when we added that last question to the registration form, we anticipated responses that would give us insight and understanding into the campers' gender identities or maybe even struggles they had experienced when it came to trauma or mental health. Given the statistics from the Trevor Project,[2] we knew that many of our campers would be carrying scars both visible and invisible.

What I did not anticipate was the overwhelming number of responses that revealed an intersectional identity represented by more than 60 percent of our campers: **neurodivergence** and queerness. Our staff had both lived and learned experience with this specific intersection, so we could adapt, but the process of adapting an already specialized camp to be even more specialized felt a bit overwhelming.

While members of the staff worked to build the programs and schedule, I began trying to learn whatever I could about how to safely, earnestly, and fully welcome neurodivergent campers. All of a sudden, we were asking questions about accessibility, mobility, noise levels, adaptive tools, and sensory safe options for as many aspects of camp that we could find.

Thankfully, the Trevor Project has fantastic resources online that helped me understand the intersection between queer and disabled identities and the spectrum that exists within them. I had known about the importance of person-first versus identity-first language, but to see it so clearly explained as a means of affirming a person in the fullness of who they are expanded my understanding of how inclusion wasn't just about being ready to welcome the queer parts of our campers. We were preparing a space that would welcome the whole of our campers' identities—visible, invisible, diagnosed, undiagnosed, named, unnamed. We were preparing to welcome and nurture whole people, and while I had understood that on the surface, I was grateful for the resources that expanded and stretched me to challenge my own biases and false assumptions.

In my research I stumbled upon Dr. Nick Walker, a queer, neurodivergent author, educator, and psychologist. In writings published in *Neuroqueer Heresies*[3] and on his website,[4] Walker articulates a "neurodiversity paradigm" that helped me have language to build on. First, Walker suggests that neurodiversity affirms natural human variation, and, in reflecting on that I came to understand that therefore, that variation is reflected back to us in God's creation.

While I had always believed this, it had not previously dawned on me that neurodiversity was part of God's diverse creation. I thought about the creation story and how God created land and sea and marshes, wetlands, deserts, forests, lakes, and beaches. God created night and day and dusk, dawn, twilight, and so forth. So it is no wonder that God created each individual and our brains to be different and unique! When I started to think about each of our campers as unique expressions of God's creation, I found that my own anxiety about "doing camp right" shifted into a deep hope to provide a place where campers would experience the abiding love of God. And my job, as it was with every youth I had ever worked with, was to make sure I did what I could to remove any barriers that were in my control to remove. I shifted from anxious to advocate.

In the second point of the neurodiversity paradigm, Dr. Walker asserts that there is no single "right way" of thinking or learning. This allowed me to seek access to training and resources to equip my team and volunteers to be more broadly mindful of the ways that we imagine hospitality and how to expand our understanding of what it would look like to fully welcome campers. It also inspired me to get curious to hear stories from the people in my life who live at the intersection of LBGTQIA+ and neurodivergent. I realized my own need for ally training!

Knowing that most of our campers had already experienced some level of "othering" because of their sexuality or gender identity, we were now being given the opportunity to make sure that they were not "othered" at camp for the ways that their brains and bodies function. The world is not ordered for neurodivergent brains and processes, and many camp activities are equally unordered. Once we confronted that fact, we worked hard to create access in all spaces by promoting equity and prioritizing agency.

From there, we got to action. We began the work of gathering items for the creation of a sensory room (many of these items are listed at the end of this chapter). We expanded our staff volunteer list to include behavioral, occupational, and family therapists. We began talking with people who had experience in this work and could help us think about the things we wouldn't otherwise think about. We ordered fidget toys, multiple pairs of noise-canceling headphones, sensory safe snacks, small notebooks, and other tools that would help maximize an experience of welcome for all our campers. We made phone calls to each camper's family to talk about what might be causing anxiety or worry, we asked about how we could make campers feel more welcome and secure and how we could support the families who were preparing to send their youth to camp, often for the first time. We prayed and planned and prayed some more. And then it was the first day of camp.

ROLLING OUT THE RAINBOW CARPET

In late July of 2022, we bravely donned our "gay apparel," did some team cheers, and took our stations to open the gates to kin-dom camp. We had people stationed at the gate to check ID against our registration list and designated guardian list. We had staff outside our registration room to welcome campers and their families and to show them where to go. We had people ready to take campers and families to their cabins to get settled. We had lined all our paths with various LBGTQIA+ flags, including various forms of the neurodiversity pride flag, and for over four hours we welcomed campers and their families, one by one, to the first faith-based camp specifically for LBGTQIA+ youth in the state.

We watched as campers and their families went step by step through the welcome and registration and were greeted with smiles, friendly faces, and expressions of excitement over their arrival. Throughout the week we watched campers feel safe and empowered enough to advocate for themselves. They asked to go to the sensory room when they needed a break, and they used their notebooks to communicate when words could not be spoken. They taught us all how to clap our hands without making the noise of clapping and encouraged us to praise and celebrate in ways that allowed everyone to participate fully. For a week we got to watch in wonder as these young people lived into the expansive freedom of a place designed for them. We experienced the joy of being invited in learning how to love each of them well, and to see life lived through their eyes. And we rejoiced. With arms held high, noise-canceling headphones on, some seated, some standing, many **stimming**, many doodling, all of us rejoiced. Without shame and without abandon, we rejoiced.

For a week, we saw the power of what intentionality, care, and a whole lot of love can do for the lives of young people. While it would be nice to say that we all rode off into the gay sunset with rainbow boas and lived queerfully ever after, that also wouldn't paint the whole picture. As any youth worker could probably anticipate, as idyllic as the week was, there were also moments of frustration and of feeling helpless. The truth is that while we had licensed professionals, nurses, specialized staff, and an abundance of training, there were moments that brought the staff to our knees as we were confronted with the trauma and pain that many of our campers were living with. There were moments where we managed the reality of teenagers being teenagers and moments when many of the staff had to find ways to care for themselves when their own histories were triggered and they found themselves overstimulated.

We battled through fatigue and the growing pains that are inevitable when you are trying something for the first time. It is safe to say we learned a *lot* in that first week, so much so that the staff all had notes in our phones that we used to capture everything we learned in real time to help us put our learning into action for camp in 2023, like adding to our intake forms, "Do you have food allergies *and* are there food textures you prefer to avoid?" We learned we needed to do a lot of research about how to offer trauma-informed care and learn about the ways that internalized homophobia and transphobia could be triggered in spaces where unconditional affirmation is aspired to.

As the week carried on, I reflected on the last point of Dr. Walker's neurodiversity paradigm: The social dynamics that manifest with neurodiversity are much like the ones experienced in other forms of human diversity. On the surface that is easy to accept as true, but after living with over fifty youth who lived at the intersection of neurodivergence and queer identities, I learned that just as we can miss so much of God's creation if we only tell the story of creation in binary terms—"God created day and night, land and sea"—we miss seeing the majesty of a whole person if we don't consider the ways that the multitudes of their identities shape a whole person.

These campers were on the spectrum of LGBTQIA+ and they were *also* on the spectrums of neurodiversity and mental illness. And because we fostered an awareness of these important intersections, we were also able to foster a camp culture of mutual care and curiosity. Because we left space for the intersections to not only be seen but affirmed, we got the gift of bearing witness to these campers thriving.

Much as many of these youth wondered if they would have to choose to embrace their queerness *or* their faith at camp, the campers we welcomed with intersectional identities all expressed relief when we let them know that our hope was that they could be fully integrated. We assured them that we would not ask them to abandon or lessen any part of who they are. We did our best to celebrate the unique expressions of humanity found in each of our campers. And while some of the expressions were challenging to our own experiences or understandings, we prioritized hospitality, care, and helping these youth see that they have lives worth living and a community that supports and loves them.

To experience these young people coming to see their identities, their stories, their differences, and their dreams reflected back to them in the lives of other campers, to see them find common ground in what was so often used to keep them separated or considered "less than," to watch them come to understand that their differences are their superpowers, was nothing short of miraculous. To watch each camper come to love themselves for who they are and who they are becoming is something that inspires me to sing praise to God for the ways that God used this camp to create a sense of belonging and care in each and all of the campers.

UNEXPECTED AFFIRMATION, UNABANDONED PRAISE

For the last night of camp we had planned a drag performance. We had waivers from all the parents and guardians to make sure that everyone offered consent, and we worked to bring in performers who were *also* educators. Each of our performers embodied intersectional identities that we knew would provide inspirational representation for our campers. And no drag show is complete without tips, so we got creative and modeled appropriate drag culture by giving the adults dollars and the campers sticky notes and pens for tips. During the performances the campers showered the performers with sticky notes of affirmation and celebration. They wrote their "tips" to the kings and queens, and to this day, I know that some of those performers carry sticky notes with them to their performances.

At kin-dom camp we always asked how we could make things better (or gayer), and how we could adapt activities so that as many campers that wanted to participate could. (Everything at kin-dom camp was "challenge by choice.") The drag performance was no different. Just as we adapted to make sure that youth could participate in the drag culture of tipping, we also made sure that the performances were varied so different sensory needs could be considered. We prepared youth ahead of time to know that there might be singing and dancing, and we assured them that that it was all part of the act. We handed out headphones and put chairs just outside the room and on the porch where campers could watch and not be overstimulated. As the campers danced and waved their hands, and as I watched them hand note after note to the performers, I turned my eyes to the rainbow-draped cross on the wall behind the stage and joy-filled tears began to fall. I was bearing witness to a holy moment, and I was standing on holy ground.

What a gift it has been to be entrusted with the fullness of each of these young people—as diverse and unique as their Creator intended. LBGTQIA+ *and* neurodivergent, LBGTQIA+ *and* neurotypical, LBGTQIA+ *and* multiracial *and*. . . . I could write over seventy-five individual and intersectional identities represented by our campers. Each of them is a reflection of the God who loves them, the God who numbered their hairs on their heads and sanctified them in the womb. Each of them is a living testimony to the Cole Arthur Riley's words, "We need more diversity of people to reflect God more fully." Each of them, all of them, queerfully, neurodivergently, and wholly, wonderfully made.

REFLECTION QUESTIONS

1. What ways can church, youth group, or any ministry with young people in your setting be made more accessible and sensory friendly?
2. How can you make space for young people's free expression of their neurodiverse, LGBTQIA+ identities as part of God's diverse creation and model self-love and self-advocacy in the body of Christ?
3. How can your work create more space for young people to praise God and celebrate themselves as God's creation?

PRACTICAL TOOL: A GUIDE FOR CREATING A SENSORY ROOM

Practical questions to ask your leaders and to ask of your programs:

- Do your registration forms ask questions about accommodations and leave room for people to explain the ways their identities might be intersectional?
- Do your forms create opportunities for you and your community to become more hospitable?
- Does your program offer and support multiple styles of learning?
    - Learn more in this article: https://teachable.com/blog/types-of-learning-styles
- Do you have resources or accommodations to help support people who get overstimulated easily?
    - Noise-canceling headphones
    - A room for people to experience worship that isn't loud or in direct flashing light
    - Handheld grounding tools or fidget toys
- Are all your youth programs geared toward being noisy or based on assumed abilities to move, hear, speak, and comprehend quickly?
- Does your website have accessibility options?
- Do you have behavioral specialists, therapists, or other folks in your congregation/setting that are trained in supporting needed accommodations to create a more welcoming environment?
    - Can you involve them in doing a programmatic inventory of the space, the bulletin, the offerings, and available resources?
- Do you have neurodivergent leaders on staff or as volunteers? That is a great way to cue that representation matters to your congregation.
- Have you asked neurodivergent people (especially youth!) directly what they need to feel more welcome? And have you taken steps to make those things possible? It is important to create means of agency and to give voice to lived experience. Neurodivergent individuals are experts on neurodivergence!

Some ideas for getting started:

- Gather a group of youth to brainstorm about a sensory space: What do they want, what do they need, and what do they envision the space being used for? Is there already a designated youth space? Could this space be adapted to become more sensory friendly?

- Ask youth to imagine who else might benefit from a sensory room in your context? Could this be a place for children, youth, and adults to participate in a Sunday-morning setting more fully?
- Who needs to be involved in the conversation before action is taken?
    - Pastor and leadership board
    - Building and grounds staff
    - Any people in the congregation who are passionate about inclusion and accessibility
    - Youth themselves!
- What is the budget impact of a space like this?
    - Dream with the youth about how they could fundraise for this space.
    - Have youth make a dream list and prioritize what things they would like in the space to maximize impact.
    - Who in the community do the youth and congregation know that could help offset costs with donations of time or materials?

Suggested materials:

- Yoga mats
- Shag throw carpet
- Noise-canceling headphones
- Fabric to cover overhead lighting (especially if fluorescent)
    - Talk to the building manager or facilities team to make sure all are on board and can prevent fire danger
- If fabric is not workable, see about light filters like the ones used in theater programs
- Fabric or adhesive window clings to diffuse natural light and reduce visual stimulation
- Single-person pop-up tents to provide isolation and darkness
- Lights on a dimmer switch
- Twinkle lights for the walls
- Fidget toys

- Sensory-friendly snacks (chewing and sucking are often forms of self-regulation); make sure to record and confirm any food allergies before offering
    - Crunchy snacks provide a lot of pressure input to the jaw
        - thick or hard granola bars, apples, pears, carrot sticks, cucumbers, pretzels, goldfish or saltine crackers, ice chips, rice cakes, bagel or pita chips, Graham crackers, dry cereal
    - Chewy snacks promote an increased rate of chewing as well as a lot of sensory input
        - fruit snacks, fruit leather, dried fruit, raisins, chewy mini bagels, gum, sausage sticks, beef jerky
    - Sucking on snacks and drinks also provides great resistance in the mouth for sensory seekers.
        - crazy straws or coffee stirrer straws
        - applesauce or yogurt pouches
        - hard candy or mints
- Coloring sheets and a variety of coloring objects (colored pencils, crayons, chalk, watercolor, felt pens, gel pens, etc.)

A PRAYER OF PRAISE FOR YOUTH

CARMELLE BEAUGELIN CALDWELL

God, I praise you because you are ________________.
I thank you for ______________.
I feel such _________________________ when I think about how you
 _________________.
Even though ___________________, I am filled with hope that you will
 ________________.
Help me to share this joy with others around me today. Amen.

God, I praise you because *(a quality of God: love, just, kind, present etc.)*.
I thank you for *(something good in your life or in the world)*.
I feel such *(emotion: joy, peace, gratitude, etc.)* when I think about how you *(a way God has worked in your life or in the world)*.
Even though *(a challenge or struggle)*, I am filled with hope that you will *(a promise or belief about God's work in the future)*.
Help me to share this joy with others around me today. Amen.

INTERLUDE: INTRODUCTION TO BODY+MIND+SPIRIT

ERIN RAFFETY

The term **bodymind**, which seeks to emphasize the intersectional and interdependent nature of bodies and minds, has appeared in **disability studies** and **disability justice** circles in just the last decade. The combined wording aims to confront a false Cartesian dualism, a hierarchy often found in Western culture, between the mind and the body as well as the patriarchal undermining of women, children, and disabled people's pain and its comprehensive effects. In conversation with movements such as neurodiversity and disability pride and disability justice, the term also asserts that there is wisdom in disabled bodies and experiences and that it has always been there. However, our inability to perceive it stems from the pervasive effects of **ableism**: We're all so busy trying to push through harmful systems that these massive insights from our bodies often fail to register or we deny them, as our culture both demands and glorifies.

At the outset of the **COVID-19 pandemic**, for instance, disabled activists were asserting that folks already living with chronic illness had insights for how we could care and protect one another by wearing masks, staying home when we were sick, adopting accommodations to allow us to work from home, even advocating online from our beds, as many in the disability justice movement have done. But just a few years out from the acute onset of the pandemic, one can see an unwillingness to accept and make space for the hybridity of our bodyminds. Many pandemic accommodations have been deemed unnecessary and removed, despite the fact that immunocompromised people are still susceptible to COVID and according to the Centers for Disease Control an estimated seventeen million Americans, or around 7 percent of people who have had COVID, are reportedly experiencing long COVID symptoms and disabilities.

As pastors, theologians, and faith leaders, we wonder if the term's hybridity could benefit from even a third addition: mind+body+spirit. In this volume there is so much evidence for how not just disabled bodies but also minds and spirits are affected and intertwined in the beliefs and the practices of faith that we inhabit. But whereas disabled folks have had to think through these connections to fight against harmful interpretations of scripture or gain access to pulpits, ordination exams, and youth groups, just to name a few, perhaps such a concept is not only meaningful but faithful, even biblical, for a fuller understanding of humanity and human flourishing for nondisabled folks, too?

An exhaustive biblical analysis is not possible in this excursus, but a few main points deserve illumination. For one, Old Testament scholars make much of the way some of the words translated as "heart" more accurately refer to the guts as the birthplace of emotions, speaking to embodied knowledge. Further, the Hebrew words *leb* and *lebab* more accurately encompass both the heart and the mind as a vision of the whole person. Although New Testament scriptures are often permeated with the mind-body dualism characteristic of Greek culture (think Paul's conflict with his flesh), as disability theologians have shown us, Paul's acceptance of his flesh is what leads to wholeness, and even Jesus's body is resurrected with his scars intact. We would do well to explore the provisional thesis that not just our bodies are temples, but our temples are made of body+mind+spirits too often denied their wholistic trinity of meaning-making.

Much as LGBTQIA+ advocates have reclaimed the term "**queer**," disability activists and scholars have reinterpreted "crip" to foreground disabled ways of doing things and being in the world that critique ableist culture. One example is "**crip time**," a term that acknowledges that disabled people often need more time to complete tasks because they are forced to go up ramps and practice all kinds of accommodations to inhabit an ableist world. The term also acknowledges the way in which disabled people's approach to time, like a subculture, offers a more dignifying, humanizing way of being in the world that acknowledges the time and space different bodies need to and do take up. Crip time appreciates the ways our bodies make and break conventions of time. But disabled activists and scholars take the concept of "**cripping**," asserting disabled ways of doing things and being in the world, to not just acknowledge and adjust but to carve out more just and hospitable places for disabled bodyminds in the world.

In short, we hope this volume and the leaders in it are cripping youth ministry not just by making space for disabled body+mind+spirits, including them where they have been previously excluded, but by actually altering the spaces and the practices of ministry in needed, prophetic ways. What we often see when we bring crip practices into youth ministry spaces—for instance, moving our meetings to visible and accessible spaces; allowing youth to attend to their bodies, minds, and spirits not as an exception but as the center of what we're about; and encouraging youth to trust and value the wisdom of their body+mind+spirits—is that not just disabled youth but all youth thrive. This is because capitalism, sexism, and ableism wreak havoc on all of us, and they pervert the gospel with their emphases on production, binaries, and perfection.

So when we crip youth ministry, we are prophesying a new kingdom reality in which disabled and neurodivergent youth, in all of their intersectional experiences, can be regarded as more than just marginal minds or bodies. As advocates for our body+mind+spirits, youth workers, alongside disabled youth, model and envision a future of thriving for all people, a broader dream for who the church can be in the world.

PART 4

PROPHECY

A PRAYER OF PROPHECY

A Prayer Against Internalized Ableism

LETIAH FRASER[1]

Incarnate God, who inhabited a human body and was not accepted by religious institutions and by the larger society,
Grant us the courage to live in a way that prophetically challenges the inaccessibility of our streets, sidewalks, and buildings, our educational systems, legal systems, housing, and healthcare.
Have mercy on those who continue to make church inaccessible and paint God as disability phobic.
Let us not be conformed to distorted healing narratives, linking our humanity to productivity or the myth of the exceptional disabled person.
God, root out anything that seeks to separate us from our disabled bodies where God is pleased to dwell. In the name of God, who became disabled.
Amen.

HOW I BECOME THE HEAD PASTOR OF MY CHURCH SOMEDAY

Supporting the Dreams of Disabled Youth

CHRIS LAROCQUE WITH ZACH GRANT

> ***Guiding Question:*** *How can you walk with young people with disabilities as they follow God's calling?*

"Chris, what do you want to be called? How do you want me to introduce you in your chapter? Chris, Chris Larocque, Pastor Chris?"

"I like that."

"Ok, Pastor Chris it is. How about me? What should I say about myself? I'm going to be helping write some—"

"I need help writing my chapter. I'm nervous for that."

"Yah?"

"It's my first time. I've never done that. It's my first book."

Left, Zach Grant; *right*, Chris Larocque

"Mine, too. What should I say about who I am? Just Zach, Zach Grant, a friend helping you write? Zach Grant, your partner in ministry and church planting?"

Double thumbs up.

"Ok, when I told you that I was nervous to write my chapter, what did you tell me? You said, 'Just relax. Take your time.'"

We have followed Pastor Chris Larocque's leadership in writing this chapter. Over the course of a number of Zoom calls, which are the primary context of our relationship since I moved away from St. Augustine, Florida, seven years ago, we have taken our time and tried to have a relaxed conversation about Chris's experience in the church and Christian ministry and his experience of disability. The italics show where Zach is thinking and writing with Chris in mind, but we hope the chapter suggests a vision for working and dreaming together.

". . . This feels awkward because we don't talk much about Down syndrome or disability, and I've asked you a few times, but you haven't seemed to want to answer. But how would you talk about disabilities in leadership?"

"What do you mean?"

I struggle for a few minutes to explain something that is pretty fundamental to the model and mission of the church Chris and I have planted together before Chris interrupts.

"I want to lead. I want to lead in everything. I want to share my heart. I want to share my heart. I want to share my good God and I want to share the Bible. I want to help the Bible. Learn the Bible. See the Bible. I want them to know I'm a good person. I learn about everything."

"Ok. What should I say about the ministries you're involved with at Anchor Faith Church, Grace United Methodist, and with Bethlehem Inclusive? Do you want me to summarize them or do you want to talk about them in your words?"

Emphatically, "My own words."

"I'll try to stay out of the way as much as possible. So, what are the ministries you're involved in?"

"I work hard in ministry for Young Life. For Anchor Faith. For Bethlehem Inclusive. Grace United Methodist. And St. James United Methodist. And a long time ago I did work for Valdosta Anchor Faith Church. I did that with my sister. I was working the parking lot. I was an usher. Nautilus for the kids. Both of them. Nautilus Jr. and the other one."

"Is there anything you want to say about the work we do together with Bethlehem Inclusive?"

"I want to say about my new job."

"The job you're doing now leading in the online services on Zoom, or what we've talked about trying to find you more support and office space in St. Augustine?"

"That one."

We talk across several meetings about what Chris might want this chapter of the book to look like. The thing he seems most to want to talk about is making plans to expand his work. So we determine together to make a map. We begin by talking about his destination.

"So, Chris, it seems like the thing that you're driving toward is being the head pastor."

"I like what you said there."

"Now, it's worth saying that there are at least three faith communities that call you pastor already. What would be different?"

"I'm a pastor, I want to go to the classes and teach the Bible, read the Bible."

"What else? Are there things that I get to do that you don't? Are there things that are part of my job that aren't part of yours that tell you 'there's more to this'? Is it an office, is it making more money, is it—"

"Yup."

"More money? Fair. To support a family to do all the things anyone gets to do with money."

"Yup. That's all true."

MINISTRY MAPMAKING

Destination Setting

We talk out a detailed picture of Chris working as head pastor. The things that seem valuable are having office space to work out of, instead of just Zoom calls from his parents' restaurant. He wants to teach classes about the Bible. He wants to make enough money to support himself. Presently Chris leads Sunday services on Zoom. He makes an hourly wage per service instead of being on salary. He leads across three worshiping communities, but the role of a teacher and preacher is the role he is most interested in. Other things he sees as attractive are the ways that some of the pastors he knows travel and preach to other congregations in other countries. Traveling around the world, preaching, and teaching are an important part of his dream.

Some obstacles also intrude and get between Chris and the destination he is setting. He believes he would need to go to college to be a pastor. The Pentecostal church that Chris goes to does not require higher education to hold the title of pastor, but the United Methodist and Presbyterian (USA) churches do. When pressed if he would like to go to college to become a head pastor, or if he would like to become a head pastor and *go to college, he is not sure. He would not like to have to move away, and he has heard that college is expensive. However, if he could afford to go to college in town, that might appeal to him. He is also clear that he needs help. If I will not move back to St. Augustine, then he would like someone locally that can help him.*

Identifying Landmarks

Though it is not clear to us how all of these obstacles will be overcome, that does not mean that we give up on charting a course forward. Though there is some distance between where Chris is and where he would like to be, we locate some landmarks that indicate he is going in the right direction. We recall together that Chris has helped teach classes with me at churches and conferences. Chris has preached in partnership with me at Bethlehem Inclusive Church. He has selected music and crafted the liturgy at church by himself. We recall these things to affirm the value of his dream.

Forging a Path

We try to figure out together what is the smallest step forward that still feels like progress. Chris likes the idea of seeking out trips within his three communities that he can take a share of leadership in. He thinks it might help him to be a pastor if he found ways to attend classes even if he were not seeking a degree yet. We will ask the pastors he knows if there is anyone in their networks locally who can help him. Then we pray to the God who calls us to lands we cannot see, and resolve to follow up next week.

Closing Prayer

We invite you to pray along with Chris for his ministry and for yours:

"Lord God, I pray for everything today. I pray for all around us, for the book, for the people reading the book, for all the countries, for healing, for a miracle. My heart, my soul, my body, everything in my life. For everything. For everything. My church, my ministry. My joy in my life inside the book."

Chris's prayer travels on. It ranges and covers everything from his parents' falafel restaurant to my grandmother, but especially dwells on you, dear reader. Take this moment to offer your own broad prayers knowing that each particular concern is precious to God and may be mighty in God's kingdom.

"I pray for my purpose, of you, for you and for me, for the Bible. I want to teach you. My ministry. I want to be the head pastor. I want to preach in all different countries. Everything my Lord God. My ministry. Heaven, all around us, to pull you tight Lord, in Jesus's name, Amen."

THREE QUESTIONS OR THINGS I WISH ADULTS WOULD ASK OR SAY TO DISABLED YOUTH

1. Do you want to get slushies and a hot dog for lunch with me?
2. Do you want to celebrate your birthday with me and your friends?
3. How can I help you follow your dreams?

DREAMING DIVERGENT FUTURES

Prophetic Imagination and Embracing Marginalized Neurodivergent Youth

RUDOLPH P. REYES II

Guiding Question: How do we change the structures of youth ministry to embrace marginalized neurodivergent youth?

This chapter is my wild dreaming of divergent futures for marginalized neurodivergent youth. As Autistic author and activist Leah Lakshmi Piepzna-Samarasinha writes, "Sick and disabled and neurodivergent folks aren't supposed to dream, especially if we are **queer** and Black or Brown—we're just supposed to be grateful the 'normals' let us live."[1] Marginalized neurodivergent people, like others in the disability community, are prevented from dreaming when the desired future is a future devoid of **neurodivergence**. The prophetic task requires moral imagination to criticize what is and to dream of what could be. Dreaming is a prophetic act. I use the term "marginalized neurodivergent youth" to refer to neurodivergent people who are People of Color, queer, poor, undocumented, or marginalized in other ways. This chapter invites others to dream wild dreams of disability liberation where marginalized neurodivergent youth are embraced as neurodivergent youth.

NEURODIVERIFYING PROPHETIC IMAGINATION

There are two overarching acts of the prophetic task: denunciation and annunciation.[2] Denunciation is the first act. The prophetic voice denounces current oppressive realities. The prophetic is often only associated with the critique of unjust realities, but this is only half the task. There is always the need to proclaim an alternative just reality; this is the task of annunciation. It is these two acts that make up what biblical scholar Walter Bruggemann calls the prophetic imagination.[3] This emphasis on the imagination makes clear the priority of praxis (reflective action) for social transformation. Reflective action provides us with the opportunity to become aware of the blocks in our moral imagination through deeply listening to those on the margins. Similarly, reflective action provides the space for experimentation that sparks our imagination of new horizons. These two actions allow for the denunciation of oppressive realities and the annunciation of a new future.

For the church to embrace marginalized neurodivergent youth we must neurodiversify its prophetic imagination, which means to center marginalized neurodivergent voices in collective liberation. To center neurodivergent voices requires accepting the neurodiversity paradigm, which is explored later in this chapter. The neurodiversity paradigm states that neurocognitive diversity is a natural part of human diversity and should be celebrated.[4] This paradigm is essential because it is not possible to neurodiversify the prophetic imagination if neurodivergent people are pathologized as broken or defective. Additionally, the neurodiversity paradigm is not the goal but the point of departure for embracing neurodiversity. The **neurodiversity movement** asserts that normalcy should be neither the aim of medical intervention nor the requirement for social acceptance of neurodivergent people. Embracing neurodiversity necessitates centering collective liberation.

Neurodiversity scholar Alyssa Hillary provides a framing of neurodivergent cultures. Hillary has a broad concept of culture, which operates on different levels. This multifaceted concept includes "historical, linguistic, social, political, personal, and aesthetic" dimensions.[5] Culture operates at different levels: national, ethnic, and group. Neurodivergent culture operates at a group level, where cultural production is made by and for neurodivergent people,[6] and is present in various neuro-cultural practices.

Neuro-cultural practices, Hillary writes, recognize that "culture and (neuro)biology affect all human knowledge, beliefs, and actions. One aspect may be more obvious at times, but both are always present."[7] For example, how one demonstrates that one is paying attention is a neuro-cultural practice. In youth ministry, youth are expected to show they are paying attention by making eye contact with youth workers or peers. This expression of attention is a neuro-cultural practice because it is a cultural expectation that fits a neurotypical way of expressing concentration. Some ADHDers can concentrate better by doodling or fidgeting. A youth worker may misinterpret this ADHDer as not paying attention when they are, in fact, engaging in a different neuro-cultural practice. The layers of misunderstandings can be amplified when youth workers and peers do not share the same macroculture.

Neurodivergent people often engage in neuro-cultural practices related to their specific **neurotype** even before encountering broader neurodivergent communities. For example, some ADHDers may favor forms of anecdotal communication, where conversations involve sharing similar experiences. However, ADHDers may not realize this is a shared neuro-cultural practice until they connect with other ADHDers.

Collective liberation recognizes the need for solidarity and that liberation is only possible when all are liberated. Liberation starts with conscientization, the critical awareness of oppression that is needed to engage in transformative action.[8] You have begun the road to critical consciousness by picking up this edited volume or deciding to read this chapter. This liberative consciousness must lead to the social analysis of current realities and the proclamation of a new reality. Neurodivergent youth will not experience freedom if not all of them are liberated. There is no **disability justice** without racial, economic, gender, ecological, and other forms of justice. Addressing one form of oppression does not solve another form. To combat neuro-**ableism** requires resisting racism, sexism, classism, heteronormativity, and all oppressive systems. If you only address neuro-ableism, you will end up with a space that only embraces neurodivergent youth who are closest to the norms of the dominant society. The reason collective liberation is necessary is because oppressive systems overlap.

This neurodiversifying of prophetic imagination to dream of embracing marginalized neurodivergent youth leads to this chapter's guiding question: How do we change the structures of youth ministry to embrace marginalized neurodivergent youth? To neurodiversify our prophetic imagination, this chapter begins by criticizing systems that prevent neurodivergent and neurotypical youth alike from dreaming the dream of God. Next, we cover a divergent Christ who preached God's dream for humanity. Once we have criticized the rejection of the dream and encountered the one who proclaimed the dream, we can be energized to embrace marginalized neurodivergent youth.

DENOUNCING NEURONORMATIVITY AND COMPULSORY NEUROTYPICALITY

The first task of a divergent prophetic imagination is to denounce the oppressive realities that marginalized neurodivergent youth face. These youth encounter a **neuronormative** church and society. *Neuronormative* is taking neurotypicality as the norm. This normativity is generated by neuro-ableism, a system that privileges and values people based on neurocognitive ability by erasing or segregating neurodivergence. Neuro-ableism is not interpersonal malice but complicity with a system. Therefore, it is a mistake to take the bigot or what Alyssa Hillary calls neuro-bigotry[9] as the exemplar of neuro-ableism. The marker of neuro-ableism is not outright hatred for marginalized neurotypes but rather a system that maintains neurotypical dominance over neurodivergence.

Neuronormative spaces are dominated by neurotypical cultural expectations. Communications scholar Emily Stones identifies three negative neurotypical cultural assumptions of neurodivergent communication: that neurodivergent people do not communicate correctly,[10] that neurodivergent people have no desire to engage in social interaction,[11] and that neurotypical communication is the ideal way of communication that benefits all.[12] Marginalized neurodivergent youth encounter these assumptions in youth ministry. Their ways of communication and engaging in social interaction are viewed as social deficits that need correcting. This leads to neurodivergent youth being misunderstood and excluded if they do not act within the acceptable range of communication or action. These neurotypical cultural expectations are some of the ways neuronormative space reinforces neuro-ableism and **masking**.

I received my most explicit feedback about speaking more neurotypically in youth ministry. I grew up in a neurodiverse Mexican American family and gravitated toward other Brown neurodivergent kids in school. My neurodivergent way of communicating was typical for my neurodiverse family and neurodivergent friends. However, my communication was not accepted in youth ministry. I would share my experiences with others but was met with disapproval and was told I was trying to one-up others when I was only relating to them through anecdotal communication. I often stopped and started my sentences while processing my thoughts, jumping from association to association. Youth group members laughed at how I communicated. I masked through suppression to avoid disproving, confused, and laughing faces.

Masking is the process by which neurodivergent people are compelled to hide their neurodivergent traits. In a neuronormative society, traits that diverge from neurotypical expectations are moralized or pathologized. A neurodivergent person is viewed as broken, unhealthy, sick, and disordered, expressing character flaws or the result of moral or parental malformation. A neurodivergent person does not simply want to impress others but to avoid marginalization. Neurodivergent people suffer from forcing their bodies into neurotypical molds.

This process of compulsion is what French philosopher Michel Foucault called disciplinary power. Foucault viewed power not as something hoarded but as a dispersed network that is exercised. The panopticon is an example of disciplinary power. In the panopticon, the uncertainty of surveillance leads to self-disciplining. Examples of this are Zoom or Microsoft Teams meetings, where you are aware of your visibility, but do not know if anyone is watching you. Do people have speaker view or gallery view turned on? Not knowing if someone is watching you can force you to discipline your body *as if* someone were watching you. Maybe you make sure to show expressions of attention by nodding or not looking for too long. Contrast this experience with listening to a sermon or a lecture. You may not be focusing on how you are presenting but rather on listening or not listening. Any teacher or preacher can tell you people have a variety of listening faces.

For neurodivergent people, this panopticon effect lasts not just an hour but is the culmination of a lifetime of being disciplined to display neurotypicality. Power is exercised through subtle (nonphysical) and violent means to force neurodivergent people to discipline their bodies. Returning to neuronormative spaces, force is brought to bear on neurodivergent youth. A neuro-diversified prophetic imagination must denounce this neuronormativity, which compels neurodivergent youth to mask.

DIVERGENT DREAMING OF THE KIN-DOM OF GOD

Anglican theologian Verna J. Dozier writes, "The Kingdom of God is the biblical name for God's dream."[13] To neurodiversify our prophetic imagination calls us to understand how God's dream connects with the dreams of marginalized neurodivergent youth. Here I present in brief a divergent Christ whose proclamation of the kin-dom of God announces God's divergent dream for marginalized neurodivergent youth. This Christology is not prescriptive for all, nor does it assume it should be the only Christology.

The divergent Christ is unapologetically divergent. Divergence in neurodivergence is not a divergence from what is normal but a divergence from what is normative. Descriptively, neurodivergence is "sensory, affectual, and cognitive" differences.[14] Politically, neurodivergence is a marginalized neurotype that does not have a neurotypical image of itself. Divergence is diverging from compulsory neurotypicality. In this way, Jesus diverges because his communication and alternative reality diverged from the unjust structures and norms of an imperial empire.

Jesus's actions and communication diverged from the cultural norms of his day. People misunderstood who Jesus was and his message. Christ preached the kin-dom of God, an alternative world order of liberation, where people and society were in right relationship with God and each other. The kin-dom of God reimagined kinship between people. Jesus taught using parables and figurative language that his followers and the crowd misunderstood. This way of speaking also occurred in everyday social interactions with Jesus. The misunderstood Christ connects with neurodivergent people because they have similarly experienced misunderstanding due to their divergent ways of being in the world. Neurodivergent people like Jesus can encounter violence because of the misreading of others. When Black and Brown neurodivergent youths' embodiment is misread, it can result in severe punishment or police violence. When nonspeaking youth are interpreted through neurotypical cultural assumptions or denied **alternative and augmentative communication** (AAC) due to prohibitive cost, they are excluded.

Jesus was unapologetic in his divergence. Jesus did not change his way of diverging even though he was continually misunderstood. A divergent Christ is an invitation to unmask. Unmasking is the practice of embracing one's neurodivergence by no longer hiding one's neurodivergent traits.

Jesus persisted in his divergent means of communication. It is the misreading of Jesus's life and ministry that led to his crucifixion. Even after Jesus was beaten, he persisted in his divergent communication with Pilate. Jesus was misunderstood as he was dying on the cross, where the soldiers thought he was asking for a drink. Christ was misrecognized at the beginning of his resurrection appearances before his followers recognized him as Jesus.

EMBRACING MARGINALIZED NEURODIVERGENT YOUTH

The second act of a divergent prophetic imagination is to announce an alternative reality in which the church embraces marginalized neurodivergent youth. This alternative reality is embodied in space. The embracing of marginalized neurodivergent youth requires both neuro-shared and neuro-separate spaces. Neuro-shared spaces are spaces that are available for both neurotypical and neurodivergent people alike.[15] Neuro-separate spaces are those that are dominated by one neurotype.[16] The distinction between a neuro-separate and a neuro-shared space is not strictly determined by the number of neurotypical or neurodivergent people in a space. For example, there are neurodiverse spaces that function as neuro-separate spaces because they are dominated by neurotypical expectations and norms. Not all neuro-separate spaces are oppressive. Neuro-separate spaces run by neurodivergent people are necessary for them to have a space to gather outside of neurotypical norms. As mentioned above, youth ministry spaces are neurodiverse spaces with neurotypical and neurodivergent youth, but they act as neuronormative spaces. Similarly, a ministry space for neurodivergent people can be neuronormative if it is designed *for* neurodivergent people *by* neurotypical people.

How do we create a neuro-shared space? Piepzna-Samarasinha offers several ways to create a disability justice space that can inform a neuro-shared space. The first is to build relationships. Piepzna-Samarasinha notes that when people attempt to build access spaces, it is often done without first developing relationships with disabled folks.[17] Similarly, to create a neuro-shared space requires building relationships with marginalized neurodivergent youth. Due to masking, it is not a safe assumption to believe that you do not already have neurodivergent youth in your church. As someone who intentionally discloses my neurodivergence, I discover a lot more neurodivergent people in spaces I encounter. In these spaces, others would believe there are no neurodivergent people because they do not feel comfortable disclosing. Building relationships develops the trust necessary for an authentic neuro-shared space.

A neuro-shared space has a different orientation to accessibility. As disability justice activist Stacy Milbern argues, access is not the end goal but a process.[18] When access is the goal, the horizon of **belonging** is reduced to the bare minimum. There can be a tendency to focus on accessibility and not ask what is being made accessible. Similarly, when accessibility is the goal, there can be frustration that full accessibility is impossible, so why bother? However, when access is a process, accessibility becomes more collective and relational. Accessibility is collective because it becomes the responsibility of the whole community to ensure their space is accessible. Therefore, accessibility is also relational because it responds to the needs of the community.

Cross-Neurotype Communication

An essential aspect of creating neuro-shared spaces is **cross-neurotype communication.** Cross-neurotype encounters are ones where people of different neurotypes interact with one another. These interactions include neurodivergent and neurotypical encounters, as well as those between different marginalized neurotypes. Alyssa Hillary frames communication between neurotypes as cross-neurotype communication and a form of cross-cultural communication. Therefore, the issue is not that neurodivergent people have a social deficit but that both parties communicate across differences that lead to misunderstandings.

A neuronormative society makes neurotypical narratives the standard by which people come to understand their motives and desires. Hillary argues that a major source of the miscommunication between neurotypes is the lack of exposure to neurodivergent narratives. It is through encounter stories that you learn the motives behind people's actions, whether these are personal narratives or fictional stories. Without neurodivergent narratives, people do not have access to their motivations or desires, which leads to reading these actions through a neuronormative lens.

Building cross-neurotype communication skills begins with neurodivergent narratives. Several anthologies offer entry points into the diverse experiences of marginalized neurodivergent people. For example, *Autistic and Black*, edited by Kala Allen Omeiza,[19] offers accounts of Black Autistic experiences. *Black, Brilliant and Dyslexic*, edited by Marcia Brissett-Bailey and Atif Choudhury,[20] collects over twenty essays from Black Dyslexics. *Typed Words, Loud Voices*, edited by Amy Sequenzia and Elizabeth Grace,[21] gathers the stories of nonspeaking Autistics and Autistics who sometimes need typed communication. These are just a few anthologies that provide the opportunity to encounter neurodivergent narratives.

To engage in cross-neurotype communication requires several assumptions. First, neurodivergent people have a valid way of communicating. Second, neurodivergent people desire social connection. Third, neurotypical communication is not ideal or beneficial for all. These first three assumptions are the inverse of the negative neurotypical cultural assumptions of neurodivergent communication. The fourth assumption is that neurodivergent communication is dynamic and not static. For example, some Autistics need to use AAC sometimes, while others use it all the time. Finally, we must engage in cross-neurotype interactions with grace and humility. These assumptions provide an anchor to develop cross-neurotype communication skills.

Communications scholar Emily Stones argues for cross-neurotype communication competencies as an approach to engaging in cross-neurotype interaction. Stones identifies several cultural categories. She focuses on opposing orientations to show the variability of each category. Three of these cultural categories are particularly relevant: affect display, social interaction, and sensory sensitivity.

Neurodivergent people encounter criticism of their affect display. Affect display is a cultural category that refers to "verbal and nonverbal displays of emotion, ranging from facial expressions and even contact to paralinguistic cues such as vocal tone."[22] For example, some neurodivergent people are told that they have a flat affect because they are not expressive or talk in a monotone manner, while other neurodivergent people are told they are too expressive for talking too loudly or being too animated. In both instances, their affect display does not meet neuronormative expectations. Therefore, people must check their assumption that a youth's affect display means what they think it does.

The next cultural category is social interaction. Stones identifies two different orientations toward social interaction within neurodivergent narratives: unstructured and structured sociality. Unstructured sociality refers to an approach that "privileges spontaneity and responsiveness" in social interaction. This is contrasted with structured sociality that "privileges predictability and stability" (57). As Stones notes, people with this orientation to sociality "may struggle to understand social cues and find it tiring to interpret the 'unpredictable behaviors' that unstructured sociality elicits" (57). However, Stones also points out that neurodivergent individuals may switch their preference for structured or unstructured sociality based on familiarity or stress (58).

If we think of a liturgical tradition, we can see how both social orientations interact on a Sunday morning. Liturgical congregations have a very set order of worship. Those who prefer structured sociality could enjoy the service because there is a structure to the way people engage with one another. However, the coffee hour may bring opportunities for unstructured socialization. You have to choose who to sit next to if there are tables. Do other people want to talk? How long should you stay? Coffee hour allows spontaneity and unpredictability. One can relate to the anxiety and unpredictability one encounters when expecting structured social interaction. For example, the panic one may feel when encountering the invitation for visitors to introduce themselves to the congregation or other ways people are put on the spot.

Another cultural category is sensory sensitivity. Sensory sensitivity describes "the ways people experience a range of visual/tactile/olfactory/auditory stimuli in a given environment" (54). People have different levels of sensory sensitivity, from sensory seeking to sensory avoidance. These differences relate to a variety of ways that neurodivergence people regulate sensory input. This requires access to shared spaces to be collective and relational to navigate a space for different sensory needs.

These cultural categories help develop cross-neurotype communication skills. This brief overview underscores the need for more research in this area. Furthermore, cross-neurotype communication is necessary for marginalized neurodivergent people because there are frictions in cross-neurotype communications between neurodivergent people. We can foster more equitable communication in youth ministry with grace and humility.

Failure

There are two more essential aspects of embracing marginalized neurodivergent youth.[23] First, neuro-shared spaces must have neurodivergent leadership. The leadership needs to invite and model a neurodivergent embodiment. This can be done through an access invocation. . . . If we follow a divergent Christ, then we are called to model Christ as an exemplar of unmasking.

Finally, neuro-shared spaces must embrace failure. There are two aspects to failure. One way of embracing failure is through the willingness to experiment with . . .

Another way to embrace marginalized youth is to embrace failure or what Piepzna-Samarasinha calls the Crip art of failure. As she notes, disability justice may look like failure to others.[24] . . . What would failure look like? . . . There are two aspects of failure. One is embracing failure through a willingness to experiment. Sometimes, what it means is trying something that does not work. Examples of experimentation . . . : Another aspect of embracing failure is that success would look like failure to neuronormative standards . . .

Embrace looks like failure . . . from the perspective of neuronormativity.

Invitation to Co-Dreaming

Dreaming of divergent futures is not an individual endeavor but a collective one. I invite you to co-dream of a future where marginalized neurodivergent youth are embraced and can be unmasked. Let us neurodiversify the prophetic imagination. Let us dream wild dreams together.

REFLECTION QUESTIONS

1. How do we lessen the burden on youth who have been expected to conform to the norm? How do we mitigate the uneven risks of unmasking?
2. How do youth ministries cultivate cross-neurotype communications in their ministries?
3. What are your wild dreams for embracing neurodivergent youth?

BELONGING TO GOD, ONE ANOTHER, AND THE EARTH

A Prophetic Theology of Body-Mind-Spirit for Queer and Disabled Youth Ministry

CODY J. SANDERS

> ***Guiding Question:*** *What can churches learn about God, ourselves, and our practice of faith from a posture of compassionate curiosity and spiritual humility toward* ***LGBTQIA2S+*** *and disabled people as sources of sacred wisdom?*

Disabled people and LGBTQIA2S+ people—and LGBTQIA2S+ disabled people—are beloved image bearers of God and sacred sources of wisdom for our communities of faith.[1] These theological claims are the foundation of this chapter but are a minority perspective within dominant theological and ecclesial discourse. Instead, **queer**, **trans**, and disabled people have often been treated as second-class citizens in the kin-dom of God and have long endured spiritual violence emanating from theological sources and interpretation of sacred texts.[2] As disabled scholar Amy Kenny writes of churches, "They create ministries *to* disabled people, casting us as a group of second-class citizens who must be segregated from the general congregation, never considering that disabled people have something to teach the broader community about living an embodied faith, never realizing that we are not objects of pity and charity but image-bearers with our gifts to share with the beloved community."[3]

For youth workers to develop a prophetic posture in ministry with LGBTQIA2S+ disabled youth, the theologies that have most informed our sense of relationship to God, one another, and the earth need to be refashioned. Additionally, how we understand our embodied selves in relation to God—or theological anthropology—needs to reclaim a holistic and integrated body-mind-spirit perspective of human existence and experience.[4]

Toward these ends, youth workers are invited to make a prophetic move away from *accommodating* LGBTQIA2S+ and disabled youth into our theological frameworks and toward the cultivation of theological ways of knowing that are *shaped by* the inspirited **bodyminds**[5] of disabled, queer, and trans people. Making this prophetic turn requires expanding our sense of what "**belonging**" means within our faith communities, understanding the theological nature of our human beingness within that framework of belonging, and developing the spiritual humility to have our theological frameworks challenged and changed by bodies and experiences that call into question the presumed neutrality, goodness, and hierarchical value of bodies privileged by heteronormativity, cisnormativity, **neuronormativity**, and **ableism**.

A BIOPSYCHOSOCIAL-SPIRITUAL ANTHROPOLOGY OF QUEER DISABILITY

"Then the Lord God formed man from the dust of the ground and breathed into his nostrils the breath of life, and the man became a living being" (Gen. 2:7 NRSVue). You wouldn't get this from English translations of this well-known verse, but the Hebrew word for *human* or *man* in this verse bears a striking resemblance to the Hebrew word for *ground*. The Hebrew words the verse uses to describe "man" (*ha-adam*)—where we get the proper name "Adam" for the first man—are tied inextricably to the earth. Here's how it sounds, inserting the Hebrew words: it is from the dust of the ground, *ha-adamah*, that God forms the human, *ha-adam*. We might dismiss this as thousands-of-years-old mythopoetic musings on the human in relation to the earth now surely supplanted by more scientific ways of explaining our relationship to ecology. But that would be a mistake. Just take the example of the human microbiome.

The term "microbiome" was coined by molecular biologist Joshua Lederberg, who used it "to signify the ecological community of commensal, symbiotic, and pathogenic microorganisms that literally share our body space."[6] Nonhuman bacteria in our microbiome at least equals our human cells and, by some estimates, may outnumber human cells ten to one! Our microbiome, residing in exceptionally high numbers in our gastrointestinal tract, is a beneficial collection of bacteria necessary for life.

We do not *have* bodies. We *are embodied*, and our bodies are a diverse, pluriform array of earth others. Yet much of Western theology and philosophy for the last couple of millennia has worked to sever that relationship, helping us to see ourselves as more souls than bodies and bodies set in hierarchical relationships over the more extensive web of life. Theologian Mark I. Wallace writes, "In Christianity's practiced forgetfulness of its earthbound origins, it has recast itself as a footnote to Greek philosophy. As a vassal to Plato and Aristotle, it has operated within a graded hierarchy of Being in which plants and animals, rocks and rivers, are denigrated as soulless matter, while human beings are elevated as godlike, intelligent creatures—mired in the muck of corporeal existence, to be sure, but still able to shake off the mortal coil that binds them to the lower life-forms and realize their true *imago Dei* natures and destinies."[7] In this "great chain" arrangement of value and worth, all things in the universe are thought about as ordered in a linear sequence, from the inanimate world of rocks and geological formations, through plants, then animals, followed by humans, then angels, with God at the top of the great chain.[8] Importantly, humans don't just occupy one common stratum in this great chain of being. In early imaginations of this hierarchical order of nature, races were differently ordered too. And, vital to our discussion, embodiments of gender, sexuality, and ability place us on different strata in this supposed great chain.

This perspective has had a profound influence on the scientific understanding of human beings in relation to the wider web of life—later extracting the spiritual beings of angels and God, leaving humans alone at the top of the chain. It has powerfully influenced our sense of spiritual relationship with the wider creation. The lasting effects of the "great chain of being" and the persistent separation of body, mind, and spirit have led to myriad expressions of injustice, violence, colonization, and now a collapse of the climate and global ecological devastation.

Scholar and activist for queer, gender, and disability justice Rabbi Julie Watts Belser says, "Disability is spiritual dissent. Disability politics are a provocative challenge to prevailing conceptions of human value, a refusal to swallow the lie that some bodies and minds deserve to be discarded or disdained."[9] One of the lies that harm queer and disabled youth that we must refuse to swallow in our spiritual dissent is the lie of body-soul and body-mind dualism. Another is our separation from and supremacy over the wider web of life. Prophetic queer and disabled youth ministry, then, holds together in inextricable relation body, mind, and spirit and imagines our humanity not with separation from "nature" but with human-ecological entanglement. Prophetic queer and disabled youth ministry moves from upholding human supremacy in our theological narratives to narrating the human-ecological inseparability that rests at the very origin of the story, re-storying and restoring the relationship between our inspirited bodyminds and the bodies of the wider web of life—of *ha-adam* with *ha-adamah*.

A TRINITARIAN FRAMEWORK FOR QUEER DISABILITY THEOLOGY AND MINISTRY

Creator, Christ, and Holy Spirit. This is how we typically speak of the Trinity: God, the cosmic divine source of life; Jesus, the incarnation of God in human flesh who dwelled among us to show us the Way; and the Spirit hovering over the face of the waters in the primordial chaos out of which creation comes, descending in the feathery flesh of a dove at Jesus's baptism, and poured out on the church in the baptism of Pentecost at the birth of the church.

However, Creator, Christ, and Holy Spirit are bound up together in the life of the Divine, each person of the Trinity singular yet always and only sharing in a community of divine being—what theologians refer to as perichoresis. When we say we belong to God, we belong to a trinitarian relationality. And, bound up in the life of God, the church embodies that relationality. "For in the one Spirit we were all baptized into one body" (1 Cor. 12:12 NRSVue). All through scripture, though ignored and diminished by so much of contemporary theology, God and humans are also bound up together in relationship always and only in a shared community with the wider ecological web of life.

A theology of belonging for queer and disabled youth requires an expansive notion of what and with whom we are bound up in mutual communities of belonging. A trinitarian being-in-community can be imagined with the three interpenetrating, overlapping dimensions of transcendence, togetherness, and tethering. Another way of saying this is to imagine our belonging as involving our belongingness to God, our belongingness in the human community, and our belongingness through rooted entanglement with the ecological web of life. All three of these dimensions provide a way for youth workers to expand theologies and practices of belonging with queer and disabled youth and with their entire communities.

TRANSCENDENCE DIMENSION

The central focus within the transcendence dimension is our sense of belonging and relationality to an ultimate context, or what many of us would call "God." Though each of these dimensions does not neatly correspond directly to one person of the Trinity, we might think of the transcendence dimension as speaking to our sense of connection to the Divine that opens us outward beyond the "self" toward a wider awareness of relationality to an Other. Something of our belongingness is bound up with this transcendent Other beyond us, which also becomes bound up with us. A sense of wonder and awe often attends the experience of this transcendent relationality.

For queer, trans, and disabled youth, belonging to God is often an area of spiritual stress and sometimes spiritual violence and trauma. Sometimes this comes through overt theological narratives that condemn LGBTQIA2S+ sexual and gender embodiments. Other times it comes by way of theologies that see disabled bodies only as objects of pity in need of God's "healing" and not as complete image bearers of God. Restorative work in the transcendence dimension attends to the ways that our lives are bound up in the life of God forever, separated neither by things present nor things to come (Rom. 8:38). This restorative work doesn't only entail revising our theologies of belongingness but learning from LGBTQIA2S+ and disabled youth the ways that their sense of belongingness to God emerges and is maintained, even amid the toxic theologies that often attempt to sever this bond of transcendent belongingness.

TOGETHERNESS DIMENSION

The central focus within the togetherness dimension is our relationship to human communities. We come to know our sense of who we are as individuals as selves-in-relation to others. These relationships can be characterized by both warmth and wounding, relationships both helpful and harmful to our sense of belonging to and with others in human community. We might think of the trinitarian connection of the togetherness dimension as the incarnation of God in the body of Jesus, who made his dwelling in human community, and who subverted many of the norms of his own human communities by bringing those on the margins into the center and turned upside-down the status structure of the empire with images of the kingdom of God. Importantly, Jesus was also challenged by and learned from those on the margins of his own human community (see Mark 7:24–29 and 10:46–52).

Belonging in human community is also fraught for disabled and LGBTQIA2S+ people. As queer, nonbinary, femme, disabled writer, artist, and activist Leah Lakshmi Piepzna-Samarasinha argues, "Ableism isolates and keeps disabled, Deaf, and neurodivergent people from finding disabled, Deaf, and neurodivergent communities. . . . Being kept from each other also kills."[10] Similarly, queer and trans youth are often cut off from community with other queer and trans youth by parents who are nonaffirming of their LGBTQIA2S+ children, by churches that perpetuate spiritually violent anti-queer theologies, and by schools beholden to an onslaught of local and state policies and laws that make educational contexts places of marginality and often violence for queer and trans youth.[11] Repair of human communal connections requires the reversal of center and margin through our ability to learn from the sacred wisdom of queer and trans disabled youth and the opening of conduits through which our communities pass down to us the narratives of our queer, trans, and disabled ancestors to whom we are connected across time and space.

TETHERING DIMENSION

The tethering dimension invites focus on the ways are we tethered, rooted, and moored to and within the earth and the beings—animate and inanimate, biotic and abiotic—that inhabit the earth alongside us (and within us!). We are always humans in relationships of earthly entanglement with wider ecological webs, even when we mistakenly set ourselves over against "nature" or the "nonhuman" in a position of human supremacy or exceptionalism. Yet our lives could not and would not be without this multispecies, biotic and abiotic, lively and inert web of earth beings.

We might imagine the trinitarian connection to the tethering dimension to the animating power of the Spirit, alive and enlivening, and most pointedly pictured incarnate in the feathery flesh of a dove descending on Jesus at his baptism in all four Gospels. This is what theologian Mark I. Wallace calls the "*double incarnation* or what one might call *libertine* or *promiscuous incarnation* insofar as God in Jesus and the Spirit embraces the fleshly reality of all interrelated organisms."[12] And while, on the surface, it may not seem that our relationship of belonging with the wider web of earthly entanglement has much to do with queer, trans, and disabled youth, the ways we have separated our bodies from our spirits, and the ways we have separated human bodies from bodies of other-than-human beings is, as noted, at the root of hierarchical understandings of value and worth assigned to human beings.

These three dimensions—transcendence, togetherness, and tethering—form what we can think of as a divine, human, and ecological web of relationality within which our inspirited bodyminds participate in God's trinitarian life. It is an integrated, imbricated, interpenetrating network of mutual giving and receiving, co-constituting our sense of who we are as human beings in relation to others, the earth that envelops us, and the Divine.

PROPHETIC DISABLED QUEER FUTURITY

Being prophetic is often used simply to mean something like a social justice orientation toward whatever topic is under consideration. Because we are followers of the way of Jesus, these concerns of justice ought to be central to our understanding of how we go about the Christ-shaped ministry to "set free those who are oppressed" (Luke 4:18 NRSVue, citing Isa. 61:1), or they aren't sufficiently prophetic. Beyond baptizing social justice concerns, we are called into even deeper engagements of love and justice toward shaping the world as it ought to be.

To be prophetic in a fuller sense of the word we should understand **prophecy** alongside South African liberation theologian Allan Boesak as "a contradiction of the present *because* there is a vision of the future—God's future."[13] This is a theological vision of the world as it is yet to be, but with the promise of something coming that is upsetting good news: upsetting to the gatekeepers of the status quo and good news for those targeted by the violence of its systems and structures.

To pursue a truly prophetic imagination that is rooted in the not-quite-yet-but-soon-coming upturning of the status quo by the eruption of the kin-dom of God in our midst, we must center the sources of sacred wisdom found in the inspirited bodyminds of our queer, trans, and disabled youth. Centering these experiences and insights of unconventional inspirited bodyminds upturning the normative status quo leads to fuller visions of a prophetic, God-preferred future shaped by a deep trinitarian belonging to the Divine, to community, and to the earth. "It's radical to imagine that the future is disabled," Piepzna-Samarasinah says, "a deeply disabled future: a future where disabled, Deaf, Mad, neurodivergent bodyminds are both accepted without question as part of vast spectrum of human and animal ways of existing, but where our cultures, knowledge, and communities shape the world."[14] This is an image of prophetic disabled queer futurity! Further, Piepzna-Samarasinha points to the emerging realities in which "the climate crisis, pandemics, and the ongoing ecocide of settler colonialism and extractive capitalism are already creating the conditions" for what they call a "majority disabled future."[15] As the title of Piepzna-Samarasinha's book claims, *the future is disabled*. And, I would add, *the future is queer*.

We can envision a genderqueer future in which there is neither male nor female (Gal. 3:28), a disabled future where all bodies are gathered into the center of the community in Jeremiah's vision of restoration (31:8), a future in which the eunuch—long an exemplar of queer faith from Acts 8, disdained for their disfigured body, their questionable masculinity, and their sexual and gender queerness—is given "a name better than sons and daughters . . . ; an everlasting name" (Isa. 56:5 NRSVue).[16] None of these subversions of gendered and ableist hierarchies, even in scripture, come because the disabled, the queer, or the genderqueer become *more like* the dominant heteronormative, neuronormative, ableist status quo, either through some act of "healing" or through any achievement of hetero-neuro-ableist parity. Instead, they represent a vision of the future—*God's future*—in which communities of faith are caught up in this prophetic vision and are transformed by the prophetic challenge bound up within it.

REFLECTION QUESTIONS

1. When did you learn that your own body was either presumed "normal" or strange, unusual, odd, different, disabled, or queer? Whose bodies were held up to you as the "norm" against which your body was to be judged?
2. What has your inspirited bodymind taught you about God? And how have the inspirited bodyminds you've encountered different from your own taught you something important about God?

3. What could the faith communities you belong to learn from a compassionately curious, spiritually humble posture toward LGBTQIA2S+ and disabled bodies?

PRACTICAL TOOL: TELLING YOUR STORIES OF BELONGING

Either on your own, perhaps with a journal, or with a small group of trusted companions, spend some time narrating your own stories of sacred belonging within the three dimensions.

Transcendence: Tell of a time when you felt especially connected to that which transcends you, a context of ultimacy, or to God. Try to tell this story not in doctrinal language but in narrative detail—a coming to the awareness that you were beloved by God. This doesn't need to be your first experience of this sense of belonging, just a time when it became palpable for you. Tell the story that first springs to awareness. What conveyed this connection to you? Where were you? Who was with you? What did you see, hear, feel, taste, smell?

Togetherness: Tell of a time when you felt especially taken by a sense of togetherness, of belonging to others, being beloved by others. Perhaps even a time when you were taken by surprise by this sense of kinship connection. What did that belonging feel like in an embodied, sensory way—what did it taste like, smell like, look like? What helped cultivate this sense of belonging or kinship?

Tethering: Tell of a place in the natural world to which you feel a special bondedness, a place that draws you in, a landscape in which you feel most held or at home, an environment to which you have sense of belonging. Describe its detail and narrate the other inhabitants of the ecological web of life that inhabit(ed) that place alongside you. What did/does it feel like to be in relationship with the earth in this place?

If you would like to continue the storytelling, you might also take another round either solo or in your group of trusted companions to narrate stories related to ways that you've experienced your belonging in any of these dimensions—to God, to human community, to the earth—harmed, fractured, or severed in some ways in the course of your life. Then, in relation to those fracturing experiences, narrate how you sought, found, or are seeking ways of cultivating healing within that dimension of your sacred belonging and what kind of support you might need from others along the way.

THE PROPHETIC LEADERSHIP OF OUR FRIENDS WITH DISABILITIES

Following Them and Their Dreaming

ZACH GRANT

> ***Guiding Question:** Can we follow our friends with disabilities to places in ministry we would otherwise not get to?*

Ken and I were going to volunteer in the high school special education classroom that had the most support needs. The other people that we could see serving in the classroom were nurses with the knowledge and experience to change feeding tubes and make other medical interventions. There were teachers with degrees and certifications in special education. Many of the students were medically fragile. Many did not communicate with words. I felt a little anxious that my skills and experience working with kids with disabilities in churches and parachurch ministries were not going to be up to the task of being a helpful presence in the class, but I was more worried about Ken.

Part of the reason Ken was looking to volunteer with me was because his blood sugar levels were difficult to regulate and that meant he was inclined to fall asleep in the middle of volunteering. That was why he had not been asked back to volunteer at the elementary school he had volunteered at for years. He had some difficulty reading and a few other elements related to his intellectual **developmental disabilities** that might mean I would need to choose at times between supporting him and supporting the students. Some could make the argument that Ken was not the right person to choose as a partner. It was providential that they did not because Ken offered insights that were instrumental to our success. Not only that, his insights made him a bit of a prophet for me.

I remember coming out of the class on that first day. I felt tired and uneasy in the work we were doing, and as I was driving Ken back to the house I was thinking we might try some other way to meet students with disabilities, some part of me, sadly, thinking that there might be other students who would fit more easily into the programs of our church that served people with disabilities. Would the students there fit well into our adaptive Sunday School programs or our specialized worship and fellowship events? Would their greater support needs overwhelm our volunteers, who were already struggling to meet the support needs of the folks with disabilities already a part of our programs?

As we drove, Ken began talking about the students. His commentary was much different from my internal monologue, as he saw what I was unable to see. He said, "Did you notice how funny that kid was?" or "Boy! She was so smart, do you remember all the things she knew about numbers?" He talked about every student and all the gifts he saw in them. It was clear that Ken could easily see what I was struggling, or perhaps unable, to perceive. Ken saw these students in ways that their parents see them, the way that God sees them. That vision that Ken showed me on our ride home helped me reimagine the work that we were doing. It surely helped me to see the students differently and see their giftedness, but also Ken's and my own giftedness to do the work. Without Ken's prophetic reimagining, we would not have been successful or even known what success looked like. My imagination was constrained by the shape of the church that served me well, and it could not picture clearly how these students with greater support needs might fit into it. Yet Ken saw each of them as a gift from God and was leading us to a place where we could reimagine what our church might be.

Walter Brueggeman in his seminal work *The Prophetic Imagination* tries to understand prophetic activity in a way that frees prophets from just being "foretellers or social protestors."[1] Prophets are about the work of reimagining. In our **friendship** and work together with these students, Ken was reimagining the students so that they were no longer merely kids with profound needs that we could maybe (but probably not) help. Instead, they were people who had great gifts to share with us and whose lives were a beautiful privilege to behold. Brueggemann writes, "It is the task of the prophet to bring to expression the new realities against the more visible ones of the old order."[2]

Furthermore, Ken's imagination was not a contest between his imagination and the hard, down-to-brass-tacks reality of the situation. Ken's imagination contested another imagination.[3] My daunted and discouraged feelings about our work were the product of a competing imagination about what our church was and what success looked like. Even while my position at the church was geared toward developing inclusive ministries for the church, my mental picture of the work of the church was still very much informed by images that excluded the students Ken and I were working with. I wanted programs that were more flexible and supportive to include people with intellectual disabilities. However, I still wanted the model to resemble the other youth ministry going on at the church. I could imagine Bible study, professions of faith, and service projects on a slower timeline or with simpler language. I was struggling to imagine Christ proclaimed without words. I was struggling to imagine a church radically different from the world. Were the "sustainable," "dynamic," and "efficient" programs I felt that I needed to create dreamed up by the Gospels? Or were they imagined by American business models and economic pressures? I was not sure.

Just because these pictures and models of the church were imagined did not mean that they were not powerful. They certainly were, both in terms of their ability to shape my mood and feelings about the work with the students with disabilities in front of me and in their capacity to apply pressure to my activity in terms of support for my ministry. Imagination is a powerful thing, but if something is imagined, then it can also be reimagined. Over time, this realization and many friends with disabilities like Ken were leading me to ask who is imagining the church the way it is. What are the forces that are shaping that imagination? Is the gospel leading me to this model of church or is it my desire for comfort? My fear of scarcity? Is there a bigger gospel than the one I have been proclaiming?

I have been blessed to ask these questions, which are important to me and which I doubt I would have asked if not for being invited into open-hearted friendship by people with disabilities. As a minority community, folks with disabilities sit naturally in tension with the dominant models the world has imagined. Since the world and the church usually serve me well, it is more difficult for me to imagine a bigger, richer gospel than the one I have inherited. Brueggemann names this difficulty aptly: "We do not believe that there will be newness but only that there will be merely a moving of the pieces into new patterns."[4] It is incredibly difficult in our affluence, our illusion of independence and sufficiency, to believe that a gift will come from somewhere we had not already thought to extract some value.

It is one of the good ways of God that friendship is used to transform us.[5] So it's fitting that friendship would become a location where God's prophetic word can shape a community. In friendship, people from all sorts of communities and subcommunities (the term Brueggemann would use, but I do not love it for discussing people with disabilities)[6] can create a liminal space so that we can begin to travel to someplace new that we are imagining together. I think of the story from the second chapter of Mark's Gospel where four people bring their friend who is paralyzed on a mat. With their friend, they reimagine the priorities of the world even unto cutting a hole through the ceiling and disrupting Jesus's preaching. Jesus sees each person's faith, which collectively becomes something dynamic, precipitating God's transformational forgiveness and healing.

Friendship can become a place where some may gain limited access to the insights of the tensions between the community of folks with disabilities and the dominant community. This includes an articulation of pain and hope, sometimes using coded language—all the necessary things for prophetic energizing.[7] Folks with disabilities may gain limited access to the resources and voices of the dominant community inasmuch as those in their community of friendship have access and are able to act as "accomplices."[8] Benjamin T. Conner writes, "A principled commitment to the idea of ministry with adolescents with developmental disabilities, 'like-ing' the idea on your Facebook page, or believing in the value of it will not transform you or your congregation the way that participating in their lives as friends will."[9]

I have been doing ministry with teenagers with disabilities since I was a teenager myself, and growing up with them has also caused my ministry to grow up. When I first began I was sure that God was calling me to help kids who really needed it. But as time went on I felt more sure that God had brought us together as colaborers for some mission that was made better because we were *all* a part of it.[10] Furthermore, as "the prophetic witness of the church is not to be identified in some *specific functions* of ministry and not in others,"[11] so, too, it has seemed better not to do disability ministry per se, but rather to reimagine the church in such a way that people with and without disabilities might lead and serve together at every level of the church.

To that end, amid the global pandemic, Pastor Chris (whom I first met as a middle schooler and took to a summer camp for adolescents with disabilities) and I decided to plant a church, and we had our first service on Pentecost. Hopefully you will have read "How I Become the Head Pastor of My Church Someday." We named the church Bethlehem Inclusive Church—everyone liked the name Chris chose better than mine. It is an apt name because it prophetically critiques our assumptions about salvation. It is still difficult for people to determine whether the child in the manger or the child in the palace will bring God's salvation. God often works through those the world mistakes as lowly.

I find it difficult to recommend any particular feature or strategy of Bethlehem Inclusive Church as edifying for the whole church. Part of the value of our friends with disabilities is that their gifts are hidden and surprising. Chris's leadership did not look like Ken's leadership or my leadership. We did not determine that they would be a gift to the church by searching for the talents we would need to build our model. We leaned heavily on the truth of their giftedness promised in scripture and listened attentively for the ways God might use them in our midst. We had a sense that people with disabilities were already leading and that we needed to find a way to follow. If you are not sharing enough power in your ministries to let people with disabilities take things off the rails, then you will only get to the places you have been before. The people with disabilities you bring into the center of your community are the best ones to guide you to the particulars.

For the nuts and bolts of inclusion, because each person and community has so much variation, you will be best served by looking around your community and asking some particular person with disabilities, some special education teacher, or some occupational therapist about the best ways to adapt your practices to serve the people of your community and all their diverse abilities. I do not always know how to do it particularly well myself; I only know enough to insist we do it. However, one benefit to feeling drawn to a destination that you do not know how to get to is that you find ways to keep wandering in hope.

When studying pastoral counseling in seminary I was introduced to a counseling strategy called Solution-Focused Brief Therapy (SFBT), which gave me a terrible taste at first, because I thought that these "solutions" were handed down to the counselee in some paternalistic sense. Rather, the strengths of the counselee are affirmed as the therapist works under the assumption that the client is already doing things to deal with his or her problem.[12] This confidence in the person usually identified as being in "need," and the strategies of de-emphasizing the obstacles and looking toward imaginative possibilities, made me think it could be especially suitable for working with people with disabilities. Now I often employ SFBT strategies not for managing problems that I might bring to a counseling session or that someone from the congregation might bring to me, but for managing the tension between the prophetic call of my friends with disabilities and the stubborn, intractable nature of the exclusionary structures of the world we have imagined.

My friends with disabilities have hopes, needs, and dreams, and we all share a dream for this church together. Yet sometimes I do not know what to do with those dreams. Pastor Chris dreams of a more robust ministry, not just with equal time leading from the front, but equality of salary, office space, and all the trappings of his title. I do not know just where those resources will come from. The systems of power and scarcity sometimes feel very real, and the world seems indifferent to the prophetic reimagining of my friends like Chris and Ken. Sometimes I feel that only a fool would think to do church this way, and I, Zach Grant, am that fool. It would take a miracle for this to work.

If you, as you walk deeper and deeper with your friends with disabilities into God's calling, ever feel that same way, I recommend to you the "miracle question." It is a thought experiment that imagines whatever goal or problem you hope to solve was achieved overnight by a miracle. It then invites you to imagine what the details are that would give away the fact that the miracle had occurred.[13]

What small details would let you know that your youth group had miraculously become a place where people with disabilities were well included?

They would be invited to every birthday party.

What else?

You would see them surrounded by people and they would all be smiling.

What else?

Every Sunday you would see people with and without disabilities leading from the front.

Once you have a lot of these little details, it is easy to think of small, concrete ways that we could achieve those outcomes, or at least move the scale by one degree. Pastor Chris, whose narrative opens this section of the book, has bigger dreams than I do for his ministry and for our church. I appreciate them and do my best to be led by them, but sometimes I am daunted by the need to fulfill or manage them. When these problems seem too oppressive, I try to see what the solution looks like, and then move toward them in the smallest, most concrete steps.

Chris is a pastor. He wants to be the *head* pastor of a church. Chris dreams about preaching the gospel in Brazil, Israel, Albania, Puerto Rico, and Valdosta, Georgia. Chris dreams about mission trips to Israel and Gaza. I ask Chris, "Is it anything that we started a church and that you have opportunities to preach at Bethlehem Inclusive, and that you lead us through our services in powerful ways?" But I don't really mean, "Is it anything?" What I mean is, "Is it enough?" When will it be enough for Chris, and when will his dreaming be satisfied? Is "How much is enough?" a question I am led to by the Spirit? Is capacity the province of visions and dreams of God's calling?

If three hundred neurotypical youth were to descend on your youth group or Young Life club or congregation, longing to be involved, would that be seen as a problem? Would we find any way possible to connect them to the life of the church? If they wanted to serve in our ministries for their long lives, would we tax our imaginations to see the throughlines between their gifts and the ministries we were involved in? I think we would. How about if three hundred youth with intellectual disabilities were to do the same thing? What would our ministries have to be to meet that surge of gifts, needs, and wild difference? We would have to be humbler, more aware of our interdependence, more loving, more courageous, more unified, and deeper in every dimension. I pray that we would be led by our friends with disabilities into those ministries and meet God there.

REFLECTION QUESTIONS

1. Suppose every person with disabilities who came to your church or community felt a deep sense of **belonging** and had everything they needed to lead in any ministry you offered. What would have to be true about your church?
2. How would your church get to that place?
3. If a 10 means that people with disabilities are leading in your church at the highest level, and a 0 means they are not leading at all, what rating would you give? What would help your church go up one point?

PRACTICAL TOOL: THE MIRACLE QUESTION

The miracle question from SFBT can be a useful tool to help a young person with or without disabilities engage their imagination and envision their ministry, and then begin to move past the obstacles to it. You can follow these steps to lead them through it.

1. **Identify the problem**: As the relationships you form with youth with disabilities awaken you to their hopes, dreams, and longings, the future you are beginning to imagine together likely will find itself in tension with our world and churches as they have been imagined. Once you have something that can be solved with a miracle (an unrealized dream, an obstacle to inclusion, a calling that seems hopeless) then you're ready to ask the question. This is a way to start with the solution rather than with the problems.[14]
2. **Ask them the question**: Start by explaining what the miracle question is. You might say, "I'm going to ask you a strange question. Tonight, after you brush your teeth, everything is silent and a miracle happens while you sleep. You are leading and serving in just the ways you want to be. When you wake up, how would you know that the miracle occurred?"
3. **Encourage them to drill down into details**: Ask them to describe the changes they would notice. For example, "What would be different each Sunday? Each Wednesday night youth group? How would your interactions with others change? Where would you go during the week? What new activities would fill your time?"
4. **Find the exceptions:** Looking for the small ways our youth show promise for leadership in the present can awaken us to unnoticed strengths. As they describe their ideal future in ministry, help them identify moments when they are already exhibiting glimpses of this future.[15] You might ask, "What gifts, talents, or resources do you have that would help make this vision a reality?" or, "What would someone important to you tell me about your gifts for ministry?"[16]
5. **Scaling questions:** Help them to anchor their vision in measurable increments. It empowers them to see the next step toward their goal. You might ask, "If a 10 means that you are leading in just the way you want to be, and a 0 means you are not leading at all, what rating would you give? What would help you go up one point? How can you contribute to that?"[17]

6. **Make a plan together**: Collaboratively develop a plan that outlines the steps they and accomplices in your community can take. You might identify necessary supports or resources to gather. Are there mentors, drivers, or teachers you can invite into the gospel work you are being called into together? How might your needs helpfully shape your community to be faithful in new ways? What practices might have to be reimagined to support the leadership of every member of the church regardless of ability?
7. **Revisit this question**: It is often true that people need more time than we give them, and this is often true for your friends with disabilities. Do not be surprised if this question must be asked over many different encounters or does not progress easily in the sequence ascribed. The most important thing is to attend closely to the communication of your conversation partner and take seriously whatever they find important to share. Schedule time to double back and see how things are going. Try to respond flexibly to what opportunities present themselves and lift up any wins or forward progress toward their imagined ministry.[18]

If someone communicates without verbal language, adapting the miracle question using alternative communication methods is wholly appropriate. You might try visual aids (pictures, vision boards, drawing, emotion cards), storytelling or roleplay (puppets or action figures to act out scenarios and imagine the future), body language (attend to their gestures, expressions, and movements; embodying the discussion by going to the physical places the leadership will happen), any assistive technologies they normally use to communicate, or collaborative art (a collage that illustrates the future they hope for).

These steps will not go neatly in the way they are arranged. Your friends will have their own paths through it, and you may find you are the expert on how to communicate with your friend and help them navigate it. I have not found two people, with or without disabilities, who work through this process in exactly the same way. Attempting to define SFBT in a sentence, its founders described it as "the pragmatics of hope and respect."[19] Listening deeply and trusting the uncommon wisdom of our friends with disabilities ought to determine the details of this practice.

A PROPHETIC PRAYER FOR YOUTH

CARMELLE BEAUGELIN CALDWELL

God, I often wonder about the future.
Sometimes, others assume that my future will be____________________.
These assumptions make me feel_________________________.
Still, I know You have lovingly created me to be __________________.
Could You help me be who I am?
God, I trust You with my story even if __________________.
Amen.

God, I often wonder about the future.
Sometimes, others often assume that my future will be *(a false assumption others place on you: limited, broken, unsuccessful, etc., or a hopeful assumption: strength, healing, etc.)*.
These assumptions make me feel *(an emotion: frustrated, hurt, understood/misunderstood, hopeful, curious, etc.)*.
Still, I know You have lovingly created me to be *(a God-inspired truth about yourself: strong, creative, beloved, etc.)*
Could You help me be who I am?
God, I trust You with my story even if *(a fear, uncertainty, or challenge in living authentically)*.
Amen.

CONCLUSION

ERIN RAFFETY

In our roundtable introduction, when we asked our contributors about what they were most excited about for this book, Rev. Sarah Griffith Lund shared that she believes that this book is "the right book at the right place at the right time." Sarah's words are humbling, because, of course, this is my hope for the book as well—that it will get into the hands of disabled youth and the ministers and youth workers, as well as the future ministers and youth workers, who hope to serve them, and make a difference in the lives of young people. But this hope is somewhat tempered by the **lament** and **protest** that ring poignantly from the pages of this book. If this is truly "the right book at the right place at the right time," this is also because disabled youth, especially those with intersectional identities, have been too long ignored and misunderstood and now find themselves in crises and at crossroads. There is a lamenting and protesting energy to even the praises and the prophecies that our authors lift. There is an already-but-not-yet testimony for those who so boldly share of their lives, all the while knowing they have been rejected and ridiculed by the very church they still seek to serve.

And yet I am so grateful that these young people and those who love them have had the courage to tell the truth. It would have been easier to elide the trauma and pain, not to take the time to explain complex identities, experiences, and stories, and not to use words like **ableism**, sexism, and racism, because it makes people uncomfortable. At yet another moment in that roundtable discussion, youth advocate Morrigan Clarke spoke up to say that as much as they want to say that **praise** is the word that comes to mind when they think about disabled youth, they feel that they, their family, and youth like them still have to fight so hard in this world for understanding. As I write this conclusion, the Trump administration, in office for all but a matter of months, is targeting migrant children, **transgender** youth, and disabled people, so protest becomes not just an act of faith but survival.

How will the church respond, not just to these assaults on our common humanity and sacred lives, but to the laments, protests, praises, and prophecies shared on these pages? Will these prayers and testimonies fall upon good soil, or will they be cast upon the rocks or plucked up by the birds? Will this be the "right time" in the sense that these stories are not just told but honored, not just listened to, but acted upon? It may just be my optimism or my bias, but I can't think of more challenging, worthy prophets to call us in. My prayer and supplication is that the time will be right not because the book has been written, but because it will be used for ministry, for such a time as this.

GLOSSARY

COMPILED BY ERIN RAFFETY

ableism: A system of assigning values to people's bodies based on socially constructed ideas of normalcy, intelligence, excellence, and productivity.

alternative and augmentative communication (AAC): Technology that facilitates language and communication for nonspeaking people.

Americans with Disabilities Act of 1990 (ADA): The major civil rights legislation passed by disability rights activists in 1990 (amended in 2008), which prohibits discrimination against disabled people, requires employers to make reasonable accommodations to employees with disabilities, and provides accessibility standards for public accommodations.

Autism: Autism, or autism spectrum disorder (ASD) is a neurological condition that affects thinking, communication, learning, and behavior. The word "spectrum" reminds us that individuals with autism differ significantly in their experiences. The **neurodiversity movement** (see below) seeks to move away from this language of disorder or deficiency, recognizing autism as a viable and valuable, different way of being in the world.

belonging: A feeling for disabled people that goes beyond being merely included or offered participation in churches or other settings. According to researcher Erik W. Carter, belonging is experienced when disabled people are included, invited, welcomed, known, accepted, supported, heard, befriended, needed, and loved (see "Where Belonging Abounds," pp. 21–33).

BIPOC: Acronym that refers to Black, Indigenous, and/or People of Color. An umbrella term that aims to be inclusive to a wide variety of identities and experiences.

bodymind: A term used in disability studies to emphasize the intersectional and interdependent nature of the body and the mind, critique the hierarchy between the two in Western culture, and emphasize the insights disabled people have because of their unique, embodied experiences in the world.

brainforest: A metaphor coined by educator Thomas Armstrong to move away from machine analogies for the brain and expand concepts of the brain to varied and interdependent ecosystems that emphasize the rich diversity and resilience of our brains.

COVID-19 pandemic: The fifth deadliest pandemic in history, which began in December 2019 in China with the outbreak of COVID-19, a respiratory virus that spread across the globe by March 2020 and claimed the lives of 18.5 to 33.5 million people. Vaccines were developed in 2021, though the disease continues to circulate, and a sizable population of individuals are now chronically ill and disabled as a result of lingering effects of the disease, popularly dubbed "long COVID."

cripping: Asserting disabled ways of doing things and being in the world, to not just acknowledge and accommodate, but to carve out more just and hospitable places for disabled bodyminds. Note: "Crip" and "cripping" are pejorative terms that have been reclaimed by disabled people.

crip time: A term that acknowledges that disabled people often need more time to complete tasks because they are forced to go up ramps or practice all kinds of accommodations to inhabit an ableist world. The term also serves to acknowledge the way in which disabled people's approach to time, like a subculture, offers a more dignifying, humanizing way of being in the world that acknowledges the time and space different bodies need to and do take up.

critical disability studies: An academic yet activist approach to critiquing and dismantling ways in which ableism is tied into other forms of intersectional oppression such as racism, sexism, capitalism, etc.

cross-neurotype communication: Communication across neurotypes, which scholar Alyssa Hillary names as a form of cross-cultural communication, because both parties are communicating across differences and those differences can often lead to misunderstandings (see Reyes's chapter, p. 161 and **neurotype**).

depression: The leading cause of disability in the world according to the World Health Organization. According to the DSM-V, depression often includes changes in weight, sleep, or activity, depressed mood or loss of interest in pleasure activities, decreased energy, or feelings of worthlessness and negative thoughts, and can include thoughts of death or **suicide** (see Cartledge's chapter, pp. 121–22).

developmental disabilities: Conditions that affect a person's physical, intellectual, or behavioral development.

(The) Disabled God: A concept pioneered by disability theologian Nancy Eiesland in her book *The Disabled God* (Abingdon, 1994), which recognizes disability as an attribute of Jesus's divine/human nature, specifically in the example of Jesus's resurrected body, which appears with wounds, and in the Christian practice of celebrating communion in Jesus's broken body through the Eucharist.

disability justice movement: Founded by queer BIPOC activists in 2005, the disability justice movement recognizes disability as an intersectional (race, gender, sexuality, age, etc.) experience of oppression, pushes beyond rights-based frameworks toward more comprehensive definitions and visions of justice, and centers the leadership of those most affected by the intersectional experience of disability in society.

disability rights movement: The disability rights movement in the United States advocates for disabled people's full rights to participation in all aspects of society and has resulted in the ADA and **IDEA** (see below).

disability studies: An academic field that examines disability from social, cultural, and political perspectives, known for its advancement of the social model of disability (also credited to activists and the disabled people's movement), which identifies barriers to access as being located largely in environments, societies, attitudes, and institutions versus individual bodies. (see also **medical model** and **social model of disability**)

disability theology (Christian): The field of study that emerged after Nancy Eiesland's 1994 book *The Disabled God,* in which disabled and nondisabled scholars have taken up limits, ethics, the Eucharist, vulnerability, friendship, and time as fruitful vantages from which disability provides valuable theological insight.

double stigma: Stigma experienced due to mental health diagnoses and disability (see Lund's chapter, p. 35).

friendship: An important practice studied in disability theology, emphasized for its transformative qualities of mutuality, love, and vulnerability (see Jacober's chapter, p. 65).

imago Dei: A Latin phrase that translates to "image of God," often invoked in Christian and Jewish theologies of disability as a baseline for our shared sacredness as humans and found in Genesis 1:26–27, where it says that humankind was made in the likeness of God.

Individualized Education Plan (IEP): A written document that outlines a student's special education services, goals, and accommodations. IEPs are created for children with disabilities, learning challenges, or emotional and behavioral problems.

Individuals with Disabilities Education Act (IDEA): A federal law that guarantees free and appropriate public education for children with disabilities. It also protects the rights of disabled children and their families.

inspiration porn: Popularized by the late disability activist Stella Young, this term describes how the ordinary lives and actions of disabled people are often sensationalized by the media and nondisabled people to make nondisabled people feel good or better about themselves.

intersectionality: A term coined by Kimberlé Crenshaw in 1989 to illuminate the ways in which multiple forms of inequality compound and create additional obstacles that disadvantage people in ways that are not always visible. In this volume we also use the term to identify some of the subordinated knowledges that form and flourish precisely at the multidimensional margins of intersectionality (see Raffety's introduction to this volume, pp. xi–xii).

Joyful Noise: A worship service popularized by the Evangelical Lutheran Church of America in New Jersey, which offers a no-boundaries, multisensory, multimodal opportunity for families with disabled children to worship together one Sunday afternoon a month (see Clarke's chapter, pp. 61–63).

lament: The biblical practice of pouring out one's grief, sorrow, and pain before God as an act of faith that God can hold and honor it and transform mourning into dancing.

LGBTQIA2S+: An acronym that stands for for lesbian, gay, bisexual, **trans**, queer, intersex, asexual, and Two-Spirit (an identity label created by and for Native American and Indigenous people). Often used interchangeably with "queer and trans," though this more thorough acronym is liberative in that it specifically names sexual, affectional, and gender identities and embodied experience (see Sanders's chapter, pp. 165–66).

masking: Disabled people's attempts to cover up their disabilities in public to blend in and avoid ridicule (see Williams's chapter, pp. 18–20).

medical model of disability: A heavily critiqued model of disability that locates impairments in individual bodies, often pathologizing them as problems that need to be fixed (see also **disability studies** and **social model of disability**).

(Autistic) meltdown: An autistic person's involuntary, embodied response to stressful situations like sensory overload.

mental health disabilities: Mental health diagnoses that can be considered disabilities, such as bipolar and ADHD (see Lund's chapter, pp. 38–39).

mental health justice: The movement toward combating the stigma of mental health diagnoses and seeking justice for individuals with mental health diagnoses in all aspects of life (see Lund's chapter, p. 34).

multidimensionality: A concept emerging from the fields of disability studies and critical disability studies that highlights the interconnected memberships (including race, gender, and disability) with which all people live their lives and the subordinated knowledges that emerge from such experiences, much like the inverse of intersectionality.

neurodivergence: Neurodivergent behaviors or experiences, such as traits characteristic to those with autism, ADHD, sensory perception conditions, high sensitivity, synesthesia, or other emotional or behavioral conditions (see Raffety, "Introduction to Neurodiversity," pp. 102–4).

neurodiversity movement: Emerging out of the autism rights movement in the 1990s, the neurodiversity movement approaches variations in thinking, sensing, and experience among people with a broad variety of emotional and behavioral conditions as yet another element of our human diversity, and, from the standpoint of human variety, seeks to depathologize many conditions previously perceived as disorders.

neuronormativity: A form of ableism that enforces neurotypical norms; it may include assumptions and practices about attention, bodily comportment, and respectful behavior that implicitly judge or devalue neurodivergent behaviors, like stimming, fidgeting, repeated speech, and intolerance of certain foods or smells.

neurotype: A way to describe how a person's brain learns, communicates, or develops; usually distinguished by the terms "neurotypical," the default neurotype, and "neurodivergent," a neurotype that differs from the general population, though some people may prefer to further identify based on their diagnoses, such as autism, ADHD, sensory perception conditions, high sensitivity, synesthesia, or other emotional or behavioral conditions.

neuroqueer: A term coined by Nick Walker to emphasize the interrelatedness of neurodivergence and queerness and that living out these identities boldly in the world is a subversive act of disrupting neuronormativity and heteronormativity (see Arden's chapter, pp. 91–92).

praise: An act of worship, showing and giving God glory.

pronouns: Gender pronouns are part of someone's gender expression, and they can be multiple (such as using both he/him/his and they/them/theirs), varied, and changing. Although nonbinary and **trans** people pioneered the practice, identifying preferred pronouns no matter one's background, rather than expecting others to assume them, is a respectful way of cultivating communication.

prophecy: A genre of biblical literature believed to be messages communicated from God to humans and often delivered by prophets. Prophecies are often future looking and can be messages of disaster or good news, ways to make sense of history or suffering, or ways to reimagine justice.

protest: Although the colloquial meaning of protest is a demonstration of public dissent, the lament psalms in the Bible are also referred to as the protest psalms, because cries for justice and vindication directed toward God can also be understood as acts of protest.

queer: An umbrella term for those who are not cisgender and heterosexual. Although originally used as a derogatory term in the nineteenth and twentieth centuries, it was reclaimed by activists in the 1980s as neutral or positive self-expression (see also **LGBTQIA2S+**).

Section 504: Section 504 of the Rehabilitation Act of 1973 is a civil rights law that protects individuals with disabilities from discrimination in programs and activities that receive federal financial assistance.

special interest: An intense focus on a particular topic that helps autistic people rest and control and/or interpret their relationships to others and the world.

social model of disability: Created by disability activists in the 1970s, the social model of disability identifies barriers to access as being largely located in environments, society, attitudes, and institutions, versus within individual's bodies.

stim: Self-stimulatory behaviors that many neurodivergent people engage in to help manage anxiety, sensory overload, or physical discomfort. May include behaviors like rocking, finger-flicking, or hand-flapping.

suicide: The act of intentionally causing one's own death. It is the second leading cause of death for five- through twenty-four year-olds in the United States. The verb-noun phrase "committed suicide" vilifies the person. Instead, "died by suicide" is preferred (see Lund's chapter, pp. 34–44, which focuses on youth ministry as suicide prevention).

transgender: Often shortened to **trans**, a term used to describe a person whose gender identity differs from the sex they were assigned at birth. For some trans people, their gender identity also transcends the male/female binary.

universal design for learning: An educational framework that aims to create learning environments that are broadly accessible to all students by providing multiple means of engagement, representation, and expression, rather than primarily providing accommodations to disabled students.

vocational rehabilitation (VR) services: Federally funded agencies that exist in all fifty states to assist disabled people with employment services. These agencies work through partnerships with local businesses, community groups, and even churches (see Steinitz's chapter, pp. 110–11).

NOTES

INTRODUCTION

1. Bolded terms can be found in the glossary.

A PRAYER OF CONFESSION

1. Reprinted with permission from *A Liturgy for All Bodies*, ed. Kimmothy Cole (Embodied Liturgy Collective, 2022), 33.

BECOMING UNMASKED

1. Devon Price, *Unmasking Autism: Discovering the New Faces of Neurodiversity* (Harmony Books, 2022), 117.

2. Claire Jack, "How It Feels to 'Unmask' as an Autistic Woman," *Psychology Today*, February 27, 2023, https://tinyurl.com/ysm798k5.

3. Lisa Jo Ruby, "How Autistic Meltdowns Differ From Ordinary Temper Tantrums," verywellhealth, July 24, 2024, https://tinyurl.com/2e5tv2hr.

4. Emily Katy, "Autistic Special Interests: Our Brain's In-Built Coping Strategy," Authentically Emily, accessed October 19, 2024, https://tinyurl.com/yhyt3abw.

WHERE BELONGING ABOUNDS

1. Eleanor X. Liu, Erik W. Carter, Thomas L. Boehm, Naomi H. Annandale, and Courtney E. Taylor, "In Their Own Words: The Place of Faith in the Lives of Young People with Intellectual Disability and Autism," *Intellectual and Developmental Disabilities* 52, no. 5 (2014): 388–404, https://doi.org/10.1352/1934-9556-52.5.388.

2. Erik W. Carter and Thomas L. Boehm, "Religious and Spiritual Expressions of Youth with Intellectual and Developmental Disabilities," *Research and Practice for Persons with Severe Disabilities* 44, no. 1 (2019): 37–52, https://doi.org/10.1177/1540796919828082.

3. Carter and Boehm, "Religious and Spiritual Expressions," 42.

4. Erik W. Carter, Michael Tuttle, Emilee Spann, Charis Ling, and Tiffany B. Jones, "Toward Accessible Worship: The Experiences and Insights of Christians with Disabilities," *Journal of Disability and Religion* 28, no. 2 (2024): 189–219, https://doi.org/10.1080/23312521.2023.2197435.

5. Erik W. Carter, "Research on Disability and Congregational Inclusion: What We Know and Where We Might Go," *Journal of Disability and Religion* 27, no. 2 (2023): 179–209, https://doi.org/10.1080/23312521.2022.2035297.

6. Melinda Jones Ault, Belva C. Collins, and Erik W. Carter, "Congregational Participation and Supports for Children and Adults with Disabilities: Parent Perceptions," *Intellectual and Developmental Disabilities* 51, no. 1 (2013): 48–61, https://doi.org/10.1352/1934-9556-51.01.048.

7. Erik W. Carter, Elizabeth E. Biggs, and Thomas L. Boehm, "Being Present Versus Having a Presence: Dimensions of Belonging for Young People with Disabilities and Their Families," *Christian Education Journal* 13, no. 1 (2016): 127–46, https://doi.org/10.1177/073989131601300109.

8. Benjamin Zablotsky, Amanda E. Ng, Lindsey I. Black, and Stephen J. Blumberg, "Diagnosed Developmental Disabilities in Children Aged 3–17 Years: United States, 2019–2021," *NCHS Data Brief* 473 (2023): 1–8.

9. Erik W. Carter, "Dimensions of Belonging for Individuals with Intellectual and Developmental Disabilities," in *Belonging and Resilience in Individuals with Intellectual and Developmental Disabilities*, ed. Jennifer L. Jones and Kami L. Gallus (Springer, 2021), 13–34.

10. Carter, "Research on Disability."

11. Erik W. Carter, "Supporting the Social Lives of Secondary Students with Severe Disabilities: Critical Elements for Effective Intervention," *Journal of Emotional and Behavioral Disorders* 26, no. 1 (2018): 52–61, https://doi.org/10.1177/1063426617739253.

12. Karrie A. Shogren, Michael L. Wehmeyer, and Nirbhay N. Singh, *Handbook of Positive Psychology in Intellectual and Developmental Disabilities* (Springer, 2017).

13. Chimamanda Ngozi Adichie, "The Danger of a Single Story," TED Talk, TEDGlobal, July 2009, 18 min., 32 sec., https://tinyurl.com/5dx4mhj2.

14. Erik W. Carter, Jennifer L. Bumble, Brianna Griffin, and Matthew P. Curcio, "Community Conversations on Faith and Disability: Identifying New Practices, Postures, and Partners for Congregations," *Pastoral Psychology* 66, no. 5 (2017): 575–94, https://doi.org/10.1007/s11089-017-0770-4.

15. Amy Elizabeth Jacober, "Youth Ministry, Religious Education, and Adolescents with Disabilities: Insights from Parents and Guardians," *Journal of Religion, Disability, and Health* 14, no. 2 (2010): 167–81, https://doi.org/10.1080/15228961003622310.

16. Erik W. Carter, Thomas L. Boehm, Naomi H. Annandale, and Courtney E. Taylor, "Supporting Congregational Inclusion for Children and Youth with Disabilities and Their Families," *Exceptional Children* 82, no. 3 (2016): 372–89, https://doi.org/10.1177/0014402915598773.

17. Ault et al., "Congregational Participation," 55.

18. Barbara J. Newman, *Worship as One: Varied Abilities in the Body of Christ* (With Ministries, 2022), 75.

19. William M. Bukowski, Brett Laursen, and Kenneth H. Rubin, *Handbook of Peer Interactions, Relationships, and Groups*, 2nd ed. (Guilford, 2019).

20. Hans S. Reinders, "The Power of Inclusion and Friendship," *Journal of Religion, Disability, and Health* 15, no. 4 (2011): 431–36, https://doi.org/10.1080/15228967.2011.619341.

21. Stephen Lipscomb, Joshua Haimson, Albert Y. Liu, John Burghardt, David R. Johnson, and Martha L. Thurlow, *Preparing for Life After High School: The Characteristics and Experiences of Youth in Special Education* (US Department of Education, 2017), 2:41.

22. Erik W. Carter, "The Changing Landscape of Disability and Ministry in the Church," *Currents in Theology and Mission* 49, no. 3 (2022): 4–9.

MENTAL HEALTH JUSTICE

1. "Mental Health Conditions," National Alliance on Mental Illness, accessed November 4, 2024, https://tinyurl.com/44b9dm75.

2. Rachael Keefe, *The Lifesaving Church: Faith Communities and Suicide Prevention* (Chalice, 2018).

3. Rachael Keefe, "God Is Not a Fan: Talking About Suicide," in *When Kids Ask Hard Questions: Faith-Filled Responses for Tough Topics*, ed. Bromleigh McCleneghan and Karen Ware Jackson (Chalice, 2019), 48–49.

4. "Health Disparities in Suicide," Centers for Disease Control, May 16, 2024, https://tinyurl.com/ywmww5ex.

5. Nancy Eiesland, *The Disabled God: Toward a Liberatory Theology of Disability* (Abingdon, 1994), 20.

6. "Data and Statistics on Children's Mental Health," Centers for Disease Control, June 5, 2025, https://tinyurl.com/2srmwujh.

7. "Data and Statistics on Children's Mental Health," Centers for Disease Control.

8. May Wong, "What's Behind the Increase in ADHD?" Stanford Institute for Economic Policy Research, January 12, 2021, https://tinyurl.com/k64nbrwh.

9. "Facts About ADHD Throughout the Years," Centers for Disease Control, October 23, 2024, https://tinyurl.com/r74aajkm.

10. Wong, "What's Behind the Increase in ADHD?"

11. Ali Howard and Elizabeth McMeekin, "New Study to Understand the Relationship Between ADHD and Suicide Risk," *University of Glasgow University News*, September 27, 2022, https://tinyurl.com/ybze9zwb.

12. Seonaid Cleare, Nadia Belkadi, and Rory O'Connor, "Understanding the Relationship Between ADHD and Suicidal Thoughts and Behaviours," University of Glasgow Suicidal Behaviour Research Laboratory, accessed November 24, 2024, 2, https://tinyurl.com/bdenw99b.

13. Cleare et al., "Understanding the Relationship Between ADHD and Suicidal Thoughts," 5.

14. Tally Moses, "Suicide Attempts Among Adolescents with Self-Reported Disabilities," *Child Psychiatry Human Development* 49 (2018): 420–33, https://doi.org/10.1007/s10578-017-0761-9.

15. Divya Nagraj and Hatim A. Omar, "Disability and Suicide," in *Youth Suicide Prevention: Everybody's Business*, ed. Hatim A. Omar (Nova Science Publishers, 2015), 85–95.

16. Stephanie Pappas, "More Than 20% of Teens Have Seriously Considered Suicide. Psychologists and Communities Can Help Tackle the Problem," *Monitor on Psychology* 54, no. 5 (2023), https://tinyurl.com/53snp776.

17. Pappas, "More Than 20% of Teens."

18. "The Mental Health of LGBTQ+ Young People with Disabilities." The Trevor Project, December 1, 2023, https://tinyurl.com/4c58j9pt.

19. Shruti Rajkumar, "Disabled LGBTQ+ Youth at Greater Risk for Suicide Than Their Peers, Study Finds," *HuffPost*, December 1, 2023, https://tinyurl.com/4zh6d98d.

20. Pappas, "More Than 20% of Teens."

21. Pappas, "More Than 20% of Teens."

22. Rory C. O'Connor and Olivia J. Kirtley, "The Integrated Motivational-

Volitional Model of Suicidal Behaviour," *Philosophical Transactions of the Royal Society of London B* 373, no. 1754 (2018): https://doi.org/10.1098/rstb.2017.0268.

TOWARD DISABLED LEADERSHIP IN WORSHIP

1. Office of the Surgeon General, "Our Epidemic of Loneliness and Isolation: The US Surgeon General's Advisory on the Healing Effects of Social Connection and Community, 2023," US Department of Health and Human Services, 2023, 19, https://tinyurl.com/2m43bvap.

2. Office of the Surgeon General, "Our Epidemic," 19.

3. Elaine Huang and Suthi Navaratnam-Tomayko, "More Than Just a Number: Princeton's History of Tragic Loss," *The Daily Princetonian*, April 27, 2023. https://tinyurl.com/yvtmbnsc.

4. Huang and Navaratnam-Tomayko, "More Than Just a Number."

5. "About Princeton Presbyterians," Princeton Presbyterians, accessed January 26, 2025, www.princetonpresbys.org/about.

A PRAYER OF PROTEST

1. Reprinted with permission from *A Liturgy for All Bodies*, ed. Kimmothy Cole (Embodied Liturgy Collective, 2022), 35–36.

SLOW AND STEADY

1. Kenda Creasy Dean, Chap Clark, and Dave Rahn, *Starting Right: Thinking Theologically About Youth Ministry* (Youth Specialties/Zondervan, 2001).

2. Formerly the *Journal of Religion, Disability, and Health*.

3. Mike Langford and Wes Ellis, eds., *Embodying Youth: Exploring Youth Ministry and Disability* (Routledge, 2020).

4. Joni Eareckson Tada and Bev Singleton, *Friendship Unlimited: How You Can Help a Disabled Friend* (H. Shaw Publishers, 1987).

5. Joni Eareckson Tada and Steve Jensen, *Barrier-Free Friendships: Bridging the Distance Between You and Friends with Disabilities* (Zondervan, 1997).

6. Tada and Jensen, *Barrier-Free Friendships*, 30.

7. Tada and Jensen, *Barrier-Free Friendships*, 107.

8. Joni Eareckson Tada, *Beyond Suffering Bible: Where Struggles Seem Endless, God's Hope Is Infinite* (Tyndale House, 2016), 1057.

9. Jim Pierson, *Exceptional Teaching: A Comprehensive Guide for Including Students with Disabilities* (Standard Publishing, 2002).

10. Pierson, *Exceptional Teaching*, 175.

11. Pierson, *Exceptional Teaching*, 25.

12. Amy Jacober, "Ostensibly Welcome: Exploratory Research on the Youth Ministry Experiences of Teenagers with Disabilities," *Journal of Youth Ministry* 6, no. 1 (2007).

13. Seyram Amenyedzi, "'We Are Forgotten': The Plight of Persons with Disability in Youth Ministry," *Scriptura* 120, no. 1 (March 2021), https://doi.org/10.7833/120-1-1459.

14. Charmaine Manuel, "Churches as Communities of Belonging for Children of All Abilities: A Practical Theological Study" (PhD diss., University of Stollenbosch, 2024).

15. Isabella Novsima, "Decolonizing Ableist Pedagogy," *International Review of Mission* 112, no. 2 (2023): 269, https://doi.org/10.1111/irom.12480.

16. Nick Palermo, "Reflections on the Future of Youth Ministry: Streets, Alleys, Roads, and Country Lanes," *Journal of Youth and Theology* 10, nos. 1–2 (2011): 73–78.

17. Palermo, "Reflections," 78.

18. Palermo, "Reflections," 77.

19. Louise Gosbell, "Embodied Worship: Reflecting on the Inclusion of People with Disabilities in Church Communities," *Practical Theology* 12, no. 3 (2019): 250–52, https://doi.org/10.1080/1756073x.2019.1609756.

20. See Amy E. Jacober, *Redefining Perfect: The Interplay Between Theology and Disability* (Cascade, 2017). The story behind the writing includes a major ministry putting in writing that major theological concepts and practices did not apply to those with disabilities. *Redefining Perfect* looked at those same doctrinal stances through the lens of disability to include all.

21. Erik W. Carter, *Including People with Disabilities in Faith Communities: A Guide for Service Providers, Families and Congregations* (Paul H. Brookes Publishing, 2007).

22. Carter, *Including People*, 89–118.

23. Carter, *Including People*, 98.

24. Benjamin T. Conner, *Amplifying Our Witness: Giving Voice to Adolescents with Developmental Disabilities* (Eerdmans, 2012).

25. Conner, *Amplifying Our Witness*, 33.

26. Benjamin T. Conner, "Disability and Youth Ministry: The Book I'm Not Going to Write," *Journal of Disability and Religion* 27, no. 4 (2023): 508–19, https://doi.org/10.1080/23312521.2023.2257198.

27. Erin Raffety, "The God of Difference: Disability, Youth Ministry, and the Difference Anthropology Makes," *Journal of Disability and Religion* 22, no. 4 (2018): 371–89, https://doi.org/10.1080/23312521.2018.1521766.

28. Richard Parsons, *Adolescents in Turmoil, Parents Under Stress: A Pastoral Ministry Primer* (Paulist, 1987).

29. Les Parrott, *Helping the Struggling Adolescent: A Guide to Thirty-Six Common Problems for Counselors, Pastors, and Youth Workers* (Zondervan, 2014).

30. Janna Kinner, ed., *Group's Emergency Response Handbook for Youth Ministry* (Group, 2007).

31. Monica Kim and Danny Kwon, *Teenagers and Mental Health: A Handbook for Parents, Pastors, and Youth Leaders* (New Growth Press, 2025).

32. Stella Young, "I'm Not Your Inspiration, Thank You Very Much," TEDx Talk, Sydney, 9 min., 2 sec., April 2014, https://tinyurl.com/4w953mfj.

33. Michael J. Hoggatt, "Night to Shine and Inspiration Porn: An Examination of Practices in Disability Ministry," *Journal of Disability and Religion* 27, no. 2 (2022): 210–22, https://doi.org/10.1080/23312521.2022.2035885.

34. Marc Tumeinski and Jeff McNair, "What Would Be Better? Social Role Valorization and the Development of Ministry to Persons Affected by Disability," *Journal of the Christian Institute on Disability* 1, no. 1 (2012): 11–22.

35. Dennis Schurter, "Fowler's Faith Stages as a Guide for Ministry for the Mentally Retarded," *Journal of Pastoral Care and Counseling* 41, no. 3 (1987): https://doi.org/10.1177/002234098704100306.

36. Michael Langford, "Abusing Youth: Theologically Understanding Youth Through Misunderstanding Disability," *Journal of Disability and Religion* 22, no. 4 (2018): 426–51, https://doi.org/10.1080/23312521.2018.1540959.

37. "Editorial Team," *Canadian Journal of Theology, Mental Health, and Disability*, accessed September 14, 2024, https://tinyurl.com/y4kn6ste.

LEADERSHIP DEVELOPMENT FOR DISABLED BIPOC YOUTH

1. Henry H. Mitchell, *Black Preaching: The Recovery of a Powerful Art* (Abingdon, 1990), 50.

2. Mitchell, *Black Preaching*, 51.

3. "Section 504, Rehabilitation Act of 1973," US Department of Labor, accessed July 10, 2025, https://tinyurl.com/ycx4w6vj.

4. Leonard Gadzekpo, "The Black Church, the Civil Rights Movement, and the Future," *Journal of Religious Thought* 53/54, no. 2/1 (1997): 107.

5. Albert J. Raboteau, *Slave Religion: The "Invisible Institution" in the Antebellum South* (Oxford University Press, 2004), 4.

6. Raboteau, *Slave Religion*, 4.

7. Onah Gregory Ajima and Eyong Usang Ubana, "The Concept of Health and Wholeness in Traditional African Religion and Social Medicine," *Arts and Social Sciences Journal* 9, no. 4 (2018): 1, https://doi.org/10.4172/2151-6200.1000388.

8. Ajima and Ubana, "Concept of Health," 1.

9. Ajima and Ubana, "Concept of Health," 4.

MODELING POSSIBILITIES

1. "All Ages and Abilities Celebrate Disability Saints Through Art," West Concord Union Church, October 9, 2019, https://tinyurl.com/48mjtw5r.

2. "Celebrating Disability Saints in Sunday School," West Concord Union Church, September 18, 2019, https://tinyurl.com/mszzamdw.

3. Nick Walker, "Neuroqueer: An Introduction," 2021, https://tinyurl.com/3snvk3a6.

4. Dex Anderson, *Body Phobia: The Western Roots of Our Fear of Difference* (Broadleaf, 2024), 32. See also Sami Schalk, *Bodyminds Reimagined: (Dis)ability, Race, and Gender in Black Women's Speculative Fiction* (Duke University Press, 2018), 89.

5. Schalk, *Bodyminds Reimagined*, 2.

6. Damon Rose, "Stop Trying to Heal Me," *BBC*, April 27, 2019, https://tinyurl.com/mtsyvs38.

7. For simplicity's sake I stick with he/him pronouns for Joseph here, but I encourage imaginative exploration of she/her and they/them pronouns for this nonconforming figure as well.

8. Danya Ruttenberg, "(Gender)queering Joseph: Midrashic Possibilities for the Torah's Most Extra Child," *Life Is a Sacred Text*, October 25, 2021, https://tinyurl.com/4x7yfymh.

9. Michael Gill, "Already Doing It: Intellectual Disability and Sexual Agency," *Disability Studies Quarterly* 35, no. 4 (2015): 29, 38. https://doi.org/10.18061/.v35i4.4984.

10. Ruttenberg, "(Gender)queering Joseph."

11. The disabled community even has a national day of mourning for disabled victims of filicide (see https://disability-memorial.org/). LGBTQIA+ youth make up 40 percent of homeless youth in the United States, largely due to family rejection (see https://tinyurl.com/4h7rrbtr).

12. Laura Sommer, host, *The Autistic Liberation Theology Podcast*, "Joseph and the Amazing Original Neuroqueer Pride Flag—Part III," Wibbley-Wobbley Minds, n.d., https://tinyurl.com/345ypkzc. For an in-depth, neuroqueer examination of what happens when Joseph's brothers come to Egypt seeking aid, check out this podcast episode on which I was a guest.

13. More Light Presbyterians is an LGBTQIA+ advocacy organization affiliated with my denomination, the Presbyterian Church (USA).

14. Gavin Somers, "Celebrating Trans Day of Visibility," *Out on Screen*, March 31, 2020, https://tinyurl.com/yf6a69wt.

15. Jeffrey H. Tigay, "'Heavy of Mouth' and 'Heavy of Tongue': On Moses' Speech Difficulty," *Bulletin of the American Schools of Oriental Research* 231 (1978): 57–58, https://tinyurl.com/4dcdnfcp.

16. Neve Be(ast) and India Harville, interview by Alice Wong, "#CRIPWISDOM: Interview with the Artists of Sins Invalid," Disability Visibility Project, October 10, 2016, https://tinyurl.com/3m9c3wds.

17. Visit SinsInvalid.org for a wealth of performance art by queer and trans disabled BIPOC.

18. Visit https://universaldesign.ie/ for information about building environments that enable use for people of as many sizes, ages, and dis/abilities as possible.

19. Meredith Bergey, "Mapping Mental Health Inequalities: The Intersecting Effects of Gender, Race, Class, and Ethnicity on ADHD Diagnosis," *Sociology of Health and Illness* 44, no. 3 (2022): 604–23, https://doi.org/10.1111/1467-9566.13443.

20. Sara Hendren, "Clock," in *What Can a Body Do? How We Meet the Built World* (Riverhead Books, 2020), Kindle.

21. Kafer, *Feminist, Queer, Crip*, 27.

22. "Special Interest," StimPunks, accessed January 21, 2025, https://tinyurl.com/4snmcbjt.

23. Megan Anna Neff and Patrick Casale, hosts, *Divergent Conversations*, episode 51, "What Is Autism? (Part 4): Special Interests and Complex Sensory Experiences," April 25, 2024, https://tinyurl.com/3res9rmb.

24. Denita Wright Watson, "How to Respond If You've Committed a

Microagression," Penn State World Campus, January 21, 2022, https://tinyurl.com/45kbvcc3.

25. Gyasi Burks-Abbott, "A Presumption of Competence: Empowering Disability Advocacy and Independent Living," *Autism Spectrum News,* October 4, 2024, https://tinyurl.com/3zantfzf.

26. Eli Clare, *Exile and Pride: Disability, Queerness, and Liberation* (Duke University Press, 1999), 1–15.

27. Lamar Hardwick, *How Ableism Fuels Racism: Dismantling the Hierarchy of Bodies in the Church* (Brazos, 2024), chap. 1.

28. Shane Clifton, "Crippling Christian Theology as I Power My Wheelchair out the Door," *Theology Today* 77, no. 2 (2020): 124–37, https://doi.org/10.1177/004057362092.

A PRAYER OF PRAISE

1. Reprinted with permission from *A Liturgy for All Bodies,* ed. Kimmothy Cole (Embodied Liturgy Collective, 2022), 100–101.

THE WILDERNESS OF TRANSITION

1. Rehabilitation Services Administration, https://rsa.ed.gov/about/states.

2. Pennsylvania Vocational Rehabilitation Agency, https://tinyurl.com/yck8zrwk.

3. Brother André's Café, https://brotherandres.org.

CALLED?

1. Grace Block was interviewed for this chapter and chose to be identified by her name and age. Her parents affirmed her decision. Grace participated in member checking for all quotes and reviewed the content of this chapter to be sure it reflects her experiences and her voice.

2. James is a self-advocate who participated in an earlier study (Deborah W. Huggins and Susan R. Copeland, "Disability and Belonging in an Inclusive Christian Faith Community," *Inclusion* 11, no. 4 [2023]: 271–85, https://doi.org/10.1352/2326-6988-11.4.271). James chose to be identified by a pseudonym and with the age range "young adult 24–29." James receives moderate to intense support across

all domains of daily living, including attending a disability-specific school when he was in K–12 education, and ongoing support in his workplace.

3. J. T. McNeill and F. L. Battles, *Calvin: Institutes of the Christian Religion* (Westminster, 1960), book 3, ch. 24, pp. 964–87.

4. Frederick Buechner, *Wishful Thinking: A Theological ABC* (Harper & Row, 1973).

5. Benjamin T. Conner, *Disabling Mission, Enabling Witness: Exploring Missiology Through the Lens of Disability Studies* (IVP Academic, 2018).

6. Martha C. White, "5 Expert Tips for Deciding Which Charities to Support This Year," *TIME*, November 23, 2018, https://tinyurl.com/33dfcsp7.

7. Conner, *Disabling Mission, Enabling Witness*, 67.

8. McNeill and Battles, *Calvin*, book 3, ch. 24, pp. 964–87.

9. Huggins and Copeland, "Disability and Belonging."

10. Darcell Rockett, "Oral History Project by Chicago Theological Seminary Shows How It Served as Incubator for Area's Civil Rights Leaders," *Chicago Tribune*, January 31, 2024, https://tinyurl.com/bddchwur.

11. Erin Raffety, *From Inclusion to Justice: Disability, Ministry, and Congregational Leadership* (Baylor University Press, 2022).

12. Huggins and Copeland, "Disability and Belonging," 284.

13. Sydney is a self-advocate who participated in an earlier study. She chose to be identified by a pseudonym and with the age range "youth 15–18." Sydney receives moderate formal supports in her academic environment and does not yet receive adult services.

14. Huggins and Copeland, "Disability and Belonging," 284.

15. Huggins and Copeland, "Disability and Belonging," 283.

16. McNeill and Battles, *Calvin*, book 3, ch. 24, pp. 964–87.

17. Caricia Catalani and Meredith Minkler, "Photovoice: A Review of the Literature in Health and Public Health," *Health Education and Behavior* 37, no. 3 (2010): 424–51, https://doi.org/10.1177/1090198109342084.

18. Eleanor X. Liu, Erik W. Carter, Thomas L. Boehm, Naomi H. Annandale, and Courtney E. Taylor, "In Their Own Words: The Place of Faith in the Lives of Young People with Intellectual Disability and Autism," *Intellectual and Developmental Disabilities* 52, no. 5 (2014): 388–404, https://doi.org/10.1352/1934-9556-52.5.388.

19. Alison Ford et al., eds., *The Syracuse Community-Referenced Curriculum Guide for Students with Moderate and Severe Disabilities* (Paul H. Brookes Publishing, 1989), 3.

20. Douglas S. O'Donnell, "Liturgy Saved Me," Crossway, October 3, 2024, https://tinyurl.com/sbv85s9t.

21. Huggins and Copeland, "Disability and Belonging," 282–83.

SINGING THE LORD'S SONG

1. M. J. Friedrich, "Depression Is the Leading Cause of Disability Around the World," *Journal of the American Medical Association* 317, no. 15 (2017): 1517, https://doi.org/10.1001/jama.2017.3826.

2. Centers for Disease Control, *Youth Risk Behavior Survey Data Summary and Trends Report: 2013–2023* (US Department of Health and Human Services, 2024), 55–56.

3. Maddy Reinert, Danielle Fritze, and Theresa Nguyen, "State of Mental Health in America 2024," Mental Health America, July 2024, 26, https://tinyurl.com/mz74hcuc.

4. Christina Caron, "Teens Turn to TikTok in Search of a Mental Health Diagnosis," *New York Times*, October 29, 2022, https://tinyurl.com/3598y9s5.

5. For some of the theological and ministerial problems behind the modern concept of adolescence, see Wesley W. Ellis, *Youth Beyond the Developmental Lens: Being over Becoming* (Fortress, 2024).

6. William Hunter and Matthew Stanford, "Adolescent Mental Health: The Role of Youth and College Pastors," *Mental Health, Religion and Culture* 17, no. 10 (2014): 957–66, https://doi.org/10.1080/13674676.2014.966663.

7. Michael Nakkula and Eric Toshalis, *Understanding Youth: Adolescent Development for Educators* (Harvard Education Press, 2006), 6.

8. The DSM-V defines major depression as involving a primary symptom of "either depressed mood or the loss of interest or pleasure in nearly all activities," as well as "at least four additional symptoms drawn from a list that includes changes in appetite or weight, sleep, and psychomotor activity; decreased energy; feelings of worthlessness or guilt; difficulty thinking, concentrating or making decisions; or recurrent thoughts of death or suicidal ideation or suicide plans or attempts." Additionally, the symptoms must persist for at least two weeks and significantly impair a person's social or professional functioning. American Psychiatric Association, *Diagnostic and Statistical Manual of Mental Disorders*, 5th ed. (American Psychiatric Publishing, 2013), 163.

9. John Swinton, *Finding Jesus in the Storm: The Spiritual Lives of Christians with Mental Health Challenges* (Eerdmans, 2020), 77.

10. Matthew Ratcliffe, *Experiences of Depression: A Study in Phenomenology*, International Perspectives in Philosophy and Psychiatry (Oxford University Press, 2015), 15.

11. Tasia Scrutton, *Christianity and Depression: Interpretation, Meaning, and the Shaping of Experience* (SCM Press, 2020), 42.

12. Jessica Coblentz, *Dust in the Blood: A Theology of Life with Depression* (Liturgical Press Academic, 2022), 143. Hereafter, references to this work will be given parenthetically in the text.

13. Friedrich Schweitzer, "Adolescents as Theologians: A New Approach in Christian Education and Youth Ministry," *Religious Education* 109, no. 2 (2014): 184–200, https://doi.org/10.1080/00344087.2014.887927.

14. Schweitzer, "Adolescents as Theologians," 185.

15. Schweitzer, "Adolescents as Theologians," 190.

16. Schweitzer, "Adolescents as Theologians," 196.

17. Schweitzer, "Adolescents as Theologians," 195.

18. Jürgen Moltmann, *Theology and Joy* (SCM, 1973), 27.

19. Moltmann, *Theology and Joy*, 36.

20. Moltmann, *Theology and Joy*, 49.

21. Alain Ehrenberg, *The Weariness of the Self: Diagnosing the History of Depression in the Contemporary Age* (McGill-Queen's University Press, 2010).

22. J. Todd Billings, *Rejoicing in Lament: Wrestling with Incurable Cancer and Life in Christ* (Brazos, 2015), 47.

23. Billings, *Rejoicing in Lament*, 49.

24. Swinton, *Finding Jesus*, 80.

PRAISE!

1. Cole Arthur Riley, *This Here Flesh: Spirituality, Liberation, and the Stories That Make Us* (Hodder & Stoughton, 2022), 7.

2. https://www.thetrevorproject.org/research.

3. Nick Walker, *Neuroqueer Heresies: Notes on the Neurodiversity Paradigm, Autistic Empowerment, and Postnormal Possibilities* (Autonomous Press, 2021).

4. Nick Walker, *Neuroqueer: The Writings of Dr. Nick Walker*, https://www.neuroqueer.com.

A PRAYER OF PROPHECY

1. Reprinted with permission from *A Liturgy for All Bodies*, ed. Kimmothy Cole (Embodied Liturgy Collective, 2022), 157.

DREAMING DIVERGENT FUTURES

1. Leah Lakshmi Piepzna-Samarasinha, *Care Work: Dreaming Disability Justice* (Arsenal Pulp, 2018), 122.

2. Ada Maria Isasi-Diaz, *La Lucha Continues: Mujerista Theology* (Orbis, 2004), 36.

3. Walter Brueggemann, *The Prophetic Imagination*, 40th anniv. ed. (Fortress, 2018).

4. Nick Walker, *Neuroqueer Heresies: Notes on the Neurodiversity Paradigm, Autistic Empowerment, and Postnormal Possibilities* (Autonomous Press, 2021), 12–32.

5. Alyssa Hillary, "Neurodiversity and Cross-Cultural Communication," in *Neurodiversity Studies: A New Critical Paradigm*, ed. Hanna Bertilsdotter Rosqvist, Nick Chown, and Anna Stenning (Routledge, 2020), 92.

6. Hillary, "Neurodiversity," 92.

7. Hillary, "Neurodiversity," 95.

8. Beverly W. Harrison, *Making the Connections: Essays in Feminist Social Ethics*, ed. Carol S. Robb (Beacon, 1985), 249.

9. Hillary, "Neurodiversity," 95.

10. Emily Stones, "Cross-Neurotype Communication Competence," in *The Palgrave Handbook of Disability and Communication*, ed. Michael S. Jeffress et al. (Palgrave Macmillan, 2023), 49.

11. Stones, "Cross-Neurotype Communication," 50.

12. Stones, "Cross-Neurotype Communication," 50.

13. Verna J. Dozier, *The Dream of God: A Call to Return* (Cowley, 1991), 125.

14. Hanna Bertilsdotter Rosqvist, Anna Stenning, and Nick Chown, introduction to *Neurodiversity Studies: A New Critical Paradigm*, ed. Hanna Bertilsdotter Rosqvist, Nick Chown, and Anna Stenning, Routledge Advances in Sociology (Routledge, 2020), 2.

15. Hanna Bertilsdotter Rosqvist, Charlotte Brownlow, and Lindsay O'Dell, "Mapping the Social Geographies of Autism: Online and Off-Line Narratives of Neuro-Shared and Separate Spaces," *Disability and Society* 28, no. 3 (2013), 7–8.

16. Bertilsdotter Rosqvist, Brownlow, and O'Dell, "Mapping the Social Geographies of Autism," 7.

17. Piepzna-Samarasinha, *Care Work*, 126.

18. Piepzna-Samarasinha, *Care Work*, 128.

19. Kala Allen Omeiza, *Autistic and Black: Our Experiences of Growth, Progress and Empowerment* (Jessica Kingsley Publishers, 2024).

20. Marcia Brissett-Bailey and Atif Choudhury, eds., *Black, Brilliant and Dyslexic: Neurodivergent Heroes Tell Their Stories* (Jessica Kingsley Publishers, 2023).

21. Amy Sequenzia and Elizabeth Grace, eds., *Typed Words, Loud Voices* (Autonomous Press, 2017).

22. Stones, "Cross-Neurotype Communication," 55. Hereafter, references to this work will be given parenthetically in the text.

23. This section is a fragment of performative academic writing that makes an argument in the way it is written. To embrace Crip art of failure is to write a failure of a section as a fragment.

24. Piepzna-Samarasinha, *Care Work*, 123–26.

BELONGING TO GOD, ONE ANOTHER, AND THE EARTH

1. In this chapter I use the acronym "LGBTQIA2S+" and the terms "queer and trans" somewhat interchangeably, though the specificity of embodiments indicated by the growing acronym should not be erased in our minds through use of umbrella terms like "queer." Naming for ourselves the diversity of our sexual, affectional, and gender identities and embodied experiences is a liberative agential act, and the language that individual youth use to describe their embodiments should be respected and used by youth workers. For those unfamiliar with the acronym, it stands for lesbian, gay, bisexual, trans, queer, intersex, asexual, and Two-Spirit (an identity label created by and for Native American and Indigenous people).

2. For an exploration of how this spiritual violence has impacted the lives of queer people, see Cody J. Sanders, *Christianity, LGBTQ Suicide, and the Souls of Queer Folk* (Lexington, 2020).

3. Amy Kenny, *My Body Is Not a Prayer Request: Disability Justice in the Church* (Brazos, 2022), 27.

4. An even fuller theological anthropology would also consider the technological and ecological entanglements with a bio-psycho-spiritual-eco-techno-social anthropological framework. But this chapter is limited in scope to the body-mind-spirit within human social relationships, or the bio-psycho-social-spiritual.

5. I use the term "inspirited bodyminds" to name the bio-psycho-social anthropology of human beingness resting at the unifying nexus of the biological fact of

our material bodies; the psychological and social ways that our humanity is felt, understood, and lived; and the spiritual yearning of our reach outward toward that which transcends us but is immanent to humans as spiritual beings.

6. Joshua Lederberg and Alexa T. McCray, "'Ome Sweet 'Omics—a Genealogical Treasury of Words," *Scientist* 15, no. 7 (2001): 8. For more on the human microbiome, see Jane Peterson et al., "The NIH Human Microbiome Project," *Genome Research* 19, no. 12 (2009): 2317–23, https://doi.org/10.1101/gr.096651.109.

7. Mark I. Wallace, *When God Was a Bird: Christianity, Animism, and the Re-Enchantment of the World* (Fordham University Press, 2019), 4.

8. Sean Nee, "The Great Chain of Being," *Nature* 435, no. 26 (2005): 429.

9. Julia Watts Belser, *Loving Our Own Bones: Disability Wisdom and the Spiritual Subversiveness of Knowing Ourselves Whole* (Beacon, 2023), 6.

10. Leah Lakshmi Piepzna-Samarasinha, *The Future Is Disabled: Prophecies, Love Notes, and Mourning Songs* (Arsenal Pulp, 2022), 18–19.

11. For more information on the school experience of LGBTQIA2S+ youth, see the latest GLSEN School Climate Survey at https://www.glsen.org/school-climate-survey.

12. Wallace, *When God Was a Bird*, 14.

13. Allan A. Boesak, *Comfort and Protest: The Apocalypse of John from a South African Perspective* (Westminster, 1987), 42.

14. Piepzna-Samarasinha, *Future Is Disabled*, 21–22.

15. Piepzna-Samarasinha, *Future Is Disabled*, 22.

16. Other figures in the biblical tradition can also be lifted up as exemplars of faith and divine wisdom as disabled people: Moses, who led the Hebrew people with a speech impediment (Exod. 4) and Jacob, who wrestled with God and whose hip was put out of joint as he was renamed "Israel" as one of the fathers of his people (Gen. 32). Importantly, biblical study with youth should make movements back and forth between reflection on these and other biblical figures embodying queerness and disability and the inspirited bodyminds of youth who also hold sacred wisdom and experience deserving of serious theological reflection as image bearers of God. I am grateful to Luke Bitzkie for helping me flesh out this insight.

THE PROPHETIC LEADERSHIP OF OUR FRIENDS WITH DISABILITIES

1. Walter Brueggemann, *The Prophetic Imagination*, 2nd ed. (Fortress, 2001), preface to the 1st edition, xxiii.

2. Brueggemann, *Prophetic Imagination*, 14.

3. Brueggemann, *Prophetic Imagination*, v.

4. Brueggemann, *Prophetic Imagination*, 14.

5. Hans S. Reinders, *Receiving the Gift of Friendship* (Eerdmans, 2008), 164.

6. Brueggemann uses the term "subcommunity" to describe the communities that are in tension with the power and identity of the society's dominant community. While it is certainly true that the community of people with disabilities lives in tension with the dominant power and identity of American culture, the terminology does not consider how folks with disabilities have been maligned as "less than." Folks with disabilities are not lesser, though they are a subset of the dominant community.

7. Brueggemann, *Prophetic Imagination*, iv.

8. Erin Raffety, *From Inclusion to Justice* (Baylor University Press, 2022), 184.

9. Benjamin Conner, *Amplifying Our Witness* (Eerdmans, 2008), 3.

10. Erik W. Carter, "The Changing Landscape of Disability and Ministry in the Church," *Currents in Theology and Mission* 49, no. 3 (2022): 4–9, https://tinyurl.com/cn2x7hjy.

11. Brueggemann, *Prophetic Imagination*, 124.

12. Steve de Shazer et al., *More Than Miracles* (Routledge, 2007), 4.

13. Insoo Kim Berg and Yvonne Dolan, *Tales of Solutions* (Norton, 2001), 7–8.

14. Berg and Dolan, *Tales of Solutions*, 5.

15. Berg and Dolan, *Tales of Solutions*, 10.

16. Fredrike Bannink, *1001 Solution-Focused Questions*, rev. 2nd ed. (Norton, 2010), 156.

17. Berg and Dolan, *Tales of Solutions*, 9.

18. Berg and Dolan, *Tales of Solutions*, 14.

19. Berg and Dolan, *Tales of Solutions*, 1.

RESOURCES FOR FURTHER STUDY

BOOKS

Abbs, Deborah Meyer. *Belonging: Accessibility, Inclusion, and Christian Community.* IVP, 2021.

Bannink, Frederike. *1001 Solution-Focused Questions.* 2nd ed. Norton, 2010.

Bell, Christopher M., ed. *Blackness and Disability: Critical Examinations and Cultural Interventions.* Michigan State University Press, 2012.

Berg, Insoo Kim, and Yvonne Dolan. *Tales of Solutions.* Norton, 2001.

Brissett-Bailey, Marcia, and Atif Choudhury, eds. *Black, Brilliant and Dyslexic: Neurodivergent Heroes Tell Their Stories.* Jessica Kingsley Publishers, 2023.

Brueggemann, Walter. *The Prophetic Imagination.* 2nd ed. Fortress, 2001.

Buechner, Friedrich. *Wishful Thinking: A Theological ABC.* Harper & Row. 1973.

Christensen, Shelley. *From Longing to Belonging: A Practical Guide to Including People with Disabilities and Mental Health Conditions in Your Faith Community.* Inclusion Innovations, 2018.

Cole, Kimmothy, ed. *A Liturgy for All Bodies.* Embodied Liturgy Collective, 2022.

Conner, Benjamin T. *Amplifying our Witness: Giving Voice to Adolescents with Developmental Disabilities.* Eerdmans, 2012.

———. *Disabling Mission, Enabling Witness: Exploring Missiology Through the Lens of Disability Studies.* IVP Academic, 2018.

Costanza-Chock, Sasha. *Design Justice: Community-Led Practices to Build the Worlds We Need.* MIT Press, 2020.

Eiesland, Nancy. *The Disabled God: Toward a Liberatory Theology of Disability.* Abingdon, 1994.

Ellis, Wesley, and Michael Langford. *Embodying Youth: Exploring Youth Ministry and Disability.* Routledge, 2020.

Henderson, Donna, Jamell White, and Sarah Wayland. *Is This Autism? A Guide for Clinicians and Everyone Else.* Taylor & Francis, 2023.

Hull, John M. *Disability: The Inclusive Church Resource.* Darton, Longman & Todd, 2014.

Kafer, Alison. *Feminist, Queer, Crip.* Indiana University Press, 2013.

Keefe, Rachael. *The Lifesaving Church: Faith Communities and Suicide Prevention.* Chalice, 2018.

Kegler, Emmy. *All Who Are Weary: Easing the Burden on the Walk with Mental Illness.* Broadleaf, 2021.

Lave, Jean, and Etienne Wenger. *Situated Learning: Legitimate Peripheral Participation.* Cambridge University Press, 1991.

Lund, Sarah Griffith. *Blessed Minds: Breaking the Silence About Neurodiversity.* Chalice, 2025.

———. *Blessed Youth: Breaking the Silence About Mental Health with Children and Teens.* Chalice, 2022.

———. *Blessed Youth Survival Guide.* Chalice, 2022.

Milne, Cara. *Noticed, Known, and Missed: Strategies to Support Purpose and Connection for People with Disabilities.* Family Lines, 2020.

Murthy, Vivek H. *Together: The Healing Power of Human Connection in a Sometimes Lonely World.* Harper, 2020.

Neff, Megan Anna, and Mark R. McMinn. *Embodying Integration: A Fresh Look at Christianity in the Therapy Room.* IVP Academic, 2020.

Omeiza, Kala Allen. *Autistic and Black: Our Experiences of Growth, Progress and Empowerment.* Jessica Kingsley Publishers, 2024.

Piepzna-Samarasinha, Leah Lakshmi. *Care Work: Dreaming Disability Justice.* Arsenal Pulp s, 2018.

———. *The Future Is Disabled: Prophecies, Love Notes and Mourning Songs.* Arsenal Pulp, 2022.

Price, Devon. *Unmasking Autism: Discovering the New Faces of Neurodiversity.* Harmony, 2022.

Raffety, Erin. *From Inclusion to Justice.* Baylor University Press, 2022.

Reinders, Hans. *Receiving the Gift of Friendship.* Eerdmans, 2008.

Reynolds, Thomas E. *Vulnerable Communion: A Theology of Disability and Hospitality.* Brazos, 2008.

Riley, Cole Arthur. *This Here Flesh: Spirituality, Liberation, and the Stories That Make Us.* Hodder & Stoughton, 2022.

Roger, Brother of Taizé. *The Dynamic of the Provisional.* Translated by Emily Chisholm. A. R. Mowbray and Co., 1981.

Santos, Jason Brian. *A Community Called Taizé: A Story of Prayer, Worship and Reconciliation*. IVP, 2008.

Sanders, Cody J. *A Brief Guide to Ministry with LGBTQIA Youth*. Westminster John Knox, 2017.

———. *Spiritual Care First Aid: An All-Hands Approach for Church and Community*. Fortress, 2025.

Schalk, Sami. *Black Disability Politics*. Duke University Press, 2022.

Sequenza, Amy, and Elizabeth J. Grace, eds. *Typed Words, Loud Voices*. Autonomous Press, 2017.

Shazer, Steve de, Yvonne Dolan, Harry Korman, Terry Trepper, Eric McCollum, and Insoo Kim Berg. *More Than Miracles: The State of the Art Solution-Focused Brief Therapy*. Routledge, 2007.

Spink, Kathryn. *A Universal Heart: The Life and Vision of Brother Roger of Taizé*. 2nd ed. GIA Publications, 2005.

Walker, Nick. *Neuroqueer Heresies: Notes on the Neurodiversity Paradigm, Autistic Empowerment, and Postnormal Possibilities*. Autonomous Press, 2021.

Williams, Claire. *Peculiar Discipleship: An Autistic Liberation Theology*. SCM, 2023.

Wise, Susie. *Design for Belonging: How to Build Inclusion and Collaboration in Your Communities*. Ten Speed, 2022.

Wong, Alice, ed. *Disability Visibility (Adapted for Young Adults): 17 First-Person Stories for Today*. Ember, 2023.

Yong, Amos. *The Bible, Disability, and the Church*. Eerdmans, 2011.

Yu, Tiffany. *The Anti-Ableist Manifesto: How to Build a Disability-Inclusive World*. Souvenir, 2024.

SCHOLARLY AND POPULAR ARTICLES AND BOOK CHAPTERS

Carter, Erik W. "The Changing Landscape of Disability and Ministry in the Church." *Currents in Theology and Mission* 49, no. 3 (2022): 4–9. https://tinyurl.com/yykjxycv.

———. "A Place of Belonging: Including Individuals with Significant Disabilities in Faith Communities." *Inclusive Practices* 1, no. 1 (2022): 6–12.

———. "Spirituality and Supports for Individuals with Intellectual and Developmental Disabilities and Their Families." In *APA Handbook of Intellectual and Developmental Disabilities: Clinical and Educational Implications: Prevention, Intervention, and Treatment*, ed. Laraine Masters Glidden, Leonard

Abbeduto, Laura Lee McIntyre, and Marc J. Tassé. American Psychological Association, 2021. https://www.doi.org/10.1037/0000195-016.

Dingle, Shannon. "Resisting Ableism in the American Church." *Sojourners*. November 7, 2018. https://tinyurl.com/bdvccn8f.

Eurich, Johannes. "Justice for People with Disabilities: Philosophical and Theological Arguments." *Religion and Theology* 19, no. 1–2 (2012): 43–59. https://www.doi.org/10.1163/15743012-12341234.

Gaventa, Bill. "A Rising Tide Lifts All Boats." *Currents in Theology and Mission* 49, no. 3 (2022): 10–15. https://tinyurl.com/mthzdthp.

Healy, Donald E. "Rediscovering the Mysteria: Sacramental Stories from Persons with Disabilities, Their Families, and Their Faith Communities." *Journal of Religion, Disability and Health* 13, no. 3–4 (2009): 194–235. https://doi.org/10.1080/15228960902932267.

Hicks, Douglas A. "The Taizé Community: Fifty Years of Prayer and Action." *Journal of Ecumenical Studies* 29, no. 2 (1992): 202–14.

Hillary, Alyssa. "Neurodiversity and Cross-Cultural Communication." In *Neurodiversity Studies: A New Critical Paradigm*, edited by Hanna Bertilsdotter Rosqvist, Nick Chown, and Anna Stenning. Routledge, 2020.

Hughes, Jessica M. F. "Increasing Neurodiversity in Disability and Social Justice Advocacy Groups." Autistic Self Advocacy Network, 2016. https://tinyurl.com/2anj233f.

Mattlin, Ben. "What I Learned from the Generation of Disabled Activists Who Came After Me." *TIME*. December 8, 2022. https://tinyurl.com/bdw2zjb6.

Stones, Emily. "Cross-Neurotype Communication Competence." In *The Palgrave Handbook of Disability and Communication*, edited by Michael S. Jeffress, Joy M. Cypher, Jim Ferris, and Julie-Ann Scott-Pollock. Palgrave Macmillan, 2023.

Thavis, Rebecca. "Sensory Informed Teaching and the Impact on Student Learning." Master's thesis, Bethel University, 2022. https://spark.bethel.edu/etd/910.

Wang, M., F. Martin, N. Hess, S. Feldman, N. Osman, J. O'Neil, G. Freeman, and K. Mulligan. "Engaging BIPOC Out-Of-School Youth with Disabilities Through Interagency Collaborations: Lessons Learned from Centers for Independent Living." *Rehabilitation Counselors and Educators Journal* 13, no. 2 (2024). https://doi.org/10.52017/001c.124185.

WEBSITES

If you or someone you know is struggling or in crisis in the United States, call or text 988 for the Suicide & Crisis Lifeline or chat 988lifeline.org.

Ability Ministry. https://abilityministry.com.

American Psychiatric Association Foundation. "Faith and Mental Health." https://www.apaf.org/faith.

BeMe App and the BeingMe Podcast. https://www.beme.com.

BIPOC Suicide Prevention: The Mental Health Coalition. www.thementalhealthcoalition.org.

The Brain Charity. https://www.thebraincharity.org.uk/lgbtqia-neurodiversity-neurodivergent-lgbtq.

Center for Faith-Based and Neighborhood Partnerships. "Youth Mental Health and Well-Being in Faith and Community Settings: A Toolkit of the HHS Partnership Center." US Department of Health and Human Services. https://www.hhs.gov/about/agencies/iea/partnerships/index.html.

"Classroom Activities." Accessible U at the University of Minnesota. https://accessibility.umn.edu/what-you-can-do/extend-core-skills/use-inclusive-teaching-strategies/classroom-activities.

Collaborative of Faith and Disability. https://www.faithanddisability.org.

Disability Belongs (formerly RespectAbility). https://www.respectability.org.

"Disability Justice in Teaching." Center for Teaching & Learning at UC Berkeley. https://teaching.berkeley.edu/teaching-guides/advancing-equity-and-inclusion/disability-justice-teaching.

Sins Invalid. www.sinsinvalid.org.

GLAAD Resource list. https://glaad.org/resourcelist.

Mental Health America. "Supporting Young Minds" 2024. https://mhanational.org/young-minds.

Mental Health First Aid for Youth. https://www.mentalhealthfirstaid.org/population-focused-modules/youth.

National Alliance on Mental Illness. "Kids, Teens and Young Adults." https://www.nami.org/your-journey/kids-teens-and-young-adults.

"The Need: Anti-Ableist Space for Human-Centered Learning." Stimpunks Foundation. https://stimpunks.org/learning.

Neuroqueer, The Writings of Dr. Nick Walker: https://www.neuroqueer.com.

Springtide Research Institute's resources on mental health and Gen-Z. https://springtideresearch.org/gen-z-mental-health.

"Universal Design for Learning." Cornell University Center for Teaching Innovation. https://teaching.cornell.edu/teaching-resources/assessment-evaluation/inclusion-accessibility-accommodation/building-inclusive-5.

"What Is Self-Determination?" Disability Voices United. https://disabilityvoicesunited.org/interchange/self-determination/what-is-self-determination.

Queer Youth and Suicide Prevention: The Trevor Project, https://www.thetrevorproject.org.

MEDIA RESOURCES

Arden, Avery, host. *Disabled AND Blessed.* Video series. Blessed Are the Binary Breakers. Posted September 7, 2019–July 21, 2024. YouTube. https://tinyurl.com/4psfhy6e. (Video series with disabled interpretations of Jacob, eunuchs, Jesus, John the Baptist and his parents, Luke 14, and the healing narratives.)

"Assume That I Can: World Down Syndrome Day 2024." Posted March 14, 2024, by CoorDown. YouTube, https://tinyurl.com/2vj9wer3.

LeBrecht, J., and Nicole Newnham. *Crip Camp*. Higher Ground Productions, 2020.

Neff, Megan Anna, and Patrick Casale, hosts. *Divergent Conversations*. Podcast. https://www.divergentpod.com/.

Spies, Miriam, and Amy Panton, hosts. *The Mad and Crip Theology Podcast.* Podcast. https://themadandcriptheologypodcast.buzzsprout.com/.

CONTRIBUTORS

AVERY ARDEN (they/ze) has a scholar's spirit, a poet's heart, and a neuroqueer bodymind that's never still! Visit binarybreakingworship.com to connect with their ministry, which uplifts trans and disabled people of faith as both recipients and crucial agents of divine blessing.

CARMELLE BEAUGELIN CALDWELL (she/her) is a Haitian American multidisciplinary artist and curator whose work blends gestural abstraction and theology to explore diaspora, faith, and cultural memory. Beyond her studio practice, Caldwell serves as Associate Director of the Missing Voices Project at Flagler College's Center for Religion and Culture.

ERIK W. CARTER (he/him) holds the Luther Sweet Endowed Chair in Disabilities at Baylor University. His research and writing focus on fostering inclusion and belonging in schools, congregations, and communities for individuals with intellectual and developmental disabilities and their families.

MICHAEL PAUL CARTLEDGE (he/him) is a practical theologian whose research and teaching focus on neurodiversity, mental health, youth ministry, and Christian education. He currently serves as Associate Director of Grants and Projects at Flagler College's Center for Religion and Culture.

MORRIGAN CLARKE (they/them) is a high school student in Lawrenceville, New Jersey, who is an advocate for children with disabilities. They also have a younger brother with autism.

JUSTIN FORBES (he/him) is Director of the Center for Religion and Culture and Assistant Professor of Religion at Flagler College in St. Augustine, Florida. His interest in youth ministry, practical theology, and contextualized experiences of marginality have led him to working and researching with young people that have been marginalized by society and the church.

ZACH GRANT (he/him) is a Presbyterian minister and co-founder of Bethlehem Inclusive Church, an ability-inclusive worshiping community. He has been blessed to lead and be led by young people with disabilities in every stage of his career.

LAMAR HARDWICK (he/him), also known as "the autism pastor," is a pastor, cancer survivor, scholar, and award-winning author whose research is focused on the intersection of disability, race, and religion.

DEBORAH HUGGINS (she/her) serves as Associate Pastor for Christian Education at Central Presbyterian Church, where she supports families as they find connection to God and community. Her research focuses on leadership and belonging with disabled youth.

AMY JACOBER (she/her) is a theologian, pastor, professor, and caregiver. She is the author of *Redefining Perfect*, *The Adolescent Journey*, and numerous articles on youth ministry, theology, and disability.

CHRIS LAROCQUE's (he/him) ministry stretches across Pentecostal, United Methodist, and Presbyterian (USA) congregations. He is a staff member and a cofounder of Bethlehem Inclusive Church, an ability-inclusive worshiping community.

SARAH GRIFFITH LUND (she/her) is an advocate, author, and pastor who is passionate about partnering with others with hope and joy to build a more just world. She serves as senior pastor of First Congregational Church of Indianapolis and as the Minister for Disabilities and Mental Health Justice on the national staff of the United Church of Christ. Sarah is the author of several books about mental health and faith, including *Blessed Are the Crazy*, *Blessed Union*, *Blessed Youth*, *Blessed Youth Survival Guide*, and *Blessed Minds*.

PEPA PANIAGUA (she/her) is the Coordinator of Innovation and New Ministry Development for Grace Presbytery in North, Texas. Paniagua is a pastor in the Presbyterian Church (USA) and views ministry through the lenses of inclusion and abundance. Many of her understandings of ministry developed from her experience growing up with her sister, Debbie, who lived with multiple disabilities.

ERIN RAFFETY (she/her) is a practical theologian and anthropologist who teaches at Princeton University and researches Christian congregations at Princeton Theological Seminary. Raffety is a Presbyterian pastor, a disability advocate, and the author of *Families We Need* and *From Inclusion to Justice*.

RUDOLPH P. REYES II (he/him) is Assistant Professor of Christian Ethics and Latinx Studies at Garrett-Evangelical Theological Seminary. He is a multiply neurodivergent Latino social ethicist who researches how theology and ethics help or hinder liberation from interlocking systems of oppression.

CODY J. SANDERS (he/him) is Associate Professor of Congregational and Community Care Leadership at Luther Seminary in Saint Paul, MN. He has authored several books, including *A Brief Guide to Ministry with LGBTQIA Youth* and *Spiritual Care First Aid: An All-Hands Approach for Church and Community*.

LEN AND ANDREW SCALES (she/her; he/him) are the Chaplains and Executive Co-Directors with Princeton Presbyterians, a Presbyterian Church (USA) campus ministry in central New Jersey. In addition to their work as campus ministers, Andrew teaches worship and preaching courses as an adjunct professor at Princeton Theological Seminary, and Len serves as the Associate Pastor for Faith Formation, Mission, and Outreach at Nassau Presbyterian Church.

HUNTER STEINITZ (she/they) is a graduate of Pittsburgh Theological Seminary and a Co-Moderator of Presbyterians for Disability Concerns. She is also affected with Harlequin Ichthyosis, and is one of the first generation of survivors with her condition.

AVERY WILLIAMS (she/they) is an African American studies major with a minor in creative writing at Princeton University. You can read more of her writing at restandreclaimwritings.substack.com and at linktr.ee/restandreclaim writings.

ILLUSTRATION CREDITS

P. 4 *Holding the World,* Elliot Freebourn, undated, acrylic on canvas. Used with permission.

P. 15 *Watching You,* Sylvia Hemenetz, 2024, acrylic on canvas. Used with permission.

P. 59 *Melt,* Elliot Freebourn, undated, watercolor on paper. Used with permission.

P. 105 *Me on a Swing with Space Because God Made Me and Space,* Brianna Stone, undated. Used with permission.

P. 147 *Made for His Glory,* Sara Gaver, 2025, acrylic on canvas. Used with permission.

INDEX OF SUBJECTS

INDEX OF SCRIPTURE